Letters of Jane Austen

By
Jane Austen

16

EasyRead Large

RHYW

ReadHowYouWant Classics Library

TABLE OF CONTENTS

Letters to Her Sister Cassandra Austen, 1796–1816

Letter I – 1796

Steventon: Saturday (January 9).

In the first place I hope you will live twenty-three years longer. Mr. Tom Lefroy's birthday was yesterday, so that you are very near of an age.

After this necessary preamble I shall proceed to inform you that we had an exceeding good ball last night, and that I was very much disappointed at not seeing Charles Fowle of the party, as I had previously heard of his being invited. In addition to our set at the Harwoods' ball, we had the Grants, St. Johns, Lady Rivers, her three daughters and a son, Mr. and Miss Heathcote, Mrs. Lefevre, two Mr. Watkins, Mr. J. Portal, Miss Deanes, two Miss Ledgers, and a tall clergyman who came with them, whose name Mary would never have guessed.

We were so terrible good as to take James in our carriage, though there were three of us before, but indeed he deserves encouragement for the very great improvement which has lately taken place in his dancing. Miss Heathcote is pretty, but not near so handsome as I expected. Mr. H. began with Elizabeth, and afterwards danced with her again; but they do not know how *to be particular.* I flatter myself, however, that they will profit by the three successive lessons which I have given them.

You scold me so much in the nice long letter which I have this moment received from you, that I am almost afraid to tell you how my Irish friend and I behaved. Imagine to yourself everything most profligate and shocking in the way of dancing and sitting down together. I *can* expose myself however, only *once more,* because he leaves the country soon after next Friday, on which day we are to have a dance at Ashe after all. He is a very gentlemanlike, good-looking, pleasant young man, I assure you. But as to our having ever met, except at the three last balls, I cannot say much; for he is so excessively laughed at about me at Ashe, that he is ashamed of coming to Steventon, and ran away when we called on Mrs. Lefroy a few days ago.

We left Warren at Dean Gate, in our way home last night, and he is now on his road to town. He left his love, &c., to you, and I will deliver it when we meet. Henry goes to Harden to-day in his way to his Master's degree. We shall feel the loss of these two most agreeable young men exceedingly, and shall have nothing to console us till the arrival of the Coopers on Tuesday. As they will stay here till the Monday following, perhaps Caroline will go to the Ashe ball with me, though I dare say she will not.

I danced twice with Warren last night, and once with Mr. Charles Watkins, and, to my inexpressible astonishment, I entirely escaped John Lyford. I was forced to fight hard for it, however. We had a very good supper, and the greenhouse was illuminated in a very elegant manner.

We had a visit yesterday morning from Mr. Benjamin Portal, whose eyes are as handsome as ever. Everybody is extremely anxious for your return, but as you cannot come home by the Ashe ball, I am glad that I have not fed them with false hopes. James danced with Alithea, and cut up the turkey last night with great perseverance. You say nothing of the silk stockings; I flatter myself, therefore, that Charles has not purchased any, as I cannot very well afford to pay for them; all my money is spent in buying white gloves and pink persian. I wish Charles had been at Manydown, because he would have given you some description of my friend, and I think you must be impatient to hear something about him.

Henry is still hankering after the Regulars, and as his project of purchasing the adjutancy of the Oxfordshire is now over, he has got a scheme in his head about getting a lieutenancy and adjutancy in the 86th, a new-raised regiment, which he fancies will be ordered to the Cape of Good Hope. I heartily hope that he will, as usual, be disappointed in this scheme. We have trimmed up and given away all the old paper hats of Mamma's manufacture; I hope you will not regret the loss of yours.

After I had written the above, we received a visit from Mr. Tom Lefroy and his cousin George. The latter is really very well-behaved now; and as for the other, he has but one fault, which time will, I trust, entirely remove – it is that his morning coat is a great deal too light. He is a very great admirer of Tom Jones, and therefore wears the same coloured clothes, I imagine, which he did when he was wounded.

Sunday. – By not returning till the 19th, you will exactly contrive to miss seeing the Coopers, which I suppose it is your wish to do. We have heard nothing from Charles for some time. One would suppose they must have sailed by this time, as the wind is so favourable. What a funny name Tom has got for his vessel! But he has no taste in names, as we well know, and I dare say he christened it himself. I am sorry for the Beaches' loss of their little girl, especially as it is the one so much like me.

I condole with Miss M. on her losses and with Eliza on her gains, and am ever yours,

J. A.

Letter II – 1796

Steventon: Thursday (January 16).

I have just received yours and Mary's letter, and I thank you both, though their contents might have been more agreeable. I do not at all expect to see you on Tuesday, since matters have fallen out so pleasantly; and if you are not able to return till after that day, it will hardly be possible for us to send for you before Saturday, though for my own part I care so little about the ball that it would be no sacrifice to me to give it up for the sake of seeing you two days earlier. We are extremely sorry for poor Eliza's illness. I trust, however, that she has continued to recover since you wrote, and that you will none of you be the worse for your attendance on her. What a good-for-nothing fellow Charles is to bespeak the stockings! I hope he will be too hot all the rest of his life for it!

I sent you a letter yesterday to Ibthorp, which I suppose you will not receive at Kintbury. It was not very long or very witty, and therefore if you never receive it, it does not much signify. I wrote principally to tell you that the Coopers were arrived and in good health. The little boy is very like Dr. Cooper, and the little girl is to resemble Jane, they say.

Our party to Ashe to-morrow night will consist of Edward Cooper, James (for a ball is nothing without *him*), Buller, who is now staying with us, and I. I look forward with great impatience to it, as I rather expect to receive an offer from my friend in the course of the evening. I shall refuse him, however, unless he promises to give away his white coat.

I am very much flattered by your commendation of my last letter, for I write only for fame, and without any view to pecuniary emolument.

Edward is gone to spend the day with his friend, John Lyford, and does not return till to-morrow. Anna is now here; she came up in her chaise to spend the day with her young cousins, but she does not much take to them or to anything about them, except Caroline's spinning-wheel. I am very glad to find from Mary that Mr. and Mrs. Fowle are pleased with you. I hope you will continue to give satisfaction.

How impertinent you are to write to me about Tom, as if I had not opportunities of hearing from him myself! The *last* letter that I received from him was dated on Friday, 8th, and he told me that if the wind should be favourable on Sunday, which it proved to be, they were to sail from Falmouth on that day. By this time, therefore, they are at Barbadoes, I suppose. The Rivers are still at Manydown, and are to be at Ashe to-morrow. I intended to call on the Miss

Biggs yesterday had the weather been tolerable. Caroline, Anna, and I have just been devouring some cold souse, and it would be difficult to say which enjoyed it most.

Tell Mary that I make over Mr. Heartley and all his estate to her for her sole use and benefit in future, and not only him, but all my other admirers into the bargain wherever she can find them, even the kiss which C. Powlett wanted to give me, as I mean to confine myself in future to Mr. Tom Lefroy, for whom I don't care sixpence. Assure her also, as a last and indubitable proof of Warren's indifference to me, that he actually drew that gentleman's picture for me, and delivered it to me without a sigh.

Friday. – At length the day is come on which I am to flirt my last with Tom Lefroy, and when you receive this it will be over. My tears flow as I write at the melancholy idea. Wm. Chute called here yesterday. I wonder what he means by being so civil. There is a report that Tom is going to be married to a Lichfield lass. John Lyford and his sister bring Edward home today, dine with us, and we shall all go together to Ashe. I understand that we are to draw for partners. I shall be extremely impatient to hear from you again, that I may know how Eliza is, and when you are to return.

With best love, &c., I am affectionately yours,

J. AUSTEN.

Letter III – 1796

Cork Street: Tuesday morn (August).

MY DEAR CASSANDRA,

Here I am once more in this scene of dissipation and vice, and I begin already to find my morals corrupted. We reached Staines yesterday, I do not (know) when, without suffering so much from the heat as I had hoped to do. We set off again this morning at seven o'clock, and had a very pleasant drive, as the morning was cloudy and perfectly cool. I came all the way in the chaise from Hertford Bridge.

Edward and Frank are both gone out to seek their fortunes; the latter is to return soon and help us seek ours. The former we shall never see again. We are to be at Astley's to-night, which I am glad of. Edward has heard from Henry this morning. He has not been at the races at all, unless his driving Miss Pearson over to Rowling one day can be so called. We shall find him there on Thursday.

I hope you are all alive after our melancholy parting yesterday, and that you pursued your intended avocation with success. God bless you! I must leave off, for we are going out.

Yours very affectionately,

J. AUSTEN.

Everybody's love.

Letter IV – 1796

Rowling: Thursday (September 1).

MY DEAREST CASSANDRA,

The letter which I have this moment received from you has diverted me beyond moderation. I could die of laughter at it, as they used to say at school. You are indeed the finest comic writer of the present age.

Since I wrote last, we have been very near returning to Steventon so early as next week. Such, for a day or two, was our dear brother Henry's scheme, but at present matters are restored, not to what they were, for my absence seems likely to be lengthened still farther. I am sorry for it, but what can I do?

Henry leaves us to-morrow for Yarmouth, as he wishes very much to consult his physician there, on whom he has great reliance. He is better than he was when he first came, though still by no means well. According to his present plan, he will not return here till about the 23rd, and bring with him, if he can, leave of absence for three weeks, as he wants very much to have some shooting at Godmersham, whither Edward and Elizabeth are to remove very early in October. If this scheme holds, I shall hardly be at Steventon before the middle of that month; but if you cannot do without me, I could return, I suppose, with Frank if he ever goes back. He enjoys himself here very much, for he has just learnt to turn, and is so delighted with the employment, that he is at it all day long.

I am sorry that you found such a conciseness in the strains of my first letter. I must endeavour to make you amends for it, when we meet, by some elaborate details, which I shall shortly begin composing.

I have had my new gown made up, and it really makes a very superb surplice. I am sorry to say that my new coloured gown is very much washed out, though I charged everybody to take great care of it. I hope yours is so too. Our men had but indifferent weather for their visit to Godmersham, for it rained great part of the way there and all the way back. They found Mrs. Knight remarkably well and in very good spirits. It is imagined that she will shortly be married again. I have taken little George once in my arms since I have been here, which I thought very kind. I have told Fanny about the bead of her necklace, and she wants very much to know where you found it.

To-morrow I shall be just like Camilla in Mr. Dubster's summer-house, for my Lionel will have taken away the ladder by which I came here, or at least by which I intended to get away, and here I must stay till his return. My situation, however, is somewhat preferable to hers, for I am very happy here, though I should be glad to get home by the end of the month. I have no idea that Miss Pearson will return with me.

What a fine fellow Charles is, to deceive us into writing two letters to him at Cork! I admire his ingenuity extremely, especially as he is so great a gainer by it.

Mr. and Mrs. Cage and Mr. and Mrs. Bridges dined with us yesterday. Fanny seemed as glad to see me as anybody, and inquired very much after you, whom she supposed to be making your wedding-clothes. She is as handsome as ever, and somewhat fatter. We had a very pleasant day, and some *liqueurs* in the evening. Louisa's figure is very much improved; she is as stout again as she was. Her face, from what I could see of it one evening, appeared not at all altered. She and the gentlemen walked up here on Monday night – she came in the morning with the Cages from Hythe.

Lady Hales, with her two youngest daughters, have been to see us. Caroline is not grown at all coarser than she was, nor Harriet at all more delicate. I am glad to hear so good an account of Mr. Charde, and only fear that my long absence may occasion his relapse. I practise every day as much as I can – I wish it were more for his sake. I have heard nothing of Mary Robinson since I have been (here). I expect to be well scolded for daring to doubt, whenever the subject is mentioned.

Frank has turned a very nice little butterchurn for Fanny. I do not believe that any of the party were aware of the valuables they had left behind; nor can I hear anything of Anna's gloves. Indeed I have not inquired at all about them hitherto.

We are very busy making Edward's shirts, and I am proud to say that I am the neatest worker of the party. They say that there are a prodigious number of birds hereabouts this year, so that perhaps *I* may kill a few. I am glad to hear so good an account of Mr. Limprey and J. Lovett. I know nothing of my mother's handkerchief, but I dare say I shall find it soon.

I am very affectionately yours,

JANE.

Letter V – 1796

Rowling: Monday (September 5).

MY DEAR CASSANDRA,

I shall be extremely anxious to hear the event of your ball, and shall hope to receive so long and minute an account of every particular that I shall be tired of reading it. Let me know how many, besides their fourteen selves and Mr. and Mrs. Wright, Michael will contrive to place about their coach, and how many of the gentlemen, musicians, and waiters, he will have persuaded to come in their shooting-jackets. I hope John Lovett's accident will not prevent his attending the ball, as you will otherwise be obliged to dance with Mr. Tincton the whole evening. Let me know how J. Harwood deports himself without the Miss Biggs, and which of the Marys will carry the day with my brother James.

We were at a ball on Saturday, I assure you. We dined at Goodnestone, and in the evening danced two country-dances and the Boulangeries. I opened the ball with Edward Bridges; the other couples were Lewis Cage and Harriet, Frank and Louisa, Fanny and George. Elizabeth played one country-dance, Lady Bridges the other, which she made Henry dance with her, and Miss Finch played the Boulangeries.

In reading over the last three or four lines, I am aware of my having expressed myself in so doubtful a manner that, if I did not tell you to the contrary, you might imagine it was Lady Bridges who made Henry dance with her at the same time that she was playing, which, if not impossible, must appear a very improbable event to you. But it was Elizabeth who danced. We supped there, and walked home at night under the shade of two umbrellas.

To-day the Goodnestone party begins to disperse and spread itself abroad. Mr. and Mrs. Cage and George repair to Hythe. Lady Waltham, Miss Bridges, and Miss Mary Finch to Dover, for the health of the two former. I have never seen Marianne at all. On Thursday Mr. and Mrs. Bridges return to Danbury; Miss Harriet Hales accompanies them to London on her way to Dorsetshire.

Farmer Claringbould died this morning, and I fancy Edward means to get some of his farm, if he can cheat Sir Brook enough in the agreement.

We have just got some venison from Godmersham, which the two Mr. Harveys are to dine on to-morrow, and on Friday or Saturday the Goodnestone people are to finish their scraps. Henry went away on Friday, as he purposed, *without fayl.* You will hear from him soon, I imagine, as he talked of writing to Steventon shortly. Mr. Richard Harvey is going to be married;

but as it is a great secret, and only known to half the neighbourhood, you must not

I am in great distress. I cannot determine whether I shall give Richis half a guinea or only five shillings when I go away. Counsel me, amiable Miss Austen, and tell me which will be the most.

We walked Frank last night to Crixhall Ruff, and he appeared much edified. Little Edward was breeched yesterday for good and all, and was whipped into the bargain.

Pray remember me to everybody who does not inquire after me; those who do, remember me without bidding. Give my love to Mary Harrison, and tell her I wish, whenever she is attached to a young man, some *respectable* Dr. Marchmont may keep them apart for five volumes.

Letter VI – 1796

Rowling: Thursday (September 15).

MY DEAR CASSANDRA,

We have been very gay since I wrote last; dining at Nackington, returning by moonlight, and everything quite in style, not to mention Mr. Claringbould's funeral which we saw go by on Sunday.

I believe I told you in a former letter that Edward had some idea of taking the name of Clarmgbould; but that scheme is over, though it would be a very eligible as well as a very pleasant plan, would anyone advance him money enough to begin on. We rather expected Mr. Milles to have done so on Tuesday; but to our great surprise nothing was said on the subject, and unless it is in your power to assist your brother with five or six hundred pounds, he must entirely give up the idea.

At Nackington we met Lady Sondes' picture over the mantel-piece in the dining-room, and the pictures of her three children in an ante room, besides Mr. Scott, Miss Fletcher, Mr. Toke, Mr. J. Toke, and the Archdeacon Lynch. Miss Fletcher and I were very thick, but I am the thinnest of the two. She wore her purple muslin, which is pretty enough, though it does not become her complexion. There are two traits in her character which are pleasing – namely, she admires Camilla, and drinks no cream in her tea. If you should ever see Lucy, you may tell her that I scolded Miss Fletcher for her negligence in writing, as she desired me to do, but without being able to bring her to any proper sense of shame – that Miss Fletcher says in her defence, that as everybody whom Lucy knew when she was in Canterbury has now left it, she has nothing at all to write to her about. By *everybody,* I suppose Miss Fletcher means that a new set of officers have arrived there. But this is a note of my own.

Mrs. Milles, Mr. John Toke, and in short everybody of any sensibility inquired in tender strains after you, and I took an opportunity of assuring Mr. J. T. that neither he nor his father need longer keep themselves single for you.

We went in our two carriages to Nackington; but how we divided I shall leave you to surmise, merely observing that, as Elizabeth and I were without either hat or bonnet, it would not have been very convenient for us to go in the chaise. We went by Bifrons, and I contemplated with a melancholy pleasure the abode of him on whom I once fondly doated. We dine to-day at Goodnestone, to meet my Aunt Fielding from Margate and a Mr. Clayton, her professed admirer – at least so I imagine. Lady Bridges has received very good accounts of Marianne, who is already certainly the better for her bathing.

So His Royal Highness Sir Thomas Williams has at length sailed; the papers say "on a cruise." But I hope they are gone to Cork, or I shall have written in vain. Give my love to Jane, as she arrived at Steventon yesterday, I dare say.

I sent a message to Mr. Digweed from Edward in a letter to Mary Lloyd which she ought to receive to-day; but as I know that the Harwoods are not very exact as to their letters, I may as well repeat it to you. Mr. Digweed is to be informed that illness has prevented Seward's coming over to look at the repairs intended at the farm, but that he will come as soon as he can. Mr. Digweed may also be informed, if you think proper, that Mr. and Mrs. Milles are to dine here to-morrow, and that Mrs. Joan Knatchbull is to be asked to meet them. Mr. Richard Harvey's match is put off till he has got a better Christian name, of which he has great hopes.

Mr. Children's two sons are both going to be married, John and George. They are to have one wife between them, a Miss Holwell, who belongs to the Black Hole at Calcutta. I depend on hearing from James very soon; he promised me an account of the ball, and by this time he must have collected his ideas enough after the fatigue of dancing to give me one.

Edward and Fly went out yesterday very early in a couple of shooting jackets, and came home like a couple of bad shots, for they killed nothing at all. They are out again to-day, and are not yet returned. Delightful sport! They are just come home, Edward with his two brace, Frank with his two and a half. What amiable young men!

Friday. – Your letter and one from Henry are just come, and the contents of both accord with my scheme more than I had dared expect. In one particular I could wish it otherwise, for Henry is very indifferent indeed. You must not expect us quite so early, however, as Wednesday, the 20th – on that day se'night, according to our present plan, we may be with you. Frank had never any idea of going away before Monday, the 26th. I shall write to Miss Mason immediately and press her returning with us, which Henry thinks very likely and particularly eligible.

Buy Mary Harrison's gown by all means. You shall have mine for ever so much money, though, if I am tolerably rich when I get home, I shall like it very much myself.

As to the mode of our travelling to town, *I* want to go in a stage-coach, but Frank will not let me. As you are likely to have the Williams and Lloyds with you next week, you would hardly find room for us then. If anyone wants anything in town, they must send their commissions to Frank, as *I* shall merely pass through it. The tallow-chandler is Penlington, at the Crown and Beehive, Charles Street, Covent Garden.

Letter VII – 1796

Rowling: Sunday (September 18).

MY DEAR CASSANDRA,

This morning has been spent in doubt and deliberation, in forming plans and removing difficulties, for it ushered in the day with an event which I had not intended should take place so soon by a week. Frank has received his appointment on board the "Captain John Gore," commanded by the "Triton," and will therefore be obliged to be in town on Wednesday; and though I have every disposition in the world to accompany him on that day, I cannot go on the uncertainty of the Pearsons being at home, as I should not have a place to go to in case they were from home.

I wrote to Miss P. on Friday, and hoped to receive an answer from her this morning, which would have rendered everything smooth and easy, and would have enabled us to leave this place to-morrow, as Frank, on first receiving his appointment, intended to do. He remains till Wednesday merely to accommodate me. I have written to her again to-day, and desired her to answer it by return of post. On Tuesday, therefore, I shall positively know whether they can receive me on Wednesday. If they cannot, Edward has been so good as to promise to take me to Greenwich on the Monday following, which was the day before fixed on, if that suits them better. If I have no answer at all on Tuesday, I must suppose Mary is not at home, and must wait till *I* do hear, as, after having invited her to go to Steventon with me, it will not quite do to go home and say no more about it.

My father will be so good as to fetch home his prodigal daughter from town, I hope, unless he wishes me to walk the hospitals, enter at the Temple, or mount guard at St. James'. It will hardly be in Frank's power to take me home – nay, it certainly will not. I shall write again as soon as I get to Greenwich.

What dreadful hot weather we have! It keeps one in a continual state of inelegance.

If Miss Pearson should return with me, pray be careful not to expect too much beauty. I will not pretend to say that *on a first view* she quite answered the opinion I had formed of her. My mother, I am sure, will be disappointed if she does not take great care. From what I remember of her picture, it is no great resemblance.

I am very glad that the idea of returning with Frank occurred to me; for as to Henry's coming into Kent again, the time of its taking place is so very uncertain that I should be waiting for *dead men's shoes*. I had once determined to go with Frank to-morrow and take my chance, &c., but they dissuaded me from so rash a step, as I really think on consideration it would have been; for if the Pearsons were not at home, I should inevitably fall a sacrifice to the arts of some fat woman who would make me drunk with small beer.

Mary is brought to bed of a boy – both doing very well. I shall leave you to guess what Mary I mean. Adieu, with best love to all your agreeable inmates. Don't let the Lloyds go on any account before I return, unless Miss P. is of the party. How ill I have written! I begin to hate myself.

Yours ever,

J. AUSTEN.

The "Triton" is a new 32 frigate just launch at Deptford. Frank is much pleased with the prospect of having Captain Gore under his command.

Letter VIII – 1798

"Bull and George," Dartford,
Wednesday (October 24).

MY DEAR CASSANDRA,

You have already heard from Daniel, I conclude, in what excellent time we reached and quitted Sitting-bourne, and how very well my mother bore her journey thither. I am now able to send you a continuation of the same good account of her. She was very little fatigued on her arrival at this place, has been refreshed by a comfortable dinner, and now seems quite stout. It wanted five minutes of twelve when we left Sittingbourne, from whence we had a famous pair of horses, which took us to Rochester in an hour and a quarter; the postboy seemed determined to show my mother that Kentish drivers were not always tedious, and really drove as fast as *Cax.*

Our next stage was not quite so expeditiously performed; the road was heavy and our horses very indifferent. However, we were in such good time, and my mother bore her journey so well, that expedition was of little importance to us; and as it was, we were very little more than two hours and a half coming hither, and it was scarcely past four when we stopped at the inn. My mother took some of her bitters at

Ospringe, and some more at Rochester, and she ate some bread several times.

We have got apartments up two pair of stairs, as we could not be otherwise accommodated with a sitting-room and bed-chambers on the same floor, which we wished to be. We have one double-bedded and one single-bedded room; in the former my mother and I are to sleep. I shall leave you to guess who is to occupy the other. We sate down to dinner a little after five, and had some beefsteaks and a boiled fowl, but no oyster sauce.

I should have begun my letter soon after our arrival but for a little adventure which prevented me. After we had been here a quarter of an hour it was discovered that my writing and dressing boxes had been by accident put into a chaise which was just packing off as we came in, and were driven away towards Gravesend in their way to the West Indies. No part of my property could have been such a prize before, for in my writing-box was all my worldly wealth, £7, and my dear Harry's deputation. Mr. Nottley immediately despatched a man and horse after the chaise, and in half an hour's time I had the pleasure of being as rich as ever; they were got about two or three miles off.

My day's journey has been pleasanter in every respect than I expected. I have been very little crowded and by no means unhappy. Your watchfulness with regard to the weather on our accounts was very kind and very effectual. We had one heavy shower on leaving Sittingbourne, but afterwards the clouds cleared away, and we had a very bright *chrystal* afternoon.

My father is now reading the "Midnight Bell," which he has got from the library, and mother sitting by the fire. Our route to-morrow is not determined. We have none of us much inclination for London, and if Mr. Nottley will give us leave, I think we shall go to Staines through Croydon and Kingston, which will be much pleasanter than any other way; but he is decidedly for Clapham and Battersea. God bless you all!

Yours affectionately,

J. A.

I flatter myself that *itty Dordy* will not forget me at least under a week. Kiss him for me.

Letter IX – 1798

Steventon: Saturday (October 27).

MY DEAR CASSANDRA,

Your letter was a most agreeable surprise to me to-day, and I have taken a long sheet of paper to show my gratitude.

We arrived here yesterday between four and five, but I cannot send you quite so triumphant an account of our last day's journey as of the first and second. Soon after I had finished my letter from Staines, my mother began to suffer from the exercise or fatigue of travelling, and she was a good deal indisposed. She had not a very good night at Staines, but bore her journey better than I had expected, and at Basingstoke, where we stopped more than half an hour, received much comfort from a mess of broth and the sight of Mr. Lyford, who recommended her to take twelve drops of laudanum when she went to bed as a composer, which she accordingly did.

James called on us just as we were going to tea, and my mother was well enough to talk very cheerfully to him before she went to bed. James seems to have taken to his old trick of coming to Steventon in spite of Mary's reproaches, for he was here before breakfast and is now paying us a second visit. They were to have dined here to-day, but the weather is too bad. I have had the pleasure of hearing that Martha is with them. James fetched her from Ibthorp on Thursday, and she will stay with them till she removes to Kintbury.

We met with no adventures at all in our journey yesterday, except that our trunk had once nearly slipped off, and we were obliged to stop at Hartley to have our wheels greased.

Whilst my mother and Mr. Lyford were together I went to Mrs. Ryder's and bought what I intended to buy, but not in much perfection. There were no narrow braces for children and scarcely any notting silk; but Miss Wood, as usual, is going to town very soon, and will lay in a fresh stock. I gave 2s. 3d. a yard for my flannel, and I fancy it is not very good, but it is so disgraceful and contemptible an article in itself that its being comparatively good or bad is of little importance. I bought some Japan ink likewise, and next week shall begin my operations on my hat, on which you know my principal hopes of happiness depend.

I am very grand indeed; I had the dignity of dropping out my mother's laudanum last night. I carry about the keys of the wine and closet, and twice since I began this letter have had orders to give in the kitchen. Our dinner was very good yesterday, and the chicken boiled perfectly tender; therefore I shall not be obliged to dismiss Nanny on that account.

Almost everything was unpacked and put away last night. Nanny chose to do it, and I was not sorry to be busy. I have unpacked the gloves and placed yours in your drawer. Their colour is light and pretty, and I believe exactly what we fixed on.

Your letter was chaperoned here by one from Mrs. Cooke, in which she says that "Battleridge" is not to come out before January, and she is so little satisfied with Cawthorn's dilatoriness that she never means to employ him again.

Mrs. Hall, of Sherborne, was brought to bed yesterday of a dead child, some weeks before she expected, owing to a fright. I suppose she happened unawares to look at her husband.

There has been a great deal of rain here for this last fortnight, much more than in Kent, and indeed we found the roads all the way from Staines most disgracefully dirty. Steventon lane has its full share of it, and I don't know when I shall be able to get to Deane.

I hear that Martha is in better looks and spirits than she has enjoyed for a long time, and I flatter myself she will now be able to jest openly about Mr. W.

The spectacles which Molly found are my mother's, the scissors my father's. We are very glad to hear such a good account of your patients, little and great. My dear itty Dordy's remembrance of me is very pleasing to me – foolishly pleasing, because I know it will be over so soon. My attachment to him will be more durable. I shall think with tenderness and delight on his beautiful and smiling countenance and interesting manner until a few years have turned him into an ungovernable, ungracious fellow.

The books from Winton are all unpacked and put away; the binding has compressed them most conveniently, and there is now very good room in the bookcase for all that we wish to have there. I believe the servants were very glad to see us. Nanny was, I am sure. She confesses that it was very dull, and yet she had her child with her till last Sunday. I understand that there are some grapes left, but I believe not many; they must be gathered as soon as possible, or this rain will entirely rot them.

I am quite angry with myself for not writing closer; why is my alphabet so much more sprawly than yours? Dame Tilbury's daughter has lain in. Shall I give her any of your baby clothes? The laceman was here only a few days ago. How unfortunate for both of us that he came so soon! Dame Bushell washes for us only one week more, as Sukey has got a place. John Steevens' wife undertakes our purification. She does not look as if anything she touched would ever be clean, but who knows? We do not seem likely to have any other maidservant at present, but Dame Staples will supply the place of one. Mary has hired a young girl from Ashe who has never been out to service to be her scrub, but James fears her not being strong enough for the place.

Earle Harwood has been to Deane lately, as I think Mary wrote us word, and his family then told him that they would receive his wife, if she continued to behave well for another year. He was very grateful, as well he might, their behaviour throughout the whole affair has been particularly kind. Earle and his wife live in the most private manner imaginable at Portsmouth, without keeping a servant of any kind. What a prodigious innate love of virtue she must have, to marry under such circumstances!

It is now Saturday evening, but I wrote the chief of this in the morning. My mother has not been down at all to-day; the laudanum made her sleep a good deal, and upon the whole I think she is better. My father and I dined by ourselves. How strange! He and John Bond are now very happy together for I have just heard the heavy step of the latter along the passage.

James Digweed called to-day, and I gave him his brother's deputation. Charles Harwood, too, has just called to ask how we are, in his way from Dummer, whither he has been conveying Miss Garrett, who is going to return to her former residence in Kent. I will leave off, or I shall not have room to add a word to-morrow.

I am very grand indeed; I had the dignity of dropping out my mother's laudanum last night. I carry about the keys of the wine and closet, and twice since I began this letter have had orders to give in the kitchen. Our dinner was very good yesterday, and the chicken boiled perfectly tender; therefore I shall not be obliged to dismiss Nanny on that account.

Almost everything was unpacked and put away last night. Nanny chose to do it, and I was not sorry to be busy. I have unpacked the gloves and placed yours in your drawer. Their colour is light and pretty, and I believe exactly what we fixed on.

Your letter was chaperoned here by one from Mrs. Cooke, in which she says that "Battleridge" is not to come out before January, and she is so little satisfied with Cawthorn's dilatoriness that she never means to employ him again.

Mrs. Hall, of Sherborne, was brought to bed yesterday of a dead child, some weeks before she expected, owing to a fright. I suppose she happened unawares to look at her husband.

There has been a great deal of rain here for this last fortnight, much more than in Kent, and indeed we found the roads all the way from Staines most disgracefully dirty. Steventon lane has its full share of it, and I don't know when I shall be able to get to Deane.

I hear that Martha is in better looks and spirits than she has enjoyed for a long time, and I flatter myself she will now be able to jest openly about Mr. W.

The spectacles which Molly found are my mother's, the scissors my father's. We are very glad to hear such a good account of your patients, little and great. My dear itty Dordy's remembrance of me is very pleasing to me – foolishly pleasing, because I know it will be over so soon. My attachment to him will be more durable. I shall think with tenderness and delight on his beautiful and smiling countenance and interesting manner until a few years have turned him into an ungovernable, ungracious fellow.

The books from Winton are all unpacked and put away; the binding has compressed them most con-veniently, and there is now very good room in the bookcase for all that we wish to have there. I be-lieve the servants were very glad to see us. Nanny was, I am sure. She confesses that it was very dull, and yet she had her child with her till last Sunday. I understand that there are some grapes left, but I believe not many; they must be gathered as soon as possible, or this rain will entirely rot them.

I am quite angry with myself for not writing closer; why is my alphabet so much more sprawly than yours? Dame Tilbury's daughter has lain in. Shall I give her any of your baby clothes? The laceman was here only a few days ago. How unfortunate for both of us that he came so soon! Dame Bushell washes for us only one week more, as Sukey has got a place. John Steevens' wife undertakes our purification. She does not look as if anything she touched would ever be clean, but who knows? We do not seem likely to have any other maidservant at present, but Dame Staples will supply the place of one. Mary has hired a young girl from Ashe who has never been out to service to be her scrub, but James fears her not being strong enough for the place.

Earle Harwood has been to Deane lately, as I think Mary wrote us word, and his family then told him that they would receive his wife, if she continued to behave well for another year. He was very grateful, as well he might, their behaviour throughout the whole affair has been particularly kind. Earle and his wife live in the most private manner imaginable at Portsmouth, without keeping a servant of any kind. What a prodigious innate love of virtue she must have, to marry under such circumstances!

It is now Saturday evening, but I wrote the chief of this in the morning. My mother has not been down at all to-day; the laudanum made her sleep a good deal, and upon the whole I think she is better. My father and I dined by ourselves. How strange! He and John Bond are now very happy together for I have just heard the heavy step of the latter along the passage.

James Digweed called to-day, and I gave him his brother's deputation. Charles Harwood, too, has just called to ask how we are, in his way from Dummer, whither he has been conveying Miss Garrett, who is going to return to her former residence in Kent. I will leave off, or I shall not have room to add a word to-morrow.

Sunday. – My mother has had a very good night, and feels much better to-day.

I have received my Aunt's letter, and thank you for your scrap. I will write to Charles soon. Pray give Fanny and Edward a kiss from me, and ask George if he has got a new song for me. 'Tis really very kind of my Aunt to ask us to Bath again; a kindness that deserves a better return than to profit by it.

Yours ever,

J. A.

Letter X – 1798

Saturday, (November 17).

MY DEAR CASSANDRA,

If you paid any attention to the conclusion of my last letter, you will be satisfied, before you receive this, that my mother has had no relapse, and that Miss Debary comes. The former continues to recover, and though she does not gain strength very rapidly, my expectations are humble enough not to outstride her improvements. She was able to sit up nearly eight hours yesterday, and to-day I hope we shall do as much...

So much for my patient – now for myself.

Mrs. Lefroy did come last Wednesday, and the Harwoods came likewise, but very considerately paid their visit before Mrs. Lefroy's arrival, with whom, in spite of interruptions both from my father and James, I was enough alone to hear all that was interesting, which you will easily credit when I tell you that of her nephew she said nothing at all, and of her friend very little. She did not once mention the name of the former to *me,* and I was too proud to make any inquiries; but on my father's afterwards asking where he was, I learnt that he was gone back to London in his way to Ireland, where he is called to the Bar and means to practise.

She showed me a letter which she had received from her friend a few weeks ago (in answer to one written by her to recommend a nephew of Mrs. Russell to his notice at Cambridge), towards the end of which was a sentence to this effect:

> "I am very sorry to hear of Mrs. Austen's illness. It would give me particular pleasure to have an opportunity of improving my acquaintance with that family – with a hope of creating to myself a nearer interest. But at present I cannot indulge any expectation of it."

This is rational enough; there is less love and more sense in it than sometimes appeared before, and I am very well satisfied. It will all go on exceedingly well, and decline away in a very reasonable manner. There seems no likelihood of his coming into Hampshire this Christmas, and it is therefore most probable that our indifference will soon be mutual, unless his regard, which appeared to spring from knowing nothing of me at first, is best supported by never seeing me.

Mrs. Lefroy made no remarks in the letter, nor did she indeed say anything about him as relative to me. Perhaps she thinks she has said too much already.

She saw a great deal of the Mapletons while she was in Bath. Christian is still in a very bad state of health, consumptive, and not likely to recover.

Mrs. Portman is not much admired in Dorsetshire; the good-natured world, as usual, extolled her beauty so highly, that all the neighbourhood have had the pleasure of being disappointed.

My mother desires me to tell you that I am a very good housekeeper, which I have no reluctance in doing, because I really think it my peculiar excellence, and for this reason – I always take care to provide such things as please my own appetite, which I consider as the chief merit in housekeeping. I have had some ragout veal, and I mean to have some haricot mutton to-morrow. We are to kill a pig soon.

There is to be a ball at Basingstoke next Thursday. Our assemblies have very kindly declined ever since we laid down the carriage, so that dis-convenience and dis-inclination to go have kept pace together.

My father's affection for Miss Cuthbert is as lively as ever, and he begs that you will not neglect to send him intelligence of her or her brother, whenever you have any to send. I am likewise to tell you that one of his Leicestershire sheep, sold to the butcher last week, weighed 27 lb. and 1/4 per quarter.

I went to Deane with my father two days ago to see Mary, who is still plagued with the rheumatism, which she would be very glad to get rid of, and still more glad to get rid of her child, of whom she is heartily tired. Her nurse is comes and has no particular charm either of person or manner; but as all the Hurstbourne world pronounce her to be the best nurse that ever was, Mary expects her attachment to increase.

What fine weather this is! Not very becoming perhaps early in the morning, but very pleasant out of doors at noon, and very wholesome – at least everybody fancies so, and imagination is everything. To Edward, however, I really think dry weather of importance. I have not taken to fires yet.

I believe I never told you that Mrs. Coulthard and Anne, late of Manydown, are both dead, and both died in childbed. We have not regaled Mary with this news. Harry St. John is in Orders, has done duty at Ashe, and performs very well.

I am very fond of experimental housekeeping, such as having an ox-cheek now and then, I shall have one next week, and I mean to have some little dumplings put into it, that I may fancy myself at Godmersham.

I hope George was pleased with my designs. Perhaps they would have suited him as well had they been less elaborately finished; but an artist cannot do anything slovenly. I suppose baby grows and improves.

Sunday. – I have just received a note from James to say that Mary was brought to bed last night, at eleven o'clock, of a fine little boy, and that everything is going on very well. My mother had desired to know nothing of it before it should be all over, and we were clever enough to prevent her having any suspicion of it, though Jenny, who had been left here by her mistress, was sent for home...

I called yesterday on Betty Londe, who inquired particularly after you, and said she seemed to miss you very much, because you used to call in upon her very often. This was an oblique reproach at me, which I am sorry to have merited, and from which I will profit. I shall send George another picture when I write next, which I suppose will be soon, on Mary's account. My mother continues well.

Yours,

J. A.

Letter XI – 1798

Steventon: Sunday (November 25).

MY DEAR SISTER,

I expected to have heard from you this morning, but no letter is come. I shall not take the trouble of announcing to you any more of Mary's children, if, instead of thanking me for the intelligence, you always sit down and write to James. I am sure nobody can desire your letters so much as I do, and I don't think anybody deserves them so well.

Having now relieved my heart of a great deal of malevolence, I will proceed to tell you that Mary continues quite well, and my mother tolerably so. I saw the former on Friday, and though I had seen her comparatively hearty the Tuesday before, I was really amazed at the improvement which three days had made in her. She looked well, her spirits were perfectly good, and she spoke much more vigorously than Elizabeth did when we left Godmersham. I had only a glimpse at the child, who was asleep; but Miss Debary told me that his eyes were large, dark, and handsome. *She* looks much as she used to do, is netting herself a gown in worsteds, and wears what Mrs. Birch would call a *pot hat.* A short and compendious history of Miss Debary!

I suppose you have heard from Henry himself that his affairs are happily settled. We do not know who furnishes the qualification. Mr. Mowell would have readily given it, had not all his Oxfordshire property been engaged for a similar purpose to the Colonel. Amusing enough!

Our family affairs are rather deranged at present, for Nanny has kept her bed these three or four days, with a pain in her side and fever, and we are forced to have two charwomen, which is not very comfortable. She is considerably better now, but it must still be some time, I suppose, before she is able to do anything. You and Edward will be amused, I think, when you know that Nanny Littlewart dresses my hair.

The ball on Thursday was a very small one indeed, hardly so large as an Oxford smack. There were but seven couples, and only twenty-seven people in the room.

The Overton Scotchman has been kind enough to rid me of some of my money, in exchange for six shifts and four pair of stockings. The Irish is not so fine as I should like it; but as I gave as much money for it as I intended, I have no reason to complain. It cost me 3*s.* 6*d.* per yard. It is rather finer, however, than our last, and not so harsh a cloth.

We have got *"Fitz-Albini";* my father has bought it against my private wishes, for it does not quite satisfy my feelings that we should purchase the only one of Egerton's works of which his family are ashamed. That these scruples, however, do not at all interfere with my reading it, you will easily believe. We have neither of us yet finished the first volume. My father is disappointed – *I* am not, for I expected nothing better. Never did any book carry more internal evidence of its author. Every sentiment is completely Egerton's. There is very little story, and what there is, is told in a strange, unconnected way. There are many characters introduced, apparently merely to be delineated. We have not been able to recognise any of them hitherto, except Dr. and Mrs. Hey and Mr. Oxenden, who is not very tenderly treated.

You must tell Edward that my father gives 25*s.* apiece to Seward for his last lot of sheep, and, in return for this news, my father wishes to receive some of Edward's pigs.

We have got Boswell's *"Tour to the Hebrides,"* and are to have his *"Life of Johnson"*; and, as some money will yet remain in Burdon's hands, it is to be laid out in the purchase of Cowper's works. This would please Mr. Clarke, could he know it.

By the bye, I have written to Mrs. Birch among my other writings, and so I hope to have some account of all the people in that part of the world before long. I have written to Mrs. E. Leigh, too, and Mrs. Heathcote has been ill-natured enough to send me a letter of inquiry; so that altogether I am tolerably tired of letter-writing, and, unless I have anything new to tell you of my mother or Mary, I shall not write again for many days; perhaps a little repose may restore my regard for a pen. Ask little Edward whether Bob Brown wears a great coat this cold either.

Letter XII – 1798

Steventon: December 1.

MY DEAR CASSANDRA,

I am so good as to write to you again thus speedily, to let you know that I have just heard from Frank. He was at Cadiz, alive and well, on October 19, and had then very lately received a letter from you, written as long ago as when the "London" was at St. Helen's. But his *raly* latest intelligence of us was in one from me of September 1, which I sent soon after we got to Godmersham. He had written a packet full for his dearest friends in England, early in October, to go by the "Excellent"; but the "Excellent" was not sailed, nor likely to sail, when he despatched this to me. It comprehended letters for both of us, for Lord Spencer, Mr. Daysh, and the East India Directors. Lord St. Vincent had left the fleet when he wrote, and was gone to Gibraltar, it was said to superintend the fitting out of a private expedition from thence against some of the enemies' ports; Minorca or Malta were conjectured to be the objects.

Frank writes in good spirits, but says that our correspondence cannot be so easily carried on in future as it has been, as the communication between Cadiz and Lisbon is less frequent than formerly. You and my mother, therefore, must not alarm yourselves at the long intervals that may divide his letters. I address this advice to you two as being the most tender-hearted of the family.

My mother made her *entrée* into the dressing-room through crowds of admiring spectators yesterday afternoon, and we all drank tea together for the. first time these five weeks. She has had a tolerable night, and bids fair for a continuance in the same brilliant course of action to-day...

Mr. Lyford was here yesterday; he came while we were at dinner, and partook of our elegant entertainment. I was not ashamed at asking him to sit down to table, for we had some pease-soup, a sparerib, and a pudding. He wants my mother to look yellow and to throw out a rash, but she will do neither.

I was at Deane yesterday morning. Mary was very well, but does not gain bodily strength very fast. When I saw her so stout on the third and sixth days, I expected to have seen her as well as ever by the end of a fortnight.

James went to Ibthorp yesterday to see his mother and child. Letty is with Mary at present, of course exceedingly happy, and in raptures with the child. Mary does not manage matters in such a way as to make me want to lay in myself. She is not tidy enough in her appearance; she has no dressing-gown to sit up in; her curtains are all too thin, and things are not in that comfort and style about her which are necessary to make such a situation an enviable one. Elizabeth was really a pretty object with her nice clean cap put on so tidily and her dress so uniformly white and orderly. We live entirely in the dressing-room now, which I like very much; I always feel so much more elegant in it than in the parlour.

No news from Kintbury yet. Eliza sports with our impatience. She was very well last Thursday. Who is Miss Maria Montresor going to marry, and what is to become of Miss Mulcaster?

I find great comfort in my stuff gown, but I hope you do not wear yours too often. I have made myself two or three caps to wear of evenings since I came home, and they save me a world of torment as to hair-dressing, which at present gives me no trouble beyond washing and brushing, for my long hair is always plaited up out of sight, and my short hair curls well enough to want no papering. I have had it cut lately by Mr. Butler.

There is no reason to suppose that Miss Morgan is dead after all. Mr. Lyford gratified us very much yesterday by his praises of my father's mutton, which they all think the finest that was ever ate. John Bond begins to find himself grow old, which John Bonds ought not to do, and unequal to much hard work; a man is therefore hired to supply his place as to labour, and John himself is to have the care of the sheep. There are not more people engaged than before, I believe; only men instead of boys. I fancy so at least, but you know my stupidity as to such matters. Lizzie Bond is just apprenticed to Miss Small, so we may hope to see her able to spoil gowns in a few years.

My father has applied to Mr. May for an alehouse for Robert, at his request, and to Mr. Deane, of Winchester, likewise. This was my mother's idea, who thought he would be proud to oblige a relation of Edward in return for Edward's accepting his money. He sent a very civil answer indeed, but has no house vacant at present. May expects to have an empty one soon at Farnham, so perhaps Nanny may have the honour of drawing ale for the Bishop. I shall write to Frank to-morrow.

Charles Powlett gave a dance on Thursday, to the great disturbance of all his neighbours, of course, who, you know, take a most lively interest in the state of his finances, and live in hopes of his being soon ruined.

We are very much disposed to like our new maid; she knows nothing of a diary, to be sure, which, in our family, is rather against her, but she is to be taught it all. In short, we have felt the inconvenience of being without a maid so long, that we are determined to like her, and she will find it a hard matter to displease us. As yet, she seems to cook very well, is uncommonly stout, and says she can work well at her needle.

Sunday. – My father is glad to hear so good an account of Edward's pigs, and desires he may be told, as encouragement to his taste for them, that Lord Bolton is particularly curious in his pigs, has had pigstyes of a most elegant construction built for them, and visits them every morning as soon as he rises.

Affectionately yours,

J. A.

Letter XIII – 1798

Steventon: Tuesday (December 18).

MY DEAR CASSANDRA,

Your letter came quite as soon as I expected, and so your letters will always do, because I have made it a rule not to expect them till they come, in which I think I consult the ease of us both.

It is a great satisfaction to us to hear that your business is in a way to be settled, and so settled as to give you as little inconvenience as possible. You are very welcome to my father's name and to his services if they are ever required in it. I shall keep my ten pounds too, to wrap myself up in next winter.

I took the liberty a few days ago of asking your black velvet bonnet to lend me its cawl, which it very readily did, and by which I have been enabled to give a considerable improvement of dignity to cap, which was before too *nidgetty* to please me. I shall wear it on Thursday, but I hope you will not be offended with me for following your advice as to its ornaments only in part. I still venture to retain the narrow silver round it, put twice round without any bow, and instead of the black military feather shall put in the coquelicot one as being smarter, and besides coquelicot is to be all the fashion this winter. After the ball I shall probably make it entirely black.

I am sorry that our dear Charles begins to feel the dignity of ill-usage. My father will write to Admiral Gambier. He must have already received so much satisfaction from his acquaintance and patronage of rank, that he will be delighted, I dare say, to have another of the family introduced to him. I think it would be very right in Charles to address Sir Thomas on the occasion, though I cannot approve of *your* scheme of writing to him (which you communicated to me a few nights ago) to request him to come home and convey you to Steventon. To do you justice, however, you had some doubts of the propriety of such a measure yourself.

I am very much obliged to my dear little George for his message – for his *love* at least; his *duty,* I suppose, was only in consequence of some hint of my favourable intentions towards him from his father or mother. I am sincerely rejoiced, however, that I ever was born, since it has been the means of procuring him a dish of tea. Give my best love to him.

This morning has been made very gay to us by visits from our two lively neighbours, Mr. Holder and Mr. John Harwood.

I have received a very civil note from Mrs. Martin, requesting my name as a subscriber to her library which opens January 14, and my name, or rather yours, is accordingly given. My mother finds the money. May subscribes too, which I am glad of, but hardly expected. As an inducement to subscribe, Mrs. Martin tells me that her collection is not to consist only of novels, but of every kind of literature, &c. She might have spared this pretension to *our* family, who are great novel-readers and not ashamed of being so; but it was necessary, I suppose, to the self-consequence of half her subscribers.

I hope and imagine that Edward Taylor is to inherit all Sir Edward Dering's fortune as well as all his own father's. I took care to tell Mrs. Lefroy of your calling on her mother, and she seemed pleased with it.

I enjoyed the hard black frosts of last week very much, and one day while they lasted walked to Deane by myself. I do not know that I ever did such a thing in my life before.

Charles Powlett has been very ill, but is getting well again. His wife is discovered to be everything that the neighbourhood could wish her, silly and cross as well as extravagant. Earle Harwood and his friend Mr. Bailey came to Deane yesterday, but are not to stay above a day or two. Earle has got the appointment to a prison-ship at Portsmouth, which he has been for some time desirous of having, and he and his wife are to live on board for the future.

We dine now at half-past three, and have done dinner, I suppose, before you begin. We drink tea at half-past six. I am afraid you will despise us. My father reads Cowper to us in the morning, to which I listen when I can. How do you spend your evenings? I guess that Elizabeth works, that you read to her, and that Edward goes to sleep. My mother continues hearty; her appetite and nights are very good, but she sometimes complains of an asthma, a dropsy, water in her chest, and a liver disorder.

The third Miss Irish Lefroy is going to be married to a Mr. Courteney, but whether James or Charles I do not know. Miss Lyford is gone into Suffolk with her brother and Miss Lodge. Everybody is now very busy in making up an income for the two latter. Miss Lodge has only 800*l.* of her own, and it is not supposed that her father can give her much; therefore the good offices of the neighbourhood will be highly acceptable. John Lyford means to take pupils.

James Digweed has had a very ugly cut – how could it happen? It happened by a young horse which he had lately purchased, and which he was trying to back into its stable; the animal kicked him down with his forefeet, and kicked a great hole in his head; he scrambled away as soon as he could, but was stunned for a time, and suffered a good deal of pain afterwards. Yesterday he got upon the horse again, and, for fear of something worse, was forced to throw himself off.

Wednesday. – I have changed my mind, and changed the trimmings of my cap this morning; they are now such as you suggested. I felt as if I should not prosper if I strayed from your directions, and I think it makes me look more like Lady Conyngham now than it did before, which is all that one lives for now. I believe I *shall* make my new gown like my robe, but the back of the latter is all in a piece with the tail, and will seven yards enable me to copy it in that respect?

Mary went to church on Sunday, and had the weather been smiling, we should have seen her here before this time. Perhaps I may stay at Manydown as long as Monday, but not longer. Martha sends me word that she is too busy to write to me now, and but for your letter I should have supposed her deep in the study of medicine preparatory to their removal from Ibthorp. The letter to Gambier goes to-day.

I expect a very stupid ball; there will be nobody worth dancing with, and nobody worth talking to but Catherine, for I believe Mrs. Lefroy will not be there. Lucy is to go with Mrs. Russell.

People get so horridly poor and economical in this part of the world that I have no patience with them. Kent is the only place for happiness; everybody is rich there. I must do similar justice, however, to the Windsor neighbourhood. I have been forced to let James and Miss Debary have two sheets of your drawing-paper, but they shan't have any more; there are not above three or four left, besides one of a smaller and richer sort. Perhaps you may want some more if you come through town in your return, or rather buy some more, for your wanting it will not depend on your coming through town, I imagine.

I have just heard from Martha and Frank: his letter was written on November 12. All well and nothing particular.

J. A.

Letter XIV – 1798

Steventon: Monday night (December 24).

MY DEAR CASSANDRA,

I have got some pleasant news for you which I am eager to communicate, and therefore begin my letter sooner, though I shall not *send* it sooner than usual.

Admiral Gambier, in reply to my father's application, writes as follows:–

> "As it is usual to keep young officers in small vessels, it being most proper on account of their inexperience, and it being also a situation where they are more in the way of learning their duty, your son has been continued in the 'corpion'; but I have mentioned to the Board of Admiralty his wish to be in a frigate, and when a proper opportunity offers and it is judged that he has taken his turn in a small ship, I hope he will be removed. With regard to your son now in the 'London' I am glad I can give you the assurance that his promotion is likely to take place very soon, as Lord Spencer has been so good as to say he would include him in an arrangement that he proposes making in a short time relative to some promotions in that quarter."

There! I may now finish my letter and go and hang myself, for I am sure I can neither write nor do anything which will not appear insipid to you after this. *Now* I really think he will soon be made, and only wish we could communicate our foreknowledge of the event to him whom it principally concerns. My father has written to Daysh to desire that he will inform us, if he can, when the commission is sent. Your chief wish is now ready to be accomplished; and could Lord Spencer give happiness to Martha at the same time, what a joyful heart he would make of yours!

I have sent the same extract of the sweets of Gambier to Charles, who, poor fellow, though he sinks into nothing but an humble attendant on the hero of the piece, will, I hope, be contented with the prospect held out to him. By what the Admiral says, it appears as if he had been designedly kept in the "Scorpion." But I will not torment myself with conjectures and suppositions; facts shall satisfy me.

Frank had not heard from any of us for ten weeks when he wrote to me on November 12 in consequence of Lord St. Vincent being removed to Gibraltar. When his commission is sent, however, it will not be so long on its road as our letters, because all the Government despatches are forwarded by land to his lordship from Lisbon with great regularity.

I returned from Manydown this morning, and found my mother certainly in no respect worse than when I left her. She does not like the cold weather, but that we cannot help. I spent my time very quietly and very pleasantly with Catherine. Miss Blackford is agreeable enough. I do not want people to be very agreeable, as it saves me the trouble of liking them a great deal. I found only Catherine and her when I got to Manydown on Thursday. We dined together and went together to Worting to seek the protection of Mrs. Clarke, with whom were Lady Mildmay, her eldest son, and a Mr. and Mrs. Hoare.

Our ball was very thin, but by no means unpleasant. There were thirty-one people, and only eleven ladies out of the number, and but five single women in the room. Of the gentlemen present you may have some idea from the list of my partners – Mr. Wood, G. Lefroy, Rice, a Mr. Butcher (belonging to the Temples, a sailor and not of the 11th Light Dragoons), Mr. Temple (not the horrid one of all), Mr. Wm. Orde (cousin to the Kingsclere man), Mr. John Harwood, and Mr. Calland, who appeared as usual with his hat in his hand, and stood every now and then behind Catherine and me to be talked to and abused for not dancing. We teased him, however, into it at last. I was very glad to see him again after so long a separation, and he was altogether rather the genius and flirt of the evening. He inquired after you.

There were twenty dances, and I danced them all, and without any fatigue. I was glad to find myself capable of dancing so much, and with so much satisfaction as I did; from my slender enjoyment of the Ashford balls (as assemblies for dancing) I had not thought myself equal to it, but in cold weather and with few couples I fancy I could just as well dance for a week together as for half an hour. My black cap was openly admired by Mrs. Lefroy, and secretly I imagine by everybody else in the room.

Tuesday. – I thank you for your long letter, which I will endeavour to deserve by writing the rest of this as closely as possible. I am full of joy at much of your information; that you should have been to a ball, and have danced at it, and supped with the Prince, and that you should meditate the purchase of a new muslin gown, are delightful circumstances. *I* am determined to buy a handsome one whenever I can, and I am so tired and ashamed of half my present stock, that I even blush at the sight of the wardrobe which contains them. But I will not be much longer libelled by the possession of my coarse spot; I shall turn it into a petticoat very soon. I wish you a merry Christmas, but *no* compliments of the season.

Poor Edward! It is very hard that he, who has everything else in the world that he can wish for, should not have good health too. But I hope with the assistance of stomach complaints, faintnesses, and sicknesses, he will soon be restored to that blessing likewise. If his nervous complaint proceeded from a suppression of something that ought to be thrown out, which does not seem unlikely, the first of these disorders may really be a remedy, and I sincerely wish it may, for I know no one more deserving of happiness without alloy than Edward is.

I cannot determine what to do about my new gown; I wish such things were to be bought ready-made. I have some hopes of meeting Martha at the christening at Deane next Tuesday, and shall see what she can do for me. I want to have something suggested which will give me no trouble of thought or direction.

Again I return to my joy that you danced at Ashford, and that you supped with the Prince. I can perfectly comprehend Mrs. Cage's distress and perplexity. She has all those kind of foolish and incomprehensible feelings which would make her fancy herself uncomfortable in such a party. I love her, however, in spite of all her nonsense. Pray give "t'other Miss Austen's" compliments to Edward Bridges when you see him again.

I insist upon your persevering in your intention of buying a new gown; I am sure you must want one, and as you will have 5*l.* due in a week's, time, I am certain you may afford it very well, and if you think you cannot, I will give you the body-lining.

Of my charities to the poor since I came home you shall have a faithful account. I have given a pair of worsted stockings to Mary Hutchins, Dame Kew, Mary Steevens, and Dame Staples; a shift to Hannah Staples, and a shawl to Betty Dawkins; amounting in all to about half a guinea. But I have no reason to suppose that the *Battys* would accept of anything, because I have not made them the offer.

I am glad to hear such a good account of Harriet Bridges; she goes on now as young ladies of seventeen ought to do, admired and admiring, in a much more rational way than her three elder sisters, who had so little of that kind of youth. I dare say she fancies Major Elkington as agreeable as Warren, and if she can think so, it is very well.

I was to have dined at Keane to-day, but the weather is so cold that I am not sorry to be kept at home by the appearance of snow. We are to have company to dinner on Friday: the three Digweeds and James. We shall be a nice silent party, I suppose. Seize upon the scissors as soon as you possibly can on the receipt of this. I only fear your being too late to secure the prize.

The Lords of the Admiralty will have enough of our applications at present, for I hear from Charles that he has written to Lord Spencer himself to be removed.

I am afraid his Serene Highness will be in a passion, and order some of our heads to be cut off.

My mother wants to know whether Edward has ever made the hen-house which they planned together. I am rejoiced to hear from Martha that they certainly continue at Ibthorp, and I have just heard that I am sure of meeting Martha at the christening.

You deserve a longer letter than this; but it is my unhappy fate seldom to treat people so well as they deserve. . . . God bless you!

Yours affectionately,

JANE AUSTEN.

Wednesday. – The snow came to nothing yesterday, so I *did* go to Deane, and returned home at nine o'clock at night in the little carriage, and without being very cold.

Letter XV – 1798

Steventon: Friday (December 28).

MY DEAR CASSANDRA,

Frank is made. He was yesterday raised to the rank of Commander, and appointed to the "Petterel" sloop, now at Gibraltar. A letter from Daysh has just announced this, and as it is confirmed by a very friendly one from Mr. Mathew to the same effect, transcribing one from Admiral Gambier to the General, we have no reason to suspect the truth of it.

As soon as you have cried a little for joy, you may go on, and learn farther that the India House have taken *Captain Austen's* petition into consideration – this comes from Daysh – and likewise that Lieutenant Charles John Austen is removed to the "Tamar" frigate – this comes from the Admiral. We cannot find out where the "Tamar" is, but I hope we shall now see Charles here at all events.

This letter is to be dedicated entirely to good news. If you will send my father an account of your washing and letter expenses, &c., he will send you a draft for the amount of it, as well as for your next quarter, and for Edward's rent. If you don't buy a muslin gown

now on the strength of this money and Frank's promotion, I shall never forgive you.

Mrs. Lefroy has just sent me word that Lady Dorch-
ester meant to invite me to her ball on January 8,
which, though an humble blessing compared with what
the last page records, I do not consider as any
calamity.

I cannot write any more now, but I have written
enough to make you very happy, and therefore may
safely conclude.

Yours affectionately,

JANE.

Letter XVI – 1798

Steventon: Tuesday (January 8).

MY DEAR CASSANDRA,

You must read your letters over *five* times in future before you send them, and then, perhaps, you may find them as entertaining as I do. I laughed at several parts of the one which I am now answering.

Charles is not come yet, but he must come this morning, or he shall never know what I will do to him. The ball at Kempshott is this evening, and I have got him an invitation, though I have not been so considerate as to get him a partner. But the cases are different between him and Eliza Bailey, for he is not in a dying way, and may therefore be equal to getting a partner for himself. I believe I told you that Monday was to be the ball night, for which, and for all other errors into which I may ever have led you, I humbly ask your pardon.

Elizabeth is very cruel about my writing music, and, as a punishment for her, I should insist upon always writing out all hers for her in future, if I were not punishing myself at the same time.

I am tolerably glad to hear that Edward's income is so good a one – as glad as I can be at anybody's being rich except you and me – and I am thoroughly rejoiced to hear of his present to you.

I am not to wear my white satin cap to-night. after all; I am to wear a mamalone cap instead, which Charles Fowle sent to Mary, and which she lends me. It is all the fashion now; worn at the opera, and by Lady Mildmays at Hackwood balls. I hate describing such things, and I dare say you will be able to guess what it is like. I have got over the dreadful epocha of mantua-making much better than I expected. My gown is made very much like my blue one, which you always told me sat very well, with only these variations: the sleeves are short, the wrap fuller, the apron comes over it, and a band of the same completes the whole.

I assure you that I dread the idea of going to Brighton as much as you do, but I am not without hopes that something may happen to prevent it.

F– has lost his election at B–, and perhaps they may not be able to see company for some time. They talk of going to Bath too, in the spring, and perhaps they may be overturned in their way down, and all laid up for the summer.

Wednesday. – I have had a cold and weakness in one of my eyes for some days, which makes writing neither very pleasant nor very profitable, and which will probably prevent my finishing this letter myself. My mother has undertaken to do it for me, and I shall leave the Kempshott ball for her.

You express so little anxiety about my being murdered under Ash Park Copse by Mrs. Hulbert's servant, that I have a great mind not to tell you whether I was or not, and shall only say that I did not return home that night or the next, as Martha kindly made room for me in her bed, which was the shut-up one in the new nursery. Nurse and the child slept upon the floor, and there we all were in some confusion and great comfort. The bed did exceedingly well for us, both to lie awake in and talk till two o'clock, and to sleep in the rest of the night. I love Martha better than ever, and I mean to go and see her, if I can, when she gets home. We all dined at the Harwoods' on Thursday, and the party broke up the next morning.

This complaint in my eye has been a sad bore to me, for I have not been able to read or work in any comfort since Friday, but *one advantage* will be derived from it, for I shall be such a proficient in music by the time I have got rid of my cold, that I shall be perfectly qualified in *that* science at least to take Mr. Roope's office at Eastwell next summer; and I am sure of Elizabeth's recommendation, be it only on Harriet's account. Of my talent in drawing I have given specimens in my letters to you, and I have nothing to do but to invent a few hard names for the stars.

Mary grows rather more reasonable about her child's beauty, and says that she does not think him really handsome; but I suspect her moderation to be something like that of W– W–'s mamma. Perhaps Mary has told you that they are going to enter more into dinner parties; the Biggs and Mr. Holder dine there to-morrow, and I am to meet them. I shall sleep there. Catherine has the honour of giving her name to a set, which will be composed of two Withers, two Heathcotes, a Blackford, and no Bigg except herself. She congratulated me last night on Frank's promotion, as if she really felt the joy she talked of.

My sweet little George! I am delighted to hear that he has such an inventive genius as to face-making. I admired his yellow *wafer* very much, and hope he will choose the wafer for your next letter. I wore my green shoes last night, and took my *white fan* with me; I am very glad he never threw it into the river.

Mrs. Knight giving up the Godmersham estate to Edward was no such prodigious act of generosity after all, it seems, for she has reserved herself an income out of it still; this ought to be known, that her conduct may not be overrated. I rather think Edward shows the most magnanimity of the two, in accepting her resignation with such incumbrances.

The more I write, the better my eye gets, so I shall at least keep on till it is quite well, before I give up my pen to my mother.

Mrs. Bramston's little movable apartment was tolerably filled last night by herself, Mrs. H. Blackstone, her two daughters, and me. I do not like the Miss Blackstones; indeed, I was always determined not to like them, so there is the less merit in it. Mrs. Bramston was very civil, kind, and noisy. I spent a very pleasant evening, chiefly among the Manydown party. There was the same kind of supper as last year, and the same want of chairs. There were more dancers than the room could conveniently hold, which is enough to constitute a good ball at any time.

I do not think I was very much in request. People were rather apt not to ask me till they could not help it; one's consequence, you know, varies so much at times without any particular reason. There was one gentleman, an officer of the Cheshire, a very good-looking young man, who, I was told, wanted very much to be introduced to me, but as he did not want it quite enough to take much trouble in effecting it, we never could bring it about.

I danced with Mr. John Wood again, twice with a Mr. South, a lad from Winchester, who, I suppose, is as far from being related to the bishop of that diocese as it is possible to be, with G. Lefroy, and J. Harwood, who, I think, takes to me rather more than he used to do. One of my gayest actions was sitting down two dances in preference to having Lord Bolton's eldest son for my partner, who danced too ill to be endured. The Miss Charterises were there, and played the parts of the Miss Edens with great spirit. Charles never came. Naughty Charles! I suppose he could not get superseded in time.

Miss Debary has replaced your two sheets of drawing-paper with two of superior size and quality; so I do not grudge her having taken them at all now. Mr. Ludlow and Miss Pugh of Andover are lately married, and so is Mrs. Skeete of Basingstoke, and Mr. French, chemist, of Reading.

I do not wonder at your wanting to read *"First Impressions"* again, so seldom as you have gone through it, and that so long ago. I am much obliged to you for meaning to leave my old petticoat behind you. I have long secretly wished it might be done, but had not courage to make the request.

Pray mention the name of Maria Montresor's lover when you write next. My mother wants to know it, and I have not courage to look back into your letters to find it out.

I shall not be able to send this till to-morrow, and you will be disappointed on Friday; I am very sorry for it, but I cannot help it.

The partnership between Jeffereys, Toomer, and Legge is dissolved; the two latter are melted away into nothing, and it is to be hoped that Jeffereys will soon break, for the sake of a few heroines whose money he may have. I wish you joy of your birthday twenty times over.

I *shall* be able to send this to the post to-day which exalts me to the utmost pinnacle of human felicity, and makes me bask in the sunshine of prosperity, or gives me any other sensation of pleasure in studied language which you may prefer. Do not be angry with me for not filling my sheet, and believe me yours affectionately,

J. A.

Letter XVII – 1798

Steventon: Monday (January 21).

MY DEAR CASSANDRA,

I will endeavour to make this letter more worthy your acceptance than my last, which was so shabby a one that I think Mr. Marshall could never charge you with the postage. My eyes have been very indifferent since it was written, but are now getting better once more; keeping them so many hours open on Thursday night, as well as the dust of the ball-room, injured them a good deal. I use them as little as I can, but you know, and Elizabeth knows, and everybody who ever had weak eyes knows, how delightful it is to hurt them by employment, against the advice and entreaty of all one's friends.

Charles leaves us to-night. The "Tamar" is in the Downs, and Mr. Daysh advises him to join her there directly, as there is no chance of her going to the westward. Charles does not approve of this at all, and will not be much grieved if he should be too late for her before she sails, as he may then hope to get into a better station. He attempted to go to town last night, and got as far on his road thither as Dean Gate; but both the coaches were full, and we had the pleasure of seeing him back again. He will call on Daysh to-morrow to know whether the "Tamar" has sailed or not, and if she is still at the Downs he will proceed in one of the night coaches to Deal. I want to go with him, that I may explain the country to him properly between Canterbury and Rowling, but the unpleasantness of returning by myself deters me. I should like to go as far as Ospringe with him very much indeed, that I might surprise you at Godmersham.

Martha writes me word that Charles was very much admired at Kintbury, and Mrs. Lefroy never saw anyone so much improved in her life, and thinks him handsomer than Henry. He appears to far more advantage here than he did at Godmersham, not surrounded by strangers and neither oppressed by a pain in his face or powder in his hair.

James christened Elizabeth Caroline on Saturday morning, and then came home. Mary, Anna, and Edward have left us of course; before the second went I took down her answer to her cousin Fanny.

Yesterday came a letter to my mother from Edward Cooper to announce, not the birth of a child, but of a living; for Mrs. Leigh has begged his acceptance of the Rectory of Hamstall-Ridware in Staffordshire, vacant by Mr. Johnson's death. We collect from his letter that he means to reside there, in which he shows his wisdom. Staffordshire is a good way off; so we shall see nothing more of them till, some fifteen years hence, the Miss Coopers are presented to us, fine, jolly, handsome, ignorant girls. The living is valued at 140*l.* a year, but perhaps it may be improvable. How will they be able to convey the furniture of the dressing-room so far in safety?

Our first cousins seem all dropping off very fast. One is incorporated into the family, another dies, and a third goes into Staffordshire. We can learn nothing of the disposal of the other living. I have not the smallest notion of Fulwar's having it. Lord Craven has probably other connections and more intimate ones, in that line, than he now has with the Kintbury family.

Our ball on Thursday was a very poor one, only eight couple and but twenty-three people in the room; but it was not the ball's fault, for we were deprived of two or three families by the sudden illness of Mr. Wither, who was seized that morning at Winchester with a return of his former alarming complaint. An express was sent off from thence to the family; Catherine and Miss Blackford were dining with Mrs. Russell. Poor Catherine's distress must have been very great. She was prevailed on to wait till the Heathcotes could come from Wintney, and then with those two and Harris proceeded directly to Winchester. In such a disorder his danger, I suppose, must always be great; but from this attack he is now rapidly recovering, and will be well enough to return to Manydown, I fancy, in a few days.

It was a fine thing for conversation at the ball. But it deprived us not only of the Biggs, but of Mrs. Russell too, and of the Boltons and John Harwood, who were dining there likewise, and of Mr. Lane, who kept away as related to the family. Poor man! – I mean Mr. Wither – his life is so useful, his character so respectable and worthy, that I really believe there was a good deal of sincerity in the general concern expressed on his account.

Our ball was chiefly made up of Jervoises and Terrys, the former of whom were apt to be vulgar, the latter to be noisy. I had an odd set of partners: Mr. Jenkins, Mr. Street, Col. Jervoise, James Digweed, J. Lyford, and Mr. Biggs, a friend of the latter. I had a very pleasant evening, however, though you will probably find out that there was no particular reason for it; but I do not think it worth while to wait for enjoyment until there is some real opportunity for it. Mary behaved very well, and was not at all fidgetty. For the history of her adventures at the ball I refer you to Anna's letter.

When you come home you will have some shirts to make up for Charles. Mrs. Davies frightened him into buying a piece of Irish when we were in Basingstoke. Mr. Daysh supposes that Captain Austen's commission has reached him by this time.

Tuesday. – Your letter has pleased and amused me very much. Your essay on happy fortnights is highly ingenious, and the talobert skin made me laugh a good deal. Whenever I fall into misfortune, how many jokes it ought to furnish to my acquaintance in general, or I shall die dreadfully in their debt for entertainment.

It began to occur to me before you mentioned it that I had been somewhat silent as to my mother's health for some time, but I thought you could have no difficulty in divining its exact state – you, who have guessed so much stranger things. She is tolerably well – better upon the whole than she was some weeks ago. She would tell you herself that she has a very dreadful cold in her head at present; but I have not much compassion for colds in the head without fever or sore throat.

Our own particular little brother got a place in the coach last night, and is now, I suppose, in town. I have no objection at all to your buying our gowns there, as your imagination has pictured to you exactly such a one as is necessary to make me happy. You quite abash me by your progress in notting, for I am still without silk. You must get me some in town or in Canterbury; it should be finer than yours.

I thought Edward would not approve of Charles being a crop, and rather wished you to conceal it from him at present, lest it might fall on his spirits and retard his recovery. My father furnishes him with a pig from Cheesedown; it is already killed and cut up, but it is not to weigh more than nine stone; the season is too far advanced to get him a larger one. My mother means to pay herself for the salt and the trouble of ordering it to be cured by the sparibs, the souse, and the lard. We have had one dead lamb.

I congratulate you on Mr. E. Hatton's good fortune. I suppose the marriage will now follow out of hand. Give my compliments to Miss Finch.

What time in March may we expect your return in? I begin to be very tired of answering people's questions on that subject, and, independent of *that,* I shall be very glad to see you at home again, and then if we can get Martha and shirk . . . who will be so happy as we?

I think of going to Ibthorp in about a fortnight. My eyes are pretty well, I thank you, if you please.

Wednesday, 23rd. – I wish my dear Fanny many returns of this day, and that she may on every return enjoy as much pleasure as she is now receiving from her doll's-beds.

I have just heard from Charles, who is by this time at Deal. He is to be Second Lieutenant, which pleases him very well. The "Endymion" is come into the Downs, which pleases him likewise. He expects to be ordered to Sheerness shortly, as the "Tamar" has never been refitted.

My father and mother made the same match for you last night, and are very much pleased with it. *He* is a beauty of my mother's.

Yours affectionately,

JANE.

Letter XVIII – 1799

13, Queen's Square, Friday (May 17).

MY DEAREST CASSANDRA,

Our journey yesterday went off exceedingly well; nothing occurred to alarm or delay us. We found the roads in excellent order, had very good horses all the way, and reached Devizes with ease by four o'clock. I suppose John has told you in what manner we were divided when we left Andover, and no alteration was afterwards made. At Devizes we had comfortable rooms and a good dinner, to which we sat down about five; amongst other things we had asparagus and a lobster, which made me wish for you, and some cheesecakes, on which the children made so delightful a supper as to endear the town of Devizes to them for a long time.

Well, here we are at Bath; we got here about one o'clock, and have been arrived just long enough to go over the house, fix on our rooms, and be very well pleased with the whole of it. Poor Elizabeth has had a dismal ride of it from Devizes, for it has rained almost all the way, and our first view of Bath has been just as gloomy as it was last November twelvemonth.

I have got so many things to say, so many things equally important, that I know not on which to decide at present, and shall therefore go and eat with the children.

We stopped in Paragon as we came along, but as it was too wet and dirty for us to get out, we could only see Frank, who told us that his master was very indifferent, but had had a better night last night than usual. In Paragon we met Mrs. Foley and Mrs. Dowdeswell with her yellow shawl airing out, and at the bottom of Kingsdown Hill we met a gentleman in a buggy, who, on minute examination, turned out to be Dr. Hall – and Dr. Hall in such very deep mourning that either his mother, his wife, or himself must be dead. These are all of our acquaintances who have yet met our eyes.

I have some hopes of being plagued about my trunk; I *had* more a few hours ago, for it was too heavy to go by the coach which brought Thomas and Rebecca from Devizes; there was reason to suppose that it might be too heavy likewise for any other coach, and for a long time we could hear of no waggon to convey it. At last, however, we unluckily discovered that one was just on the point of setting out for this place, but at any rate the trunk cannot be here till to-morrow; so far we are safe, and who knows what may not happen to procure a farther delay?

I put Mary's letter into the postoffice at Andover with my own hand.

We are exceedingly pleased with the house; the rooms are quite as large as we expected. Mrs. Bromley is a fat woman in mourning, and a little black kitten runs about the staircase. Elizabeth has the apartment within the drawing-room; she wanted my mother to have it, but as there was no bed in the inner one, and the stairs are so much easier of ascent, or my mother so much stronger than in Paragon as not to regard the double flight, it is settled for us to be above, where we have two very nice-sized rooms, with dirty quilts and everything comfortable. I have the outward and larger apartment, as I ought to have; which is quite as large as our bedroom at home, and my mother's is not materially less. The beds are both as large as any at Steventon, and I have a very nice chest of drawers and a closet full of shelves – so full indeed that there is nothing else in it, and it should therefore be called a cupboard rather than a closet, I suppose.

Tell Mary that there were some carpenters at work in the inn at Devizes this morning, but as I could not be sure of their being Mrs. W. Fowle's relations, I did not make myself known to them.

I hope it will be a tolerable afternoon. When first we came, all the umbrellas were up, but now the pavements are getting very white again.

My mother does not seem at all the worse for her journey, nor are any of us, I hope, though Edward seemed rather fagged last night, and not very brisk this morning; but I trust the bustle of sending for tea, coffee, and sugar, &c., and going out to taste a cheese himself, will do him good.

There was a very long list of arrivals here in the newspaper yesterday, so that we need not immediately dread absolute solitude; and there is a public breakfast in Sydney Gardens every morning, so that we shall not be wholly starved.

Elizabeth has just had a very good account of the three little boys. I hope you are very busy and very comfortable. I find no difficulty in closing my eyes. I like our situation very much; it is far more cheerful than Paragon, and the prospect from the drawing-room window, at which I now write, is rather picturesque, as it commands a prospective view of the left side of Brock Street, broken by three Lombardy poplars in the garden of the last house in Queen's Parade.

I am rather impatient to know the fate of my best gown, but I suppose it will be some days before

Frances can get through the trunk. In the meantime I am, with many thanks for your trouble in making it, as well as marking my silk stockings,

Yours very affectionately,

JANE.

A great deal of love from everybody.

Letter XIX – 1799

13, Queen's Square, Sunday (June 2).

MY DEAR CASSANDRA,

I am obliged to you for two letters, one from yourself and the other from Mary, for of the latter I knew nothing till on the receipt of yours yesterday, when the pigeon-basket was examined, and I received my due. As I have written to her since the time which ought to have brought me hers, I suppose she will consider herself, as I choose to consider, still in my debt.

I will lay out all the little judgment I have in endeavouring to get such stockings for Anna as she will approve; but I do not know that I shall execute Martha's commission at all, for I am not fond of ordering shoes; and, at any rate, they shall all have flat heels.

What must I tell you of Edward? Truth or falsehood. I will try the former, and you may choose for yourself another time. He was better yesterday than he had been for two or three days before – about as well as while he was at Steventon. He drinks at the Hetling Pump, is to bathe to-morrow, and try electricity on Tuesday. He proposed the latter himself to Dr. Fellowes, who made no objection to it, but I fancy we are all unanimous in expecting no advantage from it. At present I have no great notion of our staying here beyond the month.

I heard from Charles last week; they were to sail on Wednesday.

My mother seems remarkably well. My uncle over-walked himself at first, and can now only travel in a chair, but is otherwise very well,

My cloak is come home. I like it very much, and can now exclaim with delight, like J. Bond at hay-harvest, "This is what I have been looking for these three years." I saw some gauzes in a shop in Bath Street yesterday at only 4*d.* a yard, but they were not so good or so pretty as mine. Flowers are very much worn, and fruit is still more the thing. Elizabeth has a bunch of strawberries, and I have seen grapes, cherries, plums, and apricots. There are likewise almonds and raisins, French plums, and tamarinds at the grocers', but I have never seen any of them in hats. A plum or greengage would cost three shillings; cherries and grapes about five, I believe, but this is at some of the dearest shops. My aunt has told me of a very cheap one, near Walcot Church, to which I shall go in guest of something for you. I have never seen an old woman at the pump-room.

Elizabeth has given me a hat, and it is not only a pretty hat, but a pretty *style* of hat too. It is something like Eliza's, only, instead of being all straw, half of it is narrow purple ribbon. I flatter myself, however, that you can understand very little of it from this description. Heaven forbid that I should ever offer such encouragement to explanations as to give a clear one on any occasion myself! But I must write no more of this...

I spent Friday evening with the Mapletons, and was obliged to submit to being pleased in spite of my inclination. We took a very charming walk from six to eight up Beacon Hill, and across some fields, to the village of Charlecombe, which is sweetly situated in a little green valley, as a village with such a name ought to be. Marianne is sensible and intelligent, and even Jane, considering how fair she is, is not unpleasant. We had a Miss North and a Mr. Gould of our party; the latter walked home with me after tea. He is a very young man, just entered Oxford, wears spectacles, and has heard that *"Evelina"* was written by Dr. Johnson.

I am afraid I cannot undertake to carry Martha's shoes home, for, though we have plenty of room in our trunks when we came, we shall have many more things to take back, and I must allow besides for *my* packing.

There is to be a grand gala on Tuesday evening in Sydney Gardens, a concert, with illuminations and fireworks. To the latter Elizabeth and I look forward with pleasure, and even the concert will have more than its usual charm for me, as the gardens are large enough for me to get pretty well beyond the reach of its sound. In the morning Lady Willoughby is to present the colours to some corps, or Yeomanry, or other, in the Crescent, and that such festivities may have a proper commencement, we think of going to...

I am quite pleased with Martha and Mrs. Lefroy for wanting the pattern of our caps, but I am not so well pleased with your giving it to them. Some wish, some prevailing wish, is necessary to the animation of everybody's mind, and in gratifying this you leave them to form some other which will not probably be half so innocent. I shall not forget to write to Frank. Duty and love, &c

Yours affectionately,

JANE.

My uncle is quite surprised at my hearing from you so often; but as long as we can keep the frequency of our correspondence from Martha's uncle we will not fear our own.

Letter XX – 1799

13, Queen Square, Tuesday (June 11).

MY DEAR CASSANDRA,

Your letter yesterday made me very happy. I am heartily glad that you have escaped any share in the impurities of Deane, and not sorry, as it turns out, that our stay here has been lengthened. I feel tolerably secure of our getting away next week, though it is certainly possible that we may remain till Thursday the 27th. I wonder what we shall do with all our intended visits this summer! I should like to make a compromise with Adlestrop, Harden, and Bookham, that Martha's spending the summer at Steventon should be considered as our respective visits to them all.

Edward has been pretty well for this last week, and as the waters have never *dis*agreed with him in any respect, we are inclined to hope that he will derive advantage from them in the end. Everybody encourages us in this expectation, for they all say that the effect of the waters cannot be negative, and many are the instances in which their benefit is felt afterwards more than on the spot. He is more comfortable here than I thought he would be, and so is Elizabeth, though they will both, I believe, be very glad to get away – the latter especially, which one can't wonder at *somehow.* So much for Mrs. Piozzi. I had some thoughts of writing the whole of my letter in her style, but I believe I shall not.

Though you have given me unlimited powers concerning your sprig, I cannot determine what to do about it, and shall therefore in this and in every other future letter continue to ask your farther directions. We have been to the cheap shop, and very cheap we found it, but there are only flowers made there, no fruit; and as I could get four or five very pretty sprigs of the former for the same money which would procure only one Orleans plum – in short, could get more for three or four shillings than I could have means of bringing home – I cannot decide on the fruit till I hear from you again. Besides, I cannot help thinking that it is more natural to have flowers grow out of the head than fruit. What do you think on that subject?

I would not let Martha read *"First Impressions"* again upon any account, and am very glad that I did not leave it in your power. She is very cunning, but I saw through her design; she means to publish it from memory, and one more perusal must enable her to do it. As for "Fitzalbini," when I get home she shall have it as soon as ever she will own that Mr. Elliott is handsomer than Mr. Lance, that fair men are preferable to black; for I mean to take every opportunity of rooting out her prejudices.

Benjamin Portal is here. How charming that is! I do not exactly know why, but the phrase followed so naturally that I could not help putting it down. My mother saw him the other day, but without making herself known to him.

I am very glad you liked my lace, and so are you, and so is Martha, and we are all glad together. I have got your cloak home, which is quite delightful – as delightful at least as half the circumstances which are called so.

I do not know what is the matter with me to-day, but I cannot write quietly; I am always wandering away into some exclamation or other. Fortunately I have nothing very particular to say.

We walked to Weston one evening last week, and liked it very much. Liked *what* very much? Weston? No, *walking* to Weston. I have not expressed myself properly, but I hope you will understand me.

We have not been to any public place lately, nor performed anything out of the common daily routine of No. 13, Queen Square, Bath. But to-day we were to have dashed away at a very extraordinary rate, by dining out, had it not so happened that we did not go.

Edward renewed his acquaintance lately with Mr. Evelyn, who lives in the Queen's Parade, and was invited to a family dinner, which I believe at first Elizabeth was rather sorry at his accepting; but yesterday Mrs. Evelyn called on us, and her manners were so pleasing that we liked the idea of going very much. The Biggs would call her a nice woman. But Mr. Evelyn, who was indisposed yesterday, is worse to-day, and we are put off.

It is rather impertinent to suggest any household care to a housekeeper, but I just venture to say that the coffee-mill will be wanted every day while Edward is at Steventon, as he always drinks coffee for breakfast.

Fanny desires her love to you, her love to grandpapa, her love to Anna, and her love to Hannah; the latter is particularly to be remembered. Edward desires his love to you, to grandpapa, to Anna, to little Edward, to Aunt James and Uncle James, and he hopes all your turkeys and ducks, and chicken and guinea fowls are very well; and he wishes you very much to send him a printed letter, and so does Fanny – and they both rather think they shall answer it.

"On more accounts than one you wished our stay here to be lengthened beyond last Thursday." There is some mystery in this. What have you going on in Hampshire besides the *itch* from which you want to keep us?

Dr. Gardiner was married yesterday to Mrs. Percy and her three daughters.

Now I will give you the history of Mary's veil, in the purchase of which I have so considerably involved you that it is my duty to economise for you in the flowers. I had no difficulty in getting a muslin veil for half a guinea, and not much more in discovering afterwards that the muslin was thick, dirty, and ragged, and therefore would by no means do for a united gift. I changed it consequently as soon as I could, and, considering what a state my imprudence had reduced me to, I thought myself lucky in getting a black lace one for sixteen shillings. I hope the half of that sum will not greatly exceed what you had intended to offer upon the altar of sister-in-law affection.

Yours affectionately,

JANE.

They do not seem to trouble you much from Manydown. I have long wanted to quarrel with them, and I believe I shall take this opportunity. There is no denying that they are very capricious – for they like to enjoy their elder sister's company when they can.

Letter XXI – 1799

13, Queen Square, Wednesday (June 19).

MY DEAR CASSANDRA,

The children were delighted with your letters, as I fancy they will tell you themselves before this is concluded. Fanny expressed some surprise at the wetness of the wafers, but it did not lead to any suspicion of the truth.

Martha and you were just in time with your commissions, for two o'clock on Monday was the last hour of my receiving them. The office is now closed.

John Lyford's history is a melancholy one. I feel for his family, and when I know that his wife was really fond of him, I will feel for her too, but at present I cannot help thinking their loss the greatest.

Edward has not been well these last two days; his appetite has failed him, and he has complained of sick and uncomfortable feelings, which, with other symptoms, make us think of the gout; perhaps a fit of it might cure him, but I cannot wish it to begin at Bath. He made an important purchase yesterday: no less so than a pair of coach-horses. His friend Mr. Evelyn found them out and recommended them, and if the judgment of a Yahoo can ever be depended on, I suppose it may now, for I believe Mr. Evelyn has all his life thought more of horses than of anything else. Their colour is black and their size not large; their price sixty guineas, of which the chair mare was taken as fifteen – but this is of course to be a secret.

Mrs. Williams need not pride herself upon her knowledge of Dr. Mapleton's success here; she knows no more than everybody else knows in Bath. There is not a physician in the place who writes so many prescriptions as he does. I cannot help wishing that Edward had not been tied down to Dr. Fellowes, for, had he come disengaged, we should all have recommended Dr. Mapleton; my uncle and aunt as earnestly as ourselves. I do not see the Miss Mapletons very often, but just as often as I like; we are always very glad to meet, and I do not wish to wear out our satisfaction.

Last Sunday we all drank tea in Paragon; my uncle is still in his flannels, but is getting better again.

On Monday Mr. Evelyn was well enough for us to fulfil our engagement with him; the visit was very quiet and uneventful – pleasant enough. We met only another Mr. Evelyn, his cousin, whose wife came to tea.

Last night we were in Sydney Gardens again, as there was a repetition of the gala which went off so ill on the 4th. We did not go till nine, and then were in very good time for the fireworks, which were really beautiful, and surpassing my expectation; the illuminations, too, were very, pretty. The weather was as favourable as it was otherwise a fortnight ago. The play on Saturday is, *I hope,* to conclude our gaieties here, for nothing but a lengthened stay will make it otherwise. We go with Mrs. Fellowes.

Edward will not remain at Steventon longer than from Thursday to the following Monday, I believe, as the rent-day is to be fixed for the *consecutive* Friday.

I can recollect nothing more to say at present; perhaps breakfast may assist my ideas. I was deceived – my breakfast supplied only two ideas – that the rolls were good and the butter bad. But the post has been more friendly to me – it has brought me a letter from Miss Pearson.

You may remember that I wrote to her above two months ago about the parcel under my care; and as I had heard nothing from her since, I thought myself obliged to write again, two or three days ago, for after all that has passed I was determined that the correspondence should never cease through my means. This second letter has produced an apology for her silence, founded on the illness of several of the family. The exchange of packets is to take place through the medium of Mr. Nutt, probably one of the sons belonging to Woolwich Academy, who comes to Overton in the beginning of July. I am tempted to suspect from some parts of her letter that she has a matrimonial project in view. I shall question her about it when I answer her letter, but all this you know is *en mystère* between ourselves.

Edward has seen the apothecary to whom Dr. Millman recommended him, a sensible, intelligent man, since I began this, and he attributes his present little feverish indisposition to his having ate something unsuited to his stomach. I do not understand that Mr. Anderton suspects the gout at all; the occasional particular glow in the hands and feet, which we considered as a symptom of that disorder, he only calls the effect of the water in promoting a better circulation of the blood.

I cannot help thinking from your account of Mrs. E. H. that Earle's vanity has tempted him to invent the account of her former way of life, that his triumph in securing her might be greater; I dare say she was nothing but an innocent country girl in fact. Adieu! I shall not write again before Sunday, unless anything particular happens.

Yours ever,

JANE.

We shall be with you on Thursday to a very late dinner – later, I suppose, than my father will like for himself – but I give him leave to eat one before. You must give us something very nice, for we are used to live well.

Letter XXII – 1800

Steventon: Saturday evening (October 25).

MY DEAR CASSANDRA,

I am not yet able to acknowledge the receipt of any parcel from London, which I suppose will not occasion you much surprise. I was a little disappointed to-day, but not more so than is perfectly agreeable, and I hope to be disappointed again to-morrow, as only one coach comes down on Sundays.

You have had a very pleasant journey of course and have found Elizabeth and all the children very well on your arrival at Godmersham, and I congratulate you on it. Edward is rejoicing this evening, I dare say, to find himself once more at home, from which he fancies he has been absent a great while. His son left behind him the very fine chestnuts which had been selected for planting at Godmersham, and the drawing of his own which he had intended to carry to George; the former will therefore be deposited in the soil of Hampshire instead of Kent, the latter I have already consigned to another element.

We have been exceedingly busy ever since you went away. In the first place we have had to rejoice two or three times every day at your having such very delightful weather for the whole of your journey, and in the second place we have been obliged to take advantage of the very delightful weather ourselves by going to see almost all our neighbours.

On Thursday we walked to Deane, yesterday to Oakley Hall and Oakley, and to-day to Deane again. At Oakley Hall we did a great deal – eat some sandwiches all over mustard, admired Mr. Bramston's porter, and Mrs. Bramston's transparencies, and gained a promise from the latter of two roots of heartsease, one all yellow and the other all purple, for you. At Oakley we bought ten pair of worsted stockings and a shift; the shift is for Betty Dawkins, as we find she wants it more than a rug; she is one of the most grateful of all whom Edward's charity has reached, or at least she expresses herself more warmly than the rest, for she sends him a "sight of thanks."

This morning we called at the Harwoods', and in their dining-room found "Heathcote and Chute forever." Mrs. William Heathcote and Mrs. Chute – the first of whom took a long ride yesterday morning with Mrs. Harwood into Lord Carnarvon's park, and fainted away in the evening, and the second walked down from Oakley Hall attended by Mrs. Augusta Bramston; they had meant to come on to Steventon afterwards, but we knew a trick worth two of that. If I had thought of it in time, I would have said something civil to her about Edward's never having had any serious idea of calling on Mr. Chute while he was in Hampshire; but unluckily it did not occur to me. Mrs. Heathcote is gone home to-day; Catherine had paid her an early visit at Deane in the morning, and brought a good account of Harris.

James went to Winchester Fair yesterday, and bought a new horse, and Mary has got a new maid – two great acquisitions; one comes from Folly farm, is about five years old, used to draw, and thought very pretty, and the other is niece to Dinah at Kintbury.

James called by my father's desire on Mr. Bayle to inquire into the cause of his being so horrid. Mr. Bayle did not attempt to deny his being horrid, and made many apologies for it; he did not plead his having a drunken self, he talked only of a drunken foreman, &c., and gave hopes of the tables being at Steventon on Monday se'nnight next. We have had no letter since you left us, except one from Mr. Serle of Bishopstoke to inquire the character of James Elton.

Our whole neighbourhood is at present very busy grieving over poor Mrs. Martin, who has totally failed in her business, and had very lately an execution in her house. Her own brother and Mr. Rider are the principal creditors, and they have seized her effects in order to prevent other people's doing it. There has been the same affair going on, we are told, at Wilson's, and my hearing nothing of you makes me apprehensive that you, your fellow travellers, and all your effects, might be seized by the bailiffs when you stop at the house, and sold altogether for the benefit of the creditors.

In talking of Mr. Deedes' new house, Mrs. Bramston told us one circumstance, which, that we should be ignorant of it before, must make Edward's conscience fly into his face; she told us that one of the sitting rooms at Sandling, an oval room, with a bow at one end, has the very remarkable and singular feature of a fireplace with a window, the centre window of the bow, exactly over the mantel-piece.

Sunday. – This morning's unpromising aspect makes it absolutely necessary for me to observe once more how peculiarly fortunate you have been in your weather, and then I will drop the subject forever. Our improvements have advanced very well; the bank along the elm wall is sloped down for the reception of thorns and lilacs, and it is settled that the other side of the path is to continue turfed, and to be planted with beech, ash, and larch.

Monday. – I am glad I had no means of sending this yesterday, as I am now able to thank you for executing my commission so well. I like the gown very much, and my mother thinks it very ugly. I like the stockings also very much, and greatly prefer having two pair only of that quality to three of an inferior sort. The combs are very pretty, and I am much obliged to you for your present, but am sorry you should make me so many. The pink shoes are not particularly beautiful, but they fit me very well; the others are faultless. I am glad that I have still my cloak to expect.

Among my other obligations, I must not omit to remember your writing me so long a letter in a time of such hurry. I am amused by your going to Milgate at last, and glad that you have so charming a day for your journey home.

My father approves his stockings very highly, and finds no fault with any part of Mrs. Hancock's bill except the charge of 3*s.* 6*d.* for the packing-box.

The weather does not know how to be otherwise than fine. I am surprised that Mrs. Marriot should not be taller. Surely you have made a mistake. Did Mr. Roland make you look well?

Yours affectionately,

J. A.

Letter XXIII – 1800

Steventon: Saturday November

MY DEAR CASSANDRA,

You have written, I am sure, though I have received no letter from you since your leaving London; the post, and not yourself, must have been unpunctual.

We have at last heard from Frank; a letter from him to you came yesterday, and I mean to send it on as soon as I can get a ditto (*that* means a frank), which I hope to do in a day or two. *En attendant,* you must rest satisfied with knowing that on the 8th of July the "Petterel," with the rest of the Egyptian squadron, was off the Isle of Cyprus, whither they went from Jaffa for provisions, &c., and whence they were to sail in a day or two for Alexandria, there to wait the result of the English proposals for the evacuation of Egypt. The rest of the letter, according to the present fashionable style of composition, is chiefly descriptive. Of his promotion he knows nothing; of prizes he is guiltless.

Your letter is come; it came, indeed, twelve lines ago, but I could not stop to acknowledge it before, and I am glad it did not arrive till I had completed my first sentence, because the sentence had been made ever since yesterday, and I think forms a very good beginning.

Your abuse of our gowns amuses but does not discourage me; I shall take mine to be made up next week, and the more I look at it the better it pleases me. My cloak came on Tuesday, and, though I expected a good deal, the beauty of the lace astonished me. It is too handsome to be worn – almost too handsome to be looked at. The glass is all safely arrived also, and gives great satisfaction. The wine-glasses are much smaller than I expected, but I suppose it is the proper size. We find no fault with your manner of performing any of our commissions, but if you like to think yourself remiss in any of them, pray do.

My mother was rather vexed that you could not go to Penlington's, but she has since written to him, which does just as well. Mary is disappointed, of course, about her locket, and of course delighted about the mangle, which is safe at Basingstoke. You will thank Edward for it on their behalf, &c., &c., and, as you know how much it was wished for, will not feel that you are inventing gratitude.

Did you think of our ball on Thursday evening, and did you suppose me at it? You might very safely, for there I was. On Wednesday morning it was settled that Mrs. Harwood, Mary, and I should go together, and shortly afterwards a very civil note of invitation for me came from Mrs. Bramston, who wrote I believe as soon as she knew of the ball. I might likewise have gone with Mrs. Lefroy, and therefore, with three methods of going, I must have been more at the ball than anyone else. I dined and slept at Deane; Charlotte and I did my hair, which I fancy looked very indifferent, nobody abused it, however, and I retired delighted with my success.

It was a pleasant ball, and still more good than pleasant, for there were nearly sixty people, and sometimes we had seventeen couple. The Portsmouths, Dorchesters, Boltons, Portals, and Clerks were there, and all the meaner and more usual &c., &c.'s. There was a scarcity of men in general, and a still greater scarcity of any that were good for much. I danced nine dances out of ten – five with Stephen Terry, T. Chute, and James Digweed, and four with Catherine. There was commonly a couple of ladies standing up together, but not often any so amiable as ourselves.

I heard no news, except that Mr. Peters, who was not there, is supposed to be particularly attentive to Miss Lyford. You were inquired after very prettily, and I hope the whole assembly now understands that you are gone into Kent, which the families in general seemed to meet in ignorance of. Lord Portsmouth surpassed the rest in his attentive recollection of you, inquired more into the length of your absence, and concluded by desiring to be "remembered to you when I wrote next."

Lady Portsmouth had got a different dress on, and Lady Bolton is much improved by a wig. The three Miss Terries were there, but no Annie; which was a great disappointment to me. I hope the poor girl had not set her heart on her appearance that evening so much as I had. Mr. Terry is ill, in a very low way. I said civil things to Edward for Mr. Chute, who amply returned them by declaring that, had he known of my brother's being at Steventon, he should have made a point of calling upon him to thank him for his civility about the Hunt.

I have heard from Charles, and am to send his shirts by half-dozens as they are finished; one set will go next week. The "Endymion" is now waiting only for orders, but may wait for them perhaps a month. Mr. Coulthard[1] was unlucky in very narrowly missing another unexpected guest at Chawton, for Charles had actually set out and got half way thither in order to spend one day with Edward, but turned back on discovering the distance to be considerably more than he had fancied, and finding himself and his horse to be very much tired. I should regret it the more if his friend Shipley had been of the party, for Mr. Coulthard

---

[1] Coulthard rented Chawton House at this time.

might not have been so well pleased to see only one come at a time.

Miss Harwood is still at Bath, and writes word that she never was in better health, and never more happy. Joshua Wakeford died last Saturday, and my father buried him on Thursday. A deaf Miss Fonnereau is at Ashe, which has prevented Mrs. Lefroy's going to Worting or Basingstoke during the absence of Mr. Lefroy.

My mother is very happy in the prospect of dressing a new doll which Molly has given Anna. My father's feelings are not so enviable, as it appears that the farm cleared 300l. last year. James and Mary went to Ibthorp for one night last Monday, and found Mrs. Lloyd not in very good looks. Martha has been lately at Kintbury, but is probably at home by this time. Mary's promised maid has jilted her, and hired herself elsewhere. The Debaries persist in being afflicted at the death of their uncle, of whom they now say they saw a great deal in London. Love to all. I am glad George remembers me.

Yours very affectionately,

J. A.

I am very unhappy. In re-reading your letter I find I might have spared myself any intelligence of Charles.

To have written only what you knew before! You may guess how much I feel. I wore at the ball your favourite gown, a bit of muslin of the same round my head, bordered with Mrs. Cooper's band, and one little comb.

Letter XXIV – 1800

Steventon: Thursday (November 20).

MY DEAR CASSANDRA,

Your letter took me quite by surprise this morning; you are very welcome, however, and I am very much obliged to you. I believe I drank too much wine last night at Hurstbourne; I know not how else to account for the shaking of my hand to-day. You will kindly make allowance therefore for any indistinctness of writing, by attributing it to this venial error.

Naughty Charles did not come on Tuesday, but good Charles came yesterday morning. About two o'clock he walked in on a Gosport hack. His feeling equal to such a fatigue is a good sign, and his feeling no fatigue in it a still better. He walked down to Deane to dinner; he danced the whole evening, and to-day is no more tired than a gentleman ought to be.

Your desiring to hear from me on Sunday will, perhaps, bring you a more particular account of the ball than you may care for, because one is prone to think much more of such things the morning after they happen, than when time has entirely driven them out of one's recollection.

It was a pleasant evening; Charles found it remarkably so, but I cannot tell why, unless the absence of Miss Terry, towards whom his conscience reproaches him with being now perfectly indifferent, was a relief to him. There were only twelve dances, of which I danced nine, and was merely prevented from dancing the rest by the want of a partner. We began at ten, supped at one, and were at Deane before five. There were but fifty people in the room; very few families indeed from our side of the county, and not many more from the other. My partners were the two St. Johns, Hooper, Holder, and very prodigious Mr. Mathew, with whom I called the last, and whom I liked the best of my little stock.

There were very few beauties, and such as there were, were not very handsome. Miss Iremonger did not look well, and Mrs. Blount was the only one much admired. She appeared exactly as she did in September, with the same broad face, diamond bandeau, white shoes, pink husband, and fat neck. The two Miss Coxes were there: I traced in one the remains of the vulgar, broad-featured girl who danced at Enham eight years ago; the other is refined into a nice, composed-looking girl, like Catherine Bigg. I looked at Sir Thomas Champneys and thought of poor Rosalie; I looked at his daughter, and thought her a queer animal with a white neck. Mrs. Warren, I was constrained to think, a very fine young woman, which I much regret. She danced away with great activity Her husband is ugly enough, uglier even than his cousin John; but he does not look so *very* old. The Miss Maitlands are both prettyish, very like Anne, with brown skins, large dark eyes, and a good deal of nose. The General has got the gout, and Mrs. Maitland the jaundice. Miss Debary, Susan, and Sally, all in black, but without any stature, made their appearance, and I was as civil to them as circumstances[2] would allow me.

They told me nothing new of Martha. I mean to go to her on Thursday, unless Charles should determine on coming over again with his friend Shipley for the Basingstoke ball, in which case I shall not go till Friday. I shall write to you again, however, before I set off, and I shall hope to hear from you in the meantime. If I do not stay for the ball, I would not on any account do so uncivil a thing by the neighbourhood as to set off at that very time for another place, and shall therefore make a point of not being later than Thursday *morning.*

Mary said that I looked very well last night. I wore my aunt's gown and handkerchief, and my hair was at least tidy, which was all my ambition. I will now have done with the ball, and I will moreover go and dress for dinner.

---

2   Unexpurgated original: "their bad breath"

Thursday evening. – Charles leaves us on Saturday, unless Henry should take us in his way to the island, of which we have some hopes, and then they will probably go together on Sunday.

The young lady whom it is expected that Sir Thomas is to marry is Miss Emma Wabshaw; she lives somewhere between Southampton and Winchester, is handsome, accomplished, amiable, and everything but rich. He is certainly finishing his house in a great hurry. Perhaps the report of his being to marry a Miss Fanshawe might originate in his attentions to this very lady – the names are not unlike.

Summers has made my gown very well indeed, and I get more and more pleased with it. Charles does not like it, but my father and Mary do. My mother is very much resigned to it; and as for James, he gives it the preference over everything of the kind he ever saw, in proof of which I am desired to say that if you like to sell yours Mary will buy it.

We had a very pleasant day on Monday at Ashe, we sat down fourteen to dinner in the study, the diningroom being not habitable from the storms having blown down its chimney. Mrs. Bramston talked a good deal of nonsense, which Mr. Bramston and Mr. Clerk seemed almost equally to enjoy. There was a whist and a casino table, and six outsiders. Rice and Lucy made love, Mat. Robinson fell asleep, James and Mrs.

Augusta alternately read Dr. Finnis' pamphlet on the cow-pox, and I bestowed my company by turns on all.

On inquiring of Mrs. Clerk, I find that Mrs. Heathcote made a great blunder in her news of the Crookes and Morleys. It is young Mr. Crook who is to marry the second Miss Morley, and it is the Miss Morleys instead of the second Miss Crooke who were the beauties at the music meeting. This seems a more likely tale, a better devised imposture.

The three Digweeds all came on Tuesday, and we played a pool at commerce. James Digweed left Hampshire to-day. I think he must be in love with you, from his anxiety to have you go to the Faversham balls, and likewise from his supposing that the two elms fell from their grief at your absence. Was not it a gallant idea? It never occurred to me before, but I dare say it was so.

Hacker has been here to-day putting in the fruit trees. A new plan has been suggested concerning the plantation of the new inclosure of the right-hand side of the elm walk: the doubt is whether it would be better to make a little orchard of it by planting apples, pears, and cherries, or whether it should be larch, mountain ash, and acacia. What is your opinion? I say nothing, and am ready to agree with anybody.

You and George walking to Eggerton! What a droll party! Do the Ashford people still come to Godmersham church every Sunday in a cart? It is *you* that always disliked Mr. N. Toke so much, not I. I do not like his wife, and I do not like Mr. Brett, but as for Mr. Toke, there are few people whom I like better.

Miss Harwood and her friend have taken a house fifteen miles from Bath; she writes very kind letters, but sends no other particulars of the situation. Perhaps it is one of the first houses in Bristol.

Farewell; Charles sends *you* his best love and Edward his worst. If you think the distinction improper, you may take the worst yourself. He will write to you when he gets back to his ship, and in the meantime desires that you will consider me as

Your affectionate sister,

J. A.

Friday. – I have determined to go on Thursday, but of course not before the post comes in. Charles is in very good looks indeed. I had the comfort of finding out the other evening who all the fat girls with long noses were that disturbed me at the 1st H. ball. They all prove to be Miss Atkinsons of En–.[3]

I rejoice to say that we have just had another letter from our dear Frank. It is to you, very short, written from Larnica in Cyprus, and so lately as October 2. He came from Alexandria, and was to return there in three or four days, knew nothing of his promotion, and does not write above twenty lines, from a doubt of the letter's ever reaching you, and an idea of all letters being opened at Vienna. He wrote a few days before to you from Alexandria by the "Mercury," sent with despatches to Lord Keith. Another letter must be owing to us besides this, *one* if not *two;* because none of these are to me. Henry comes to-morrow, for one night only.

My mother has heard from Mrs. E. Leigh. Lady Saye and Seale and her daughter are going to remove to Bath. Mrs. Estwick is married again to a Mr. Sloane, a young man under age, without the knowledge of either family. He bears a good character, however.

---

3 Illegible

Letter XXV – 1800

Steventon: Saturday (January 3).

MY DEAR CASSANDRA,

As you have by this time received my last letter, it is fit that I should begin another, and I begin with the hope, which is at present uppermost in my mind, that you often wore a white gown in the morning at the time of all the gay parties being with you.

Our visit at Ash Park, last Wednesday, went off in a *come-çá* way. We met Mr. Lefroy and Tom Chute, played at cards, and came home again. James and Mary dined here on the following day, and at night Henry set off in the mail for London. He was as agreeable as ever during his visit, and has not lost anything in Miss Lloyd's estimation.

Yesterday we were quite alone – only our four selves; but to-day the scene is agreeably varied by Mary's driving Martha to Basingstoke, and Martha's afterwards dining at Deane.

My mother looks forward with as much certainty as you can do to our keeping two maids; my father is the only one not in the secret. We plan having a steady cook and a young, giddy housemaid, with a sedate, middle-aged man, who is to undertake the double office of husband to the former and sweetheart to the latter. No children, of course, to be allowed on either side.

You feel more for John Bond than John Bond deserves. I am sorry to lower his character, but he is not ashamed to own himself that he has no doubt at all of getting a good place, and that he had even an offer many years ago from a Farmer Paine of taking him into his service whenever he might quit my father's.

There are three parts of Bath which we have thought of as likely to have houses in them – Westgate Buildings, Charles Street, and some of the short streets leading from Laura Place or Pulteney Street.

Westgate Buildings, though quite in the lower part of the town, are not badly situated themselves. The street is broad, and has rather a good appearance. Charles Street, however, I think, is preferable. The buildings are new, and its nearness to Kingsmead Fields would be a pleasant circumstance. Perhaps you may remember, or perhaps you may forget, that Charles Street leads from the Queen Square Chapel to the two Green Park Streets.

The houses in the streets near Laura Place I should expect to be above our price. Gay Street would be too high, except only the lower house on the left-hand side as you ascend. Towards *that* my mother has no disinclination; it used to be lower rented than any other house in the row, from some inferiority in the apartments. But above all others her wishes are at present fixed on the corner house in Chapel Row, which opens into Prince's Street. Her knowledge of it, however, is confined only to the outside, and therefore she is equally uncertain of its being really desirable as of its being to be had. In the meantime she assures you that she will do everything in her power to avoid Trim Street, although you have not expressed the fearful presentiment of it which was rather expected.

We know that Mrs. Perrot will want to get us into Oxford Buildings, but we all unite in particular dislike of that part of the town, and therefore hope to escape. Upon all these different situations you and Edward may confer together, and your opinion of each will be expected with eagerness.

As to our pictures, the battle-piece, Mr. Nibbs, Sir William East, and all the old heterogeneous miscellany, manuscript, Scriptural pieces dispersed over the house, are to be given to James. Your own drawings will not cease to be your own, and the two paintings on tin will be at your disposal. My mother says that the French agricultural prints in the best bedroom were given by Edward to his two sisters. Do you or he know anything about it?

She has written to my aunt, and we are all impatient for the answer. I do not know how to give up the idea of our both going to Paragon in May. *Your* going I consider as indispensably necessary, and I shall not like being left behind; there is no place here or hereabouts that I shall want to be staying at, and though, to be sure, the keep of two will be more than of one, I will endeavour to make the difference less by disordering my stomach with Bath buns; and as to the *trouble* of accommodating us, whether there are one or two, it is much the same.

According to the first plan, my mother and our two selves are to travel down together, and my father follow us afterwards in about a fortnight or three weeks. We have promised to spend a couple of days at Ibthorp in our way. We must all meet at Bath, you know, before we set out for the sea, and, everything considered, I think the first plan as good as any.

My father and mother, wisely aware of the difficulty of finding in all Bath such a bed as their own, have resolved on taking it with them; all the beds, indeed, that we shall want are to be removed – viz., besides theirs, our own two, the best for a spare one, and two for servants; and these necessary articles will probably be the only material ones that it would answer to send down. I do not think it will be worth while to remove any of our chests of drawers; we shall be able to get some of a much more commodious sort, made of deal, and painted to look very neat; and I flatter myself that for little comforts of all kinds our apartment will be one of the most complete things of the sort all over Bath, Bristol included.

We have thought at times of removing the sideboard, or a Pembroke table, or some other piece of furniture, but, upon the whole, it has ended in thinking that the trouble and risk of the removal would be more than the advantage of having them at a place where everything may be purchased. Pray send your opinion.

Martha has as good as promised to come to us again in March. Her spirits are better than they were.

I have now attained the true art of letter-writing, which we are always told is to express on paper exactly what one would say to the same person by word of mouth. I have been talking to you almost as fast as I could the whole of this letter.

Your Christmas gaieties are really quite surprising; I think they would satisfy even Miss Walter herself. I hope the ten shillings won by Miss Foote may make everything easy between her and her cousin Frederick. So Lady Bridges, in the delicate language of Coulson Wallop, is *in for it!* I am very glad to hear of the Pearsons' good fortune. It is a piece of promotion which I know they looked forward to as very desirable some years ago, on Captain Lockyer's illness. It brings them a considerable increase of income and a better house.

My mother bargains for having no trouble at all in furnishing our house in Bath, and I have engaged for your willingly undertaking to do it all. I get more and more reconciled to the idea of our removal. We have lived long enough in this neighbourhood: the Basingstoke balls are certainly on the decline, there is something interesting in the bustle of going away, and the prospect of spending future summers by the sea or in Wales is very delightful. For a time we shall now possess many of the advantages which I have often thought of with envy in the wives of sailors or soldiers. It must not be generally known, however, that I am not sacrificing a great deal in quitting the country, or I can expect to inspire no tenderness, no interest, in those we leave behind.

The threatened Act of Parliament does not seem to give any alarm.

My father is doing all in his power to increase his income, by raising his tithes, &c., and I do not despair of getting very nearly six hundred a year.

In what part of Bath do you mean to place your bees? We are afraid of the South Parade's being too hot.

Monday. – Martha desires her best love, and says a great many kind things about spending some time with you in March, and depending on a large return from us both in the autumn. Perhaps I may not write again before Sunday.

Yours affectionately,

J. A.

Letter XXVI – 1800

Steventon: Thursday (January 8).

MY DEAR CASSANDRA,

The "perhaps" which concluded my last letter being only a "perhaps," will not occasion your being overpowered with surprise, I dare say, if you *should* receive this before Tuesday, which, unless circumstances are very perverse, will be the case. I received yours with much general philanthropy, and still more peculiar good will, two days ago; and I suppose I need not tell you that it was very long, being written on a foolscap sheet, and very entertaining, being written by you.

Mr. Payne has been dead long enough for Henry to be out of mourning for him before his last visit, though we knew nothing of it till about that time. Why he died, or of what complaint, or to what noblemen he bequeathed his four daughters in marriage, we have not heard.

I am glad that the Wildmans are going to give a ball, and hope you will not fail to benefit both yourself and me by laying out a few kisses in the purchase of a frank. I believe you are right in proposing to delay the cambric muslin, and I submit with a kind of voluntary reluctance.

Mr. Peter Debary has declined Deane curacy; he wishes to be settled near London. A foolish reason! as if Deane were not near London in comparison of Exeter or York. Take the whole world through, and he will find many more places at a greater distance from London than Deane than he will at a less. What does he think of Glencoe or Lake Katherine?

I feel rather indignant that any possible objection should be raised against so valuable a piece of preferment, so delightful a situation! – that Deane should not be universally allowed to be as near the metropolis as any other country villages. As this is the case, however, as Mr. Peter Debary has shown himself a Peter in the blackest sense of the word, we are obliged to look elsewhere for an heir; and my father has thought it a necessary compliment to James Digweed to offer the curacy to him, though without considering it as either a desirable or an eligible situation for him. Unless he is in love with Miss Lyford, I think he had better not be set-tled exactly in this neighbourhood; and unless he is very much in love with her indeed, he is not likely to think a salary of 50*l.* equal in value or ef-ficiency to one of 75*l.*

Were *you* indeed to be considered as one of the fixtures of the house! – but you were never actually erected in it either by Mr. Egerton Brydges or Mrs. Lloyd.

The Prices are not to have an house on Weyhill; for the present he has lodgings in Andover, and they are in view of a dwelling hereafter in Appleshaw, that village of wonderful elasticity, which stretches itself out for the reception of everybody who does not wish for a house on Speen Hill.

Martha and I dined yesterday at Deane to meet the Powletts and Tom Chute, which we did not fail to do. Mrs. Powlett was at once expensively and nakedly dressed; we have had the satisfaction of estimating her lace and her muslins; and she said too little to afford us much other amusement.

Mrs. John Lyford is so much pleased with the state of widowhood as to be going to put in for being a widow again; she is to marry a Mr. Fendall, a banker in Gloucester, a man of very good fortune, but considerably older than herself, and with three little children. Miss Lyford has never been here yet; she can come only for a day, and is not able to fix the day.

I fancy Mr. Holder will have the farm, and without being obliged to depend on the accommodating spirit of Mr. William Portal; he will probably have it for the remainder of my father's lease. This pleases us all much better than its falling into the hands of Mr. Harwood or Farmer Twitchen. Mr. Holder is to come in a day or two to talk to my father on the subject, and then John Bond's interest will not be forgotten.

I have had a letter to-day from Mrs. Cooke. Mrs. Laurel is going to be married to a Mr. Hinchman, a rich East Indian. I hope Mary will be satisfied with this proof of her cousin's existence and welfare, and cease to torment herself with the idea of his bones being bleaching in the sun on Wantage Downs.

Martha's visit is drawing towards its close, which we all four sincerely regret. The wedding day is to be celebrated on the 16th, because the 17th falls on Saturday; and a day or two before the 16th Mary will drive her sister to Ibthorp to find all the festivity she can in contriving for everybody's comfort, and being thwarted or teased by almost everybody's temper. Fulwar, Eliza, and Tom Chute are to be of the party. I know of nobody else. I was asked, but declined it.

Eliza has seen Lord Craven at Barton, and probably by this time at Kintbury, where he was expected for one day this week. She found his manners very pleasing indeed. The little flaw of having a mistress now living with him at Ashdown Park seems to be the only unpleasing circumstance about him. From

Ibthorp, Fulwar and Eliza are to return with James and Mary to Deane.

The Prices are *not* to have an house on Weyhill; for the present he has lodgings in Andover, and they are in view of a dwelling hereafter in Appleshaw, that village of wonderful elasticity, which stretches itself out for the reception of everybody who does not wish for a house on Speen Hill.

Pray give my love to George; tell him that I am very glad to hear he can skip so well already, and that I hope he will continue to send me word of his improvement in the art.

I think you judge very wisely in putting off your London visit, and I am mistaken if it be not put off for some time. You speak with such noble resignation of Mrs. Jordan and the Opera House, that it would be an insult to suppose consolation required; but to prevent you thinking with regret of this rupture of your engagement with Mr. Smithson, I must assure you that Henry suspects him to be a great miser.

Friday. – No answer from my aunt. She has no time for writing, I suppose, in the hurry of selling furniture, packing clothes, and preparing for their removal to Scarletts.

You are very kind in planning presents for me to make, and my mother has shown me exactly the same attention; but as I do not choose to have generosity dictated to me, I shall not resolve on giving my cabinet to Anna till the first thought of it has been my own.

Sidmouth is now talked of as our summer abode. Get all the information, therefore, about it that you can from Mrs. C. Cage.

My father's old ministers are already deserting him to pay their court to his son. The brown mare, which, as well as the black, was to devolve on James at our removal, has not had patience to wait for that, and has settled herself even now at Deane. The death of Hugh Capet, which, like that of Mr. Skipsey, though undesired, was not wholly unexpected, being purposely effected, has made the immediate possession of the mare very convenient, and everything else I suppose will be seized by degrees in the same manner. Martha and I work at the books every day.

Yours affectionately,

J. A.

Letter XXVII – 1800

Steventon: Wednesday (January 14).

Poor Miss Austen! It appears to me that I have rather oppressed you of late by the frequency of my letters. You had hoped not to hear from me again before Tuesday, but Sunday showed you with what a merciless sister you had to deal. I cannot recall the past, but you shall not hear from me quite so often in future.

Your letter to Mary was duly received before she left Dean with Martha yesterday morning, and it gives us great pleasure to know that the Chilham ball was so agreeable, and that you danced four dances with Mr. Kemble. Desirable, however, as the latter circumstance was, I cannot help wondering at its taking place. Why did you dance four dances with so stupid a man? Why not rather dance two of them with some elegant brother officer who was struck with your appearance as soon as you entered the room?

Martha left you her best love. She will write to you herself in a short time; but, trusting to my memory rather than her own, she has nevertheless desired me to ask you to purchase for her two bottles of Steele's lavender water when you are in town, provided you should go to the shop on your own account, otherwise you may be sure that she would not have you recollect the request.

James dined with us yesterday, wrote to Edward in the evening, filled three sides of paper, every line inclining too much towards the northeast, and the very first line of all scratched out, and this morning he joins his lady in the fields of Elysium and Ibthorp.

Last Friday was a very busy day with us. We were visited by Miss Lyford and Mr. Bayle. The latter began his operations in the house, but had only time to finish the four sitting-rooms; the rest is deferred till the spring is more advanced and the days longer. He took his paper of appraisement away with him, and therefore we only know the estimate he has made of one or two articles of furniture which my father particularly inquired into. I understand, however, that he was of opinion that the whole would amount to more than two hundred pounds, and it is not imagined that this will comprehend the brewhouse and many other, &c., &c.

Miss Lyford was very pleasant, and gave my mother such an account of the houses in Westgate Buildings, where Mrs. Lyford lodged four years ago, as made her think of a situation there with great pleasures but your opposition will be without difficulty decisive, and my father, in particular, who was very well inclined towards the Row before, has now ceased to think of it entirely. At present the environs of Laura Place seem to be his choice. His views on the subject are much advanced since I came home; he grows quite ambitious, and actually requires now a comfortable and a creditable-looking house.

On Saturday Miss Lyford went to her long home that is to say, it was a long way off – and soon afterwards a party of fine ladies issuing from a well-known commodious green vehicle, their heads full of Bantam cocks and Galinies, entered the house – Mrs. Heathcote, Mrs. Harwood, Mrs. James Austen, Miss Bigg, Miss Jane Blachford. Hardly a day passes in which we do not have some visitor or other: yesterday came Mrs. Bramstone, who is very sorry that she is to lose us, and afterwards Mr. Holder, who was shut up for an hour with my father and James in a most awful manner. John Bond est a lui.

Mr. Holder was perfectly willing to take him on exactly the same terms with my father, and John seems exceedingly well satisfied. The comfort of not changing his home is a very material one to him, and since such are his unnatural feelings, his belonging to Mr. Holder is the every thing needful; but otherwise there would have been a situation offering to him, which I had thought of with particular satisfaction, viz., under Harry Digweed, who, if John had quitted Cheesedown, would have been eager to engage him as superintendent at Steventon, would have kept a horse for him to ride about on, would probably have supplied him with a more permanent home, and I think would certainly have been a more desirable master altogether.

John and Corbett are not to have any concern with each other – there are to be two farms and two bailiffs. We are of opinion that it would be better in only one.

This morning brought my aunt's reply, and most thoroughly affectionate is its tenor. She thinks with the greatest pleasure of our being settled in Bath – it is an event which will attach her to the place more than anything else could do, &c., &c. She is, moreover, very urgent with my mother not to delay her visit in Paragon, if she should continue unwell, and even recommends her spending the whole winter with them. At present and for many days past my mother has been quite stout, and she wishes not to be obliged by any relapse to alter her arrangements.

Mr. and Mrs. Chamberlayne are in Bath, lodging at the Charitable Repository; I wish the scene may suggest to Mrs. C. the notion of selling her black beaver bonnet for the relief of the poor. Mrs. Welby has been singing duets with the Prince of Wales.

My father has got above 500 volumes to dispose of; I want James to take them at a venture at half a guinea a volume. The whole repairs of the parsonage at Deane, inside and out, coachbox, basket and dickey will not much exceed 100 *l.*

Have you seen that Major Byng, a nephew of Lord Torrington, is dead? That must be Edmund.

Friday. – I thank you for yours, though I should have been more grateful for it if it had not been charged *8d.* instead of *6d.,* which has given me the torment of writing to Mr. Lambould on the occasion. I am rather surprised at the revival of the London visit; but Mr. Doricourt has travelled – he knows best.

That James Digweed has refused Deane curacy I suppose he has told you himself, though probably the subject has never been mentioned between you. Mrs. Milles flatters herself falsely, it has never been Mrs. Rice's wish to have her son settled near herself; and there is now a hope entertained of her relenting in favour of Deane.

Mrs. Lefroy and her son-in-law were here yesterday; she tries not to be sanguine, but he was in excellent spirits. I rather wish they may have the curacy. It would be an amusement to Mary to superintend their household management, and abuse them for expense, especially as Mrs. L. means to advise them to put their washing out.

Yours affectionately,

J. A.

Letter XXVIII – 1800

Steventon: Wednesday (January 21).

Expect a most agreeable letter, for not being overburdened with subject (having nothing at all to say), I shall have no check to my genius from beginning to end. Well, and so Frank's letters has made you very happy, but you are afraid he would not have patience to stay for the "Haarlem," which you wish him to have done as being safer than the merchantman. Poor fellow! to wait from the middle of November to the end of December, and perhaps even longer, it must be sad work; especially in a place where the ink is so abominably pale. What a surprise to him it must have been on October 20, to be visited, collared, and thrust out of the "Petterell" by Captain Inglis. He kindly passes over the poignancy of his feelings in quitting his ship, his officers, and his men.

What a pity it is that he should not be in England at the time of this promotion, because he certainly would have had an appointment, so everybody says, and therefore it must be right for me to say it too. Had he been really here, the certainty of the appointment, I dare say, would not have been half so great, but as it could not be brought to the proof his absence will be always a lucky source of regret.

Eliza talks of having read in a newspaper that all the 1st lieutenants of the frigates whose captains were to be sent into line-of-battle ships were to be promoted to the rank of commanders. If it be true, Mr. Valentine may afford himself a fine Valentine's knot, and Charles may perhaps become 1st of the "Endymion," though I suppose Captain Durham is too likely to bring a villain with him under that denomination.

I dined at Deane yesterday, as I told you I should, and met the two Mr. Holders. We played at vingt-un, which, as Fulwar was unsuccessful, gave him an opportunity of exposing himself as usual.

Eliza says she is quite well, but she is thinner than when we saw her last, and not in very good looks. I suppose she has not recovered from the effects of her illness in December. She cuts her hair too short over her forehead, and does not wear her cap far enough upon her head; in spite of these many disadvantages, however, I can still admire her beauty. They all dine here to-day; much good may it do us all.

William and Tom are much as usual; Caroline is improved in her person; I think her now really a pretty child. She is still very shy, and does not talk much.

Fulwar goes next month into Gloucestershire, Leicestershire, and Warwickshire, and Eliza spends the time of his absence at Ibthorp and Deane; she hopes, therefore, to see you before it is long.

Lord Craven was prevented by company at home from paying his visit at Kintbury, but, as I told you before, Eliza is greatly pleased with him, and they seem likely to be on the most friendly terms.

Martha returns into this country next Tuesday, and then begins her two visits at Deane.

I expect to see Miss Bigg every day to fix the time for my going to Manydown; I think it will be next week, and I shall give you notice of it, if I can, that you may direct to me there.

The neighbourhood have quite recovered the death of Mrs. Rider; so much so, that I think they are rather rejoiced at it now; her things were so very dear! and Mrs. Rogers is to be all that is desirable. Not even death itself can fix the friendship of the world.

You are not to give yourself the trouble of going to Penlingtons when you are in town; my father is to settle the matter when he goes there himself; you are only to take special care of the bills of his in your hands, and I dare say will not be sorry to be excused the rest of the business.

Thursday. – Our party yesterday was very quietly pleasant. Today we all attack Ashe Park, and to-morrow I dine again at Deane. What an eventful week!

Eliza left me a message for you, which I have great pleasure in delivering: she will write to you and send you your money next Sunday. Mary has likewise a message: she will be much obliged to you if you can bring her the pattern of the jacket and trousers, or whatever it is that Elizabeth's boys wear when they are first put into breeches; so if you could bring her an old suit itself, she would be very glad, but that I suppose is hardly done.

I am happy to hear of Mrs. Knight's amendment, whatever might be her complaint.

The Wylmots being robbed must be an amusing thing to their acquaintance, and I hope it is as much their pleasure as it seems their avocation to be subjects of general entertainment.

I have a great mind not to acknowledge the receipt of your letter, which I have just had the pleasure of reading, because I am so ashamed to compare the sprawling lines of this with it. But if I say all that I have to say, I hope I have no reason to hang myself.

Caroline was only brought to bed on the 7th of this month, so that her recovery does seem pretty rapid. I have heard twice from Edward on the occasion, and his letters have each been exactly what they ought to be – cheerful and amusing. He dares not write *otherwise* to me, but perhaps he might be obliged to purge himself from the guilt of writing nonsense by filling his shoes with whole peas for a week afterwards. Mrs. G. has left him 100*l.*, his wife and son 500*l.* each.

I join with you in wishing for the environs of Laura Place, but do not venture to expect it. My mother hankers after the Square dreadfully, and it is but natural to suppose that my uncle will take *her* part. It would be very pleasant to be near Sydney Gardens; we might go into the labyrinth every day.

You need not endeavour to match my mother's morning calico; she does not mean to make it up any more.

Why did not J. D. make his proposals to you? I suppose he went to see the cathedral, that he might know how he should like to be married in it.

Fanny shall have the boarding-school, as soon as her papa gives me an opportunity of sending it; and I do not know whether I may not by that time have worked myself into so generous a fit as to give it to her forever.

We have a ball on Thursday too; I expect to go to it from Manydown. Do not be surprised, or imagine that Frank is come, if I write again soon; it will only be to say that I am going to M., and to answer your question about my gown.

Letter XXIX – 1800

Steventon: Sunday (January 25).

I have nothing to say about Manydown, but I write because you will expect to hear from me, and because if I waited another day or two, I hope your visit to Goodnestone would make my letter too late in its arrival. I dare say I shall be at M. in the course of this week, but as it is not certain you will direct to me at home.

I shall want two new coloured gowns for the summer, for my pink one will not do more than clear me from Steventon. I shall not trouble you, however, to get more than one of them, and that is to be a plain brown cambric muslin, for morning wear; the other, which is to be a very pretty yellow and white cloud, I mean to buy in Bath. Buy two brown ones, if you please, and both of a length, but one longer than the other – it is for a tall woman. Seven yards for my mother, seven yards and a half for me; a dark brown, but the kind of brown is left to your own choice, and I had rather they were different, as it will be always something to say, to dispute about which is the prettiest. They must be cambric muslin.

How do you like this cold weather? I hope you have all been earnestly praying for it as a salutary relief from the dreadful mild and unhealthy season preceding it, fancying yourself half putrified from the want of it, and that now you all draw into the fire, complain that you never felt such bitterness of cold before, that you are half starved, quite frozen, and wish the mild weather back again with all your hearts.

Your unfortunate sister was betrayed last Thursday into a situation of the utmost cruelty. I arrived at Ashe Park before the party from Deane, and was shut up in the drawing-room with Mr. Holder alone for ten minutes. I had some thoughts of insisting on the housekeeper or Mary Corbett being sent for, and nothing could prevail on me to move two steps from the door, on the lock of which I kept one hand constantly fixed. We met nobody but ourselves, played at *vingt-un* again, and were very cross.

On Friday I wound up my four days of dissipation by meeting William Digweed at Deane, and am pretty well, I thank you, after it. While I was there a sudden fall of snow rendered the roads impassable, and made my journey home in the little carriage much more easy and agreeable than my journey down.

Fulwar and Eliza left Deane yesterday. You will be glad to hear that Mary is going to keep another maid. I fancy Sally is too much of a servant to find time for everything, and Mary thinks Edward is not so much out of doors as he ought to be; there is therefore to be a girl in the nursery.

I would not give much for Mr. Price's chance of living at Deane; he builds his hope, I find, not upon anything that his mother has written, but upon the effect of what he has written himself. He must write a great deal better than those eyes indicate if he can persuade a perverse and narrow-minded woman to oblige those whom she does not love.

Your brother Edward makes very honourable mention of you, I assure you, in his letter to James, and seems quite sorry to part with you. It is a great comfort to me to think that my cares have not been thrown away, and that you are respected in the world. Perhaps you may be prevailed on to return with him and Elizabeth into Kent, when they leave us in April, and I rather suspect that your great wish of keeping yourself disengaged has been with that view. Do as you like; I have overcome my desire of your going to Bath with my mother and me. There is nothing which energy will not bring one to.

Edward Cooper is so kind as to want us all to come to Hamstall this summer, instead of going to the sea, but we are not so kind as to mean to do it. The summer after, if you please, Mr. Cooper, but for the present we greatly prefer the sea to all our relations.

I dare say you will spend a very pleasant three weeks in town. I hope you will see everything worthy of notice, from the Opera House to Henry's office in Cleveland Court; and I shall expect you to lay in a stock of intelligence that may procure me amusement for a twelvemonth to come. You will have a turkey from Steventon while you are there, and pray note down how many full courses of exquisite dishes M. Halavant converts it into.

I cannot write any closer. Neither my affection for you nor for letter-writing can stand out against a Kentish visit. For a three-months' absence I can be a very loving relation and a very excellent cor-respondent, but beyond that I degenerate into negligence and indifference.

I wish you a very pleasant ball on Thursday, and myself another, and Mary and Martha a third, but they will not have theirs till Friday, as they have a scheme for the Newbury Assembly.

Nanny's husband is decidedly against her quitting service in such times as these, and I believe would be very glad to have her continue with us. In some respects she would be a great comfort, and in some we should wish for a different sort of servant. The washing would be the greatest evil. Nothing is settled, however, at present with her, but I should think it would be as well for all parties if she could suit herself in the meanwhile somewhere nearer her husband and child than Bath. Mrs. H. Rice's place would be very likely to do for her. It is not many, as she is herself aware, that she is qualified for.

My mother has not been so well for many months as she is now.

Adieu.

Yours sincerely,

J. A.

Letter XXX – 1801

Paragon: Tuesday (May 5).

MY DEAR CASSANDRA,

I have the pleasure of writing from my *own* room up two pair of stairs, with everything very comfortable about me.

Our journey here was perfectly free from accident or event; we changed horses at the end of every stage, and paid at almost every turn-pike. We had charming weather, hardly any dust, and were exceedingly agreeable, as we did not speak above once in three miles.

Between Luggershall and Everley we made our grand meal, and then with admiring astonishment perceived in what a magnificent manner our support had been provided for. We could not with the utmost exertion consume above the twentieth part of the beef. The cucumber will, I believe, be a very acceptable present, as my uncle talks of having inquired the price of one lately, when he was told a shilling.

We had a very neat chaise from Devizes; it looked almost as well as a gentleman's, at least as a very shabby gentleman's; in spite of this advantage, however, we were above three hours coming from thence to Paragon, and it was half after seven by your clocks before we entered the house.

Frank, whose black head was in waiting in the Hall window, received us very kindly; and his master and mistress did not show less cordiality. They both look very well, though my aunt has a violent cough. We drank tea as soon as we arrived, and so ends the account of our journey, which my mother bore without any fatigue.

How do you do to-day? I hope you improve in sleeping – I think you must, because *I* fall off; I have been awake ever since five and sooner; I fancy I had too much clothes over me; I thought I *should* by the feel of them before I went to bed, but I had not courage to alter them. I am warmer here without any fire than I have been lately with an excellent one.

Well, and so the good news is confirmed, and Martha triumphs. My uncle and aunt seemed quite surprised that you and my father were not coming sooner.

I have given the soap and the basket, and each have been kindly received. *One* thing only among all our concerns has not arrived in safety: when I got into the chaise at Devizes I discovered that your drawing ruler was broke in two; it is just at the top where the cross-piece is fastened on. I beg pardon.

There is to be only one more ball – next Monday is the day. The Chamberlaynes are still here. I begin to think better of Mrs. C–, and upon recollection believe she has rather a long chin than otherwise, as she remembers us in Gloucestershire when we were very charming young women.

The first view of Bath in fine weather does not answer my expectations; I think I see more distinctly through rain. The sun was got behind everything, and the appearance of the place from the top of Kingsdown was all vapour, shadow, smoke, and confusion.

I fancy we are to have a house in Seymour Street, or thereabouts. My uncle and aunt both like the situation. I was glad to hear the former talk of all the houses in New King Street as too small; it was my own idea of them. I had not been two minutes in the dining-room before he questioned me with all his accustomary eager interest about Frank and Charles, their views and intentions. I did my best to give information.

I am not without hopes of tempting Mrs. Lloyd to settle in Bath; meat is only 8*d.* per pound, butter 12*d.*, and cheese 9 1/2 *d.* You must carefully conceal from her, however, the exorbitant price of fish: a salmon has been sold at 2 *s.* 9*d.* per pound the whole fish. The Duchess of York's removal is expected to make that article more reasonable – and till it really appears so, say nothing about salmon.

Tuesday night. – When my uncle went to take his second glass of water I walked with him, and in our morning's circuit we looked at two houses in Green Park Buildings, one of which pleased me very well. We walked all over it except into the garret; the dining-room is of a comfortable size, just as large as you like to fancy it; the second room about 14 ft. square. The apartment over the drawing-room pleased me particularly, because it is divided into two, the smaller one a very nice-sized dressing-room, which upon occasion might admit a bed. The aspect is south-east. The only doubt is about the dampness of the offices, of which there were symptoms.

Wednesday. – Mrs. Mussell has got my gown, and I will endeavour to explain what her intentions are. It is to be a round gown, with a jacket and a frock front, like Cath. Bigg's, to open at the side. The jacket is all in one with the body, and comes as far as the pocket-holes – about half a quarter of a yard deep, I suppose, all the way round, cut off straight at the corners with a broad hem. No fulness appears either in the body or the flap; the back is quite plain in this form

and the sides equally so. The front is sloped round to the bosom and drawn in, and there is to be a frill of the same to put on occasionally when all one's handkerchiefs are dirty – which frill *must* fall back. She is to put two breadths and a-half in the tail, and no gores – gores not being so much worn as they were. There is nothing new in the sleeves: they are to be plain, with a fulness of the same falling down and gathered up underneath, just like some of Martha's, or perhaps a little longer. Low in the back behind, and a belt of the same. I can think of nothing more, though I am afraid of not being particular enough.

My mother has ordered a new bonnet, and so have I; both white strip, trimmed with white ribbon. I find my straw bonnet looking very much like other people's, and quite as smart. Bonnets of cambric muslin on the plan of Lady Bridges' are a good deal worn, and some of them are very pretty; but I shall defer one of that sort till your arrival. Bath is getting so very empty that I am not afraid of doing too little. Black gauze cloaks are worn as much as anything. I shall write again in a day or two. Best love.

Yours ever,

J. A.

We have had Mrs. Lillingstone and the Chamberlaynes to call on us. My mother was very much struck with the odd looks of the two latter; *I* have only *seen her.* Mrs. Busby drinks tea and plays at cribbage here to-morrow; and on Friday, I believe, we go to the Chamberlaynes'. Last night we walked by the Canal.

Letter XXXI – 1801

Paragon: Tuesday (May 12).

MY DEAR CASSANDRA,

My mother has heard from Mary, and I have heard from Frank; we therefore know something now of our concerns in distant quarters; and you, I hope, by some means or other are equally instructed, for I do not feel inclined to transcribe the letter of either.

You know from Elizabeth, I dare say, that my father and Frank, deferring their visit to Kippington on account of Mr. M. Austen's[4] absence, are to be at Godmersham to-day; and James, I dare say, has been over to Ibthorp by this time to inquire particularly after Mrs. Lloyd's health, and forestall whatever intelligence of the sale I might attempt to give; sixty-one guineas and a-half for the three cows gives one some support under the blow of only eleven guineas for the tables. Eight for my pianoforte is about what I really expected to get; I am more anxious to know the amount of my books, especially as they are said to have sold well.

---

4 Francis Motley-Austen, who bought Kippington from Sir Chas. Farnaby.

My adventures since I wrote last have not been numerous; but such as they are, they are much at your service.

We met not a creature at Mrs. Lillingstone's, and yet were not so very stupid, as I expected, which I attribute to my wearing my new bonnet and being in good looks. On Sunday we went to church twice, and after evening service walked a little in the Crescent fields, but found it too cold to stay long.

Yesterday morning we looked into a house in Seymour Street, which there is reason to suppose will soon be empty; and as we are assured from many quarters that no inconvenience from the river is felt in those buildings, we are at liberty to fix in them if we can. But this house was not inviting; the largest room downstairs was not much more than fourteen feet square, with a western aspect.

In the evening, I hope you honoured my toilette and ball with a thought; I dressed myself as well as I could, and had all my finery much admired at home. By nine o'clock my uncle, aunt, and I entered the rooms, and linked Miss Winstone on to us. Before tea it was rather a dull affair; but then the before tea did not last long, for there was only one dance, danced by four couple. Think of four couple, surrounded by about an hundred people, dancing in the Upper Rooms at Bath.

After tea we *cheered up;* the breaking up of private parties sent some scores more to the ball, and though it was shockingly and inhumanly thin for this place, there were people enough, I suppose, to have made five or six very pretty Basingstoke assemblies.

I then got Mr. Evelyn to talk to, and Miss T. to look at; and I am proud to say that though repeatedly assured that another in the same party was the *She,* I fixed upon the right one from the first. A resemblance to Mrs. L. was my guide. She is not so pretty as I expected; her face has the same defect of baldness as her sisters, and her features not so handsome; she was highly rouged, and looked rather quietly and contentedly silly than anything else.

Mrs. B. and two young women were of the same party, except when Mrs. B. thought herself obliged to leave them to run round the room after her drunken husband. His avoidance, and her pursuit, with the probable intoxication of both, was an amusing scene.

The Evelyns returned our visit on Saturday; we were very happy to meet, and all that; they are going to-morrow into Gloucestershire to the Dolphins for ten days. Our acquaintance, Mr. Woodward, is just married to a Miss Rowe, a young lady rich in money and music.

I thank you for your Sunday's letter, it is very long and very agreeable. I fancy you know many more particulars of our sale than we do; we have heard the price of nothing but the cows, bacon, hay, hops, tables, and my father's chest of drawers and study table. Mary is more minute in her account of their own gains than in ours; probably being better informed in them. I will attend to Mrs. Lloyd's commission and to her abhorrence of musk when I write again.

I have bestowed three calls of inquiry on the Mapletons, and I fancy very beneficial ones to Marianne, as I am always told that she is better. I have not seen any of them. Her complaint is a bilious fever.

I like my dark gown very much indeed, colour, make, and everything; I mean to have my new white one made up now, in case we should go to the rooms again next Monday, which is to be really the last time.

Wednesday. – Another stupid party last night; perhaps if larger they might be less intolerable, but here there were only just enough to make one card-table, with six people to look on and talk nonsense to each other. Lady Fust, Mrs. Busby, and a Mrs. Owen sat down with my uncle to whist, within five minutes after the three old *Toughs* came in, and there they sat, with only the exchange of Adm. Stanhope for my uncle, till their chairs were announced.

I cannot anyhow continue to find people agreeable; I respect Mrs. Chamberlayne for doing her hair well, but cannot feel a more tender sentiment. Miss Langley is like any other short girl, with a broad nose and wide mouth, fashionable dress and exposed bosom. Adm. Stanhope is a gentleman-like man, but then his legs are too short and his tail too long. Mrs. Stanhope could not come; I fancy she had a private appointment with Mr. Chamberlayne, whom I wished to see more than all the rest.

My uncle has quite got the better of his lameness, or at least his walking with a stick is the only remains of it. He and I are soon to take the long-planned walk to the Cassoon, and on Friday we are all to accompany Mrs. Chamberlayne and Miss Langley to Weston.

My mother had a letter yesterday from my father; it seems as if the W. Kent Scheme was entirely given up. He talks of spending a fortnight at Godmersham, and then returning to town.

Yours ever,

> Yours ever,
> J. A.

Excepting a slight cold, my mother is very well; she has been quite free from feverish or bilious complaints since her arrival here.

Letter XXXII – 1801

Paragon: Thursday (May 21).

MY DEAR CASSANDRA,

To make long sentences upon unpleasant subjects is very odious, and I shall therefore get rid of the one now uppermost in my thoughts as soon as possible.

Our views on G. P. Buildings seem all at an end; the observation of the damps still remaining in the offices of an house which has been only vacated a week, with reports of discontented families and putrid fevers, has given the *coup de grace.* We have now nothing in view. When you arrive, we will at least have the pleasure of examining some of these putrefying houses again; they are so very desirable in size and situation, that there is some satisfaction in spending ten minutes within them.

I will now answer the inquiries in your last letter. I cannot learn any other explanation of the coolness between my aunt and Miss Bond than that the latter felt herself slighted by the former's leaving Bath last summer without calling to see her before she went. It seems the oddest kind of quarrel in the world. They never visit, but I believe they speak very civilly if they meet. My uncle and Miss Bond certainly do.

The four boxes of lozenges, at 1s. 1 1/2 *d.* per box, amount, as I was told, to 4*s.* 6*d.,* and as the sum was so trifling, I thought it better to pay at once than contest the matter.

I have just heard from Frank. My father's plans are now fixed; you will see him at Kintbury on Friday, and, unless inconvenient to you, we are to see you both here on Monday, the 1st of June. Frank has an invitation to Milgate, which I believe he means to accept.

Our party at Ly. Fust's was made up of the same set of people that you have already heard of – the Winstones, Mrs. Chamberlayne, Mrs. Busby, Mrs. Franklyn, and Mrs. Maria Somerville; yet I think it was not quite so stupid as the two preceding parties here.

The friendship between Mrs. Chamberlayne and me which you predicted has already taken place, for we shake hands whenever we meet. Our grand walk to Weston was again fixed for yesterday, and was accomplished in a very striking manner. Every one of the party declined it under some pretence or other except our two selves, and we had therefore a *tête-à-tête,* but *that* we should equally have had after the first two yards had half the inhabitants of Bath set off with us.

It would have amused you to see our progress. We went up by Sion Hill, and returned across the fields. In climbing a hill Mrs. Chamberlayne is very capital; I could with difficulty keep pace with her, yet would not flinch for the world. On plain ground I was quite her equal. And so we posted away under a fine hot sun, *she* without any parasol or any shade to her hat, stopping for nothing, and crossing the church-yard at Weston with as much expedition as if we were afraid of being buried alive. After seeing what she is equal to, I cannot help feeling a regard for her. As to agreeableness, she is much like other people.

Yesterday evening we had a short call from two of the Miss Arnolds, who came from Chippenham on business. They are very civil, and not too genteel, and upon hearing that we wanted a house, recom-mended one at Chippenham.

This morning we have been visited again by Mrs. and Miss Holder; they wanted us to fix an evening for drinking tea with them, but my mother's still remain-ing cold allows her to decline everything of the kind. As *I* had a separate invitation, however, I believe I shall go some afternoon. It is the fashion to think them both very detestable, but they are so civil, and their gowns look so white and so nice (which, by the bye, my aunt thinks an absurd pretension in this place), that I cannot utterly abhor them, especially as Miss Holder owns that she has no taste for music.

After they left us I went with my mother to help look at some houses in New King Street, towards which she felt some kind of inclination, but their size has now satisfied her. They were smaller than I expected to find them; one in particular out of the two was quite monstrously little; the best of the sitting-rooms not so large as the little parlour at Steventon, and the second room in every floor about capacious enough to admit a very small single bed.

We are to have a tiny party here to-night. I hate tiny parties, they force one into constant exertion. Miss Edwards and her father, Mrs. Busby and her nephew, Mr. Maitland, and Mrs. Lillingstone are to be the whole; and I am prevented from setting my black cap at Mr. Maitland by his having a wife and ten children.

My aunt has a very bad cough – do not forget to have heard about *that* when you come – and I think she is deafer than ever. My mother's cold disordered her for some days, but she seems now very well. Her resolution as to remaining here begins to give way a little; she will not like being left behind, and will be glad to compound matters with her enraged family.

You will be sorry to hear that Marianne Mapleton's disorder has ended fatally. She was believed out of danger on Sunday, but a sudden relapse carried her off the next day. So affectionate a family must suffer severely; and many a girl on early death has been praised into an angel, I believe, on slighter pretensions to beauty, sense, and merit than Marianne.

Mr. Bent seems *bent* upon being very detestable, for he values the books at only 70*l.* The whole world is in a conspiracy to enrich one part of our family at the expense of another. Ten shillings for Dodsley's *Poems,* however, please me to the quick, and I do not care how often I sell them for as much. When Mrs. Bramston has read them through I will sell them again. I suppose you can hear nothing of your magnesia?

Friday. – You have a nice day for your journey, in whatever way it is to be performed, whether in the Debary's coach or on your own twenty toes.

When you have made Martha's bonnet you must make her a cloak of the same sort of materials; they are very much worn here, in different forms – many of them just like her black silk spencer, with a trimming round the armholes instead of sleeves, some are long before, and some long all round, like C. Bigg's. Our party last night supplied me with no new idea for my letter.

Yours ever,

J. A.

The Pickfords are in Bath, and have called here. She is the most elegant-looking woman I have seen since I left Martha; *he* is as raffish in his appearance as I would wish every disciple of Godwin to be. We drink tea to-night with Mrs. Busby. I scandalised her nephew cruelly; he has but three children instead of ten.

Best love to everybody.

Letter XXXIII – 1805

Godmersham Park: Saturday (August 24).

MY DEAR CASSANDRA,

How do you do; and how is Harriot's cold? I hope you are at this time sitting down to answer these questions.

Our visit to Eastwell was very agreeable; I found Ly. Gordon's manners as pleasing as they had been described, and saw nothing to dislike in Sir Janison, excepting once or twice a sort of sneer at Mrs. Anne Finch. He was just getting into talk with Elizabeth as the carriage was ordered, but during the first part of the visit he said very little.

Your going with Harriot was highly approved of by everyone, and only too much applauded as an act of virtue on your part. I said all I could to lessen your merit. The Mrs. Finches were afraid you would find Goodnestone very dull; I wished when I heard them say so that they could have heard Mr. E. Bridges' solicitude on the subject, and have known all the amusements that were planned to prevent it.

They were very civil to me, as they always are; fortune was also very civil to me in placing Mr. E. Hatton by me at dinner. I have discovered that Lady Elizabeth, for a woman of her age and situation, has astonishingly little to say for herself, and that Miss Hatton has not much more. Her eloquence lies in her fingers; they were most fluently harmonious.

George is a fine boy, and well behaved, but Daniel chiefly delighted me; the good humour of his countenance is quite bewitching. After tea we had a cribbage-table, and he and I won two rubbers of his brother and Mrs. Mary. Mr. Brett was the only person there, besides our two families.

It was considerably past eleven before we were at home, and I was so tired as to feel no envy of those who were at Ly. Yates' ball. My good wishes for its being a pleasant one were, I hope, successful.

Yesterday was a very quiet day with us; my noisiest efforts were writing to Frank, and playing at battledore and shuttlecock with William; he and I have practised together two mornings, and improve a little; we have frequently kept it up three times, and once or twice six.

The two Edwards went to Canterbury in the chaise, and found Mrs. Knight, as you found her, I suppose, the day before, cheerful but weak. Fanny was met walking with Miss Sharp and Miss Milles, the happiest being in the world; she sent a private message to her mamma implying as much. "Tell mamma that I am quite Palmerstone!" If little Lizzy used the same language she would, I dare say, send the same message from Goodnestone.

In the evening we took a quiet walk round the farm, with George and Henry to animate us by their races and merriment. Little Edward is by no means better, and his papa and mamma have determined to consult Dr. Wilmot. Unless he recovers his strength beyond what is now probable, his brothers will return to school without him, and he will be of the party to Worthing. If sea-bathing should be recommended he will be left there with us, but this is not thought likely to happen.

I have been used very ill this morning: I have received a letter from Frank which I ought to have had when Elizabeth and Henry had theirs, and which in its way from Albany to Godmersham has been to Dover and Steventon. It was finished on ye 16th, and tells what theirs told before as to his present situation; he is in a great hurry to be married, and I have encouraged him in it, in the letter which ought to have been an answer to his. He must think it very strange that I do not acknowledge the receipt of his, when I speak of those of the same date to Eliz. and Henry; and to add to my injuries, I forgot to number mine on the outside.

I have found your white mittens; they were folded up within my clean nightcap, and send their duty to you.

Elizabeth has this moment proposed a scheme which will be very much for my pleasure if equally convenient to the other party; it is that when you return on Monday, I should take your place at Goodnestone for a few days. Harriot cannot be insincere, let her try for it ever so much, and therefore I defy her to accept this self-invitation of mine, unless it be really what perfectly suits her. As there is no time for an answer, I shall go in the carriage on Monday, and can return with you, if my going on to Goodnestone is at all inconvenient.

The Knatchbulls come on Wednesday to dinner, and stay only till Friday morning at the latest. Frank's letter to me is the only one that you or I have received since Thursday.

Mr. Hall walked off this morning to Ospringe, with no inconsiderable booty. He charged Elizabeth 5s. for every time of dressing her hair, and 5s. for every lesson to Sace, allowing nothing for the pleasures of his visit here, for meat, drink, and lodging, the benefit of country air, and the charms of Mrs. Salkeld's and Mrs. Sace's society.[5] Towards me he was as

---

5 The Godmersham housekeeper and lady's-maid.

considerate as I had hoped for from my relationship to you, charging me only 2*s.* 6*d.* for cutting my hair, though it was as thoroughly dressed after being cut for Eastwell as it had been for the Ashford assembly. He certainly respects either our youth or our poverty.

My writing to you to-day prevents Elizabeth writing to Harriot, for which evil I implore the latter's pardon. Give my best love to her, and kind remembrance to her brothers.

Yours very affectionately,

J. A.

You are desired to bring back with you Henry's picture of Rowling for the Misses Finches.

As I find, on looking into my affairs, that instead of being very rich I am likely to be very poor, I cannot afford more than ten shillings for Sackree; but as we are to meet in Canterbury I need not have mentioned this. It is as well, however, to prepare you for the sight of a sister sunk in poverty, that it may not overcome your spirits.

Elizabeth hopes you will not be later here on Monday than five o'clock, on Lizzy's account.

We have heard nothing from Henry since he went. Daniel told us that he went from Ospringe in one of the coaches.

Letter XXXIV – 1805

Goodnestone Farm: Tuesday (August 27).

MY DEAR CASSANDRA,

We had a very pleasant drive from Canterbury, and reached this place about half-past four, which seemed to bid fair for a punctual dinner at five; but scenes of great agitation awaited us, and there was much to be endured and done before we could sit down to table.

Harriot found a letter from Louisa Hatton, desiring to know if she and her brothers were to be at the ball at Deal on Friday, and saying that the Eastwell family had some idea of going to it, and were to make use of Rowling if they did; and while I was dressing she came to me with another letter in her hand, in great perplexity. It was from Captain Woodford, containing a message from Lady Forbes, which he had intended to deliver in person, but had been prevented from doing.

The offer of a ticket for this grand ball, with an invitation to come to her house at Dover before and after it, was Lady Forbes' message. Harriot was at first very little inclined, or rather totally disinclined, to profit by her ladyship's attention; but at length, after many debates, she was persuaded by me and herself together to accept the ticket. The offer of dressing and sleeping at Dover she determined on Marianne's account to decline, and her plan is to be conveyed by Lady Elizabeth Hatton.

I hope their going is by this time certain, and will be soon known to be so. I think Miss H. would not have written such a letter if she had not been all but sure of it, and a little more. I am anxious on the subject, from the fear of being in the way if they do not come to give Harriot a conveyance. I proposed and pressed being sent home on Thursday, to prevent the possibility of being in the wrong place, but Harriot would not hear of it.

There is no chance of tickets for the Mr. Bridgeses, as no gentlemen but of the garrison are invited.

With a civil note to be fabricated to Lady F., and an answer written to Miss H., you will easily believe that we could not begin dinner till six. We were agreeably surprised by Edward Bridges' company to it. He had been, strange to tell, too late for the cricket match, too late at least to play himself, and, not being asked to dine with the players, came home. It is impossible to do justice to the hospitality of his attentions towards me; he made a point of ordering toasted cheese for supper entirely on my account.

We had a very agreeable evening, and here I am before breakfast writing to you, having got up between six and seven; Lady Brydges' room must be good for early rising.

Mr. Sankey was here last night, and found his patient better, but I have heard from a maid-servant that she has had but an indifferent night.

Tell Elizabeth that I did not give her letter to Harriot till we were in the carriage, when she received it with great delight, and could read it in comfort.

As you have been here so lately, I need not particularly describe the house or style of living, in which all seems for use and comfort; nor need I be diffuse on the state of Lady Brydges' bookcase and corner-shelves upstairs. What a treat to my mother to arrange them!

Harriot is constrained to give up all hope of seeing Edward here to fetch me, as I soon recollected that Mr. and Mrs. Charles Knatchbull's being at Godmersham on Thursday must put it out of the question.

Had I waited till after breakfast, the chief of all this might have been spared. The Duke of Gloucester's death sets my heart at ease, though it will cause some dozens to ache. Harriot's is not among the number of the last; she is very well pleased to be spared the trouble of preparation. She joins me in best love to you all, and will write to Elizabeth soon. I shall be very glad to hear from you, that we may know how you all are, especially the two Edwards.

I have asked Sophie if she has anything to say to Lizzy in acknowledgment of the little bird, and her message is that, with her love, she is very glad Lizzy sent it. She volunteers, moreover, her love to little Marianne, with the promise of bringing her a doll the next time she goes to Godmersham.

John is just come from Ramsgate, and brings a good account of the people there. He and his brother, you know, dine at Nackington; we are to dine at four, that we may walk afterwards. As it is now two, and Harriot has letters to write, we shall probably not get out before.

Yours affectionately,

J. A.

Three o'clock. – Harriot is just come from Marianne, and thinks her upon the whole better. The sickness has not returned, and a headache is at present her chief complaint, which Henry attributes to the sick-ness.

Letter XXXV – 1805

Goodnestone Farm: Friday (August 30).

MY DEAR CASSANDRA,

The purport of Elizabeth's letter makes me anxious to hear more of what we are to do and not to do, and I hope you will be able to write me your own plans and opinions to-morrow. The journey to London is a point of the first expediency, and I am glad it is resolved on, though it seems likely to injure our Worthing scheme. I expect that we are to be at Sandling, while they are in town.

It gives us great pleasure to hear of little Edward's being better, and we imagine, from his mamma's expressions, that he is expected to be well enough to return to school with his brothers.

Marianne was equal to seeing me two days ago; we sat with her for a couple of hours before dinner, and the same yesterday, when she was evidently better, more equal to conversation, and more cheerful than during our first visit. She received me very kindly, and expressed her egret in not having been able to see you.

She is, of course, altered since we saw her in October, 1794. Eleven years could not pass away even in health without making some change, but in her case it is wonderful that the change should be so little. I have not seen her to advantage, as I understand she has frequently a nice colour, and her complexion has not yet recovered from the effects of her late illness. Her face is grown longer and thinner, and her features more marked, and the likeness which I remember to have always seen between her and Catherine Bigg is stronger than ever, and so striking is the voice and manner of speaking that I seem to be really hearing Catherine, and once or twice have been on the point of calling Harriot "Alethea." She is very pleasant, cheerful, and interested in everything about her, and at the same time shows a thoughtful, considerate, and decided turn of mind.

Edward Bridges dined at home yesterday; the day before he was at St. Albans; to-day he goes to Broome, and to-morrow to Mr. Hallett's, which latter engagement has had some weight in my resolution of not leaving Harriot till Monday.

We have walked to Rowling on each of the two last days after dinner, and very great was my pleasure in going over the house and grounds. We have also found time to visit all the principal walks of this place, except the walk round the top of the park, which we shall accomplish probably to-day.

Next week seems likely to be an unpleasant one to this family on the matter of game. The evil intentions of the Guards are certain, and the gentlemen of the neighbourhood seem unwilling to come forward in any decided or early support of their rights. Edward Bridges has been trying to arouse their spirits, but without success. Mr. Hammond, under the influence of daughters and an expected ball, declares he will do nothing.

Harriot hopes my brother will not mortify her by resisting all her plans and refusing all her invitations; she has never yet been successful with him in any, but she trusts he will now make her all the amends in his power by coming on Monday. She thanks Elizabeth for her letter, and you may be sure is not less solicitous than myself for her going to town.

Pray say everything kind for us to Miss Sharpe, who could not regret the shortness of our meeting in Canterbury more than we did. I hope she returned to Godmersham as much pleased with Mrs. Knight's beauty and Miss Milles' judicious remarks as those ladies respectively were with hers. You must send me word that you have heard from Miss Irvine.

I had almost forgot to thank you for your letter. I am glad you recommended "Gisborne," for having begun, I am pleased with it, and I had quite determined not to read it.

I suppose everybody will be black for the D. of G. Must we buy lace, or will ribbon do?

We shall not be at Worthing so soon as we have been used to talk of, shall we? This will be no evil to us, and we are sure of my mother and Martha being happy together. Do not forget to write to Charles. As I am to return so soon, we shall not send the pincush-ions.

Yours affectionately,

J. A.

You continue, I suppose, taking hartshorn, and I hope with good effect.

Letter XXXVI – 1807

Southampton: Wednesday (January 7).

MY DEAR CASSANDRA,

You were mistaken in supposing I should expect your letter on Sunday; I had no idea of hearing from you before Tuesday, and my pleasure yesterday was therefore unhurt by any previous disappointment. I thank you for writing so much; you must really have sent me the value of two letters in one. We are extremely glad to hear that Elizabeth is so much better, and hope you will be sensible of still further amendment in her when you return from Canterbury.

Of your visit there I must now speak "incessantly"; it surprises, but pleases me more, and I consider it as a very just and honourable distinction of you, and not less to the credit of Mrs. Knight. I have no doubt of your spending your time with her most pleasantly in quiet and rational conversation, and am so far from thinking her expectations of you will be deceived, that my only fear is of your being so agreeable, so much to her taste, as to make her wish to keep you with her for ever. If that should be the case, we must remove to Canterbury, which I should not like so well as Southampton.

When you receive this, our guests will be all gone or going; and I shall be left to the comfortable disposal of my time, to ease of mind from the torments of rice puddings and apple dumplings, and probably to regret that I did not take more pains to please them all.

Mrs. J. Austen has asked me to return with her to Steventon; I need not give my answer; and she has invited my mother to spend there the time of Mrs. F. A.'s confinement, which she seems half inclined to do.

A few days ago I had a letter from Miss Irvine, and as I was in her debt, you will guess it to be a remonstrance, not a very severe one, however; the first page is in her usual retrospective, jealous, inconsistent style, but the remainder is chatty and harmless. She supposes my silence may have proceeded from resentment of her not having written to inquire particularly after my hooping cough, &c. She is a funny one.

I have answered her letter, and have endeavoured to give something like the truth with as little incivility as I could, by placing my silence to the want of subject in the very quiet way in which we live. Phebe has repented, and stays. I have also written to Charles, and I answered Miss Buller's letter by return of post, as I intended to tell you in my last.

Two or three things I recollected when it was too late, that I might have told you; one is, that the Welbys have lost their eldest son by a putrid fever at Eton, and another that Tom Chute is going to settle in Norfolk.

You have scarcely ever mentioned Lizzy since your being at Godmersham. I hope it is not because she is altered for the worse.

I cannot yet satisfy Fanny as to Mrs. Foote's baby's name, and I must not encourage her to expect a good one, as Captain Foote is a professed adversary to all but the plainest; he likes only Mary, Elizabeth, Anne, &c. Our best chance is of "Caroline," which in compliment to a sister seems the only exception.

He dined with us on Friday, and I fear will not soon venture again, for the strength of our dinner was a boiled leg of mutton, underdone even for James; and Captain Foote has a particular dislike to underdone mutton, but he was so good-humoured and pleasant that I did not much mind his being starved. He gives us all the most cordial invitation to his house in the country, saying just what the Williams ought to say to make us welcome. Of them we have seen nothing since you left us, and we hear that they are just gone to Bath again, to be out of the way of further alterations at Brooklands.

Mrs. F. A. has had a very agreeable letter from Mrs. Dickson, who was delighted with the purse, and desires her not to provide herself with a christening dress, which is exactly what her young correspondent wanted; and she means to defer making any of the caps as long as she can, in hope of having Mrs. D.'s present in time to be serviceable as a pattern. She desires me to tell you that the gowns were cut out before your letter arrived, but that they are long enough for Caroline. The *Beds,* as I believe they are called, have fallen to Frank's share to continue, and of course are cut out to admiration.

"Alphonsine" did not do. We were disgusted in twenty pages, as, independent of a bad translation, it has indelicacies which disgrace a pen hitherto so pure; and we changed it for the "Female Quixotte," which now makes our evening amusement; to me a very high one, as I find the work quite equal to what I remembered it. Mrs. F. A., to whom it is new, enjoys it as one could wish; the other Mary, I believe, has little pleasure from that or any other book.

My mother does not seem at all more disappointed than ourselves at the termination of the family treaty; she thinks less of *that* just now than of the comfortable state of her own finances, which she finds on closing her year's accounts beyond her expectation, as she begins the new year with a balance of 30*l.* in her favour; and when she has written her answer to my aunt, which you know always hangs a little upon her mind, will be above the world entirely. You will have a great deal of unreserved discourse with Mrs. K., I dare say, upon this subject, as well as upon many other of our family matters. Abuse everybody but me.

Thursday. – We expected James yesterday, but he did not come; if he comes at all now, his visit will be a very short one, as he must return to-morrow, that Ajax and the chair may be sent to Winchester on Saturday. Caroline's new pelisse depended upon her mother's being able or not to come so far in the chair; how the guinea that will be saved by the same means of return is to be spent I know not. Mrs. J. A. does not talk much of poverty now, though she has no hope of my brother's being able to buy another horse *next* summer.

Their scheme against Warwickshire continues, but I doubt the family's being at Stoneleigh so early as James says he must go, which is May.

My mother is afraid I have not been explicit enough on the subject of her wealth; she began 1806 with 68*l.*, she begins 1807 with 99*l.*, and this after 32*l.* purchase of stock. Frank, too, has been settling his accounts and making calculations, and each party feels quite equal to our present expenses; but much increase of house rent would not do for either. Frank limits himself, I believe, to four hundred a year.

You will be surprised to hear that Jelmy is not yet come back; we have heard nothing of her since her reaching Itchingswell, and can only suppose that she must be detained by illness in somebody or other, and that she has been each day expecting to be able to come on the morrow. I am glad I did not know beforehand that she was to be absent during the whole or almost the whole of our friends being with us, for though the inconvenience has not been nothing, I should have feared still more. Our dinners have certainly suffered not a little by having only Molly's head and Molly's hands to conduct them; she fries better than she did, but not like Jenny.

We did *not* take our walk on Friday, it was too dirty, nor have we yet done it; we may perhaps do something like it to-day, as after seeing Frank skate, which he hopes to do in the meadows by the beech, we are to treat ourselves with a passage over the ferry. It is one of the pleasantest frosts I ever knew, so very quiet. I hope it will last some time longer for Frank's sake, who is quite anxious to get some skating; he tried yesterday, but it would not do.

Our acquaintance increase too fast. He was recognized lately by Admiral Bertie, and a few days since arrived the Admiral and his daughter Catherine to wait upon us. There was nothing to like or dislike in either. To the Berties are to be added the Lances, with whose cards we have been endowed, and whose visit Frank and I returned yesterday. They live about a mile and three-quarters from S. to the right of the new road to Portsmouth, and I believe their house is one of those which are to be seen almost anywhere among the woods on the other side of the Itchen. It is a handsome building, stands high, and in a very beautiful situation.

We found only Mrs. Lance at home, and whether she boasts any offspring besides a grand pianoforte did not appear. She was civil and chatty enough, and offered to introduce us to some acquaintance in Southampton, which we gratefully declined.

I suppose they must be acting by the orders of Mr. Lance of Netherton in this civility, as there seems no other reason for their coming near us. They will not come often, I dare say. They live in a handsome style and are rich, and she seemed to like to be rich, and we gave her to understand that we were far from being so; she will soon feel therefore that we are not worth her acquaintance.

You must have heard from Martha by this time. We have had no accounts of Kintbury since her letter to me.

Mrs. F. A. has had one fainting fit lately; it came on as usual after eating a hearty dinner, but did not last long.

I can recollect nothing more to say. When my letter is gone, I suppose I shall.

Yours affectionately,

J. A.

I have just asked Caroline if I should send her love to her godmama, to which she answered "Yes."

Letter XXXVII – 1807

Southampton: February 8.

MY DEAREST CASSANDRA,

My expectation of having nothing to say to you after the conclusion of my last seems nearer truth than I thought it would be, for I feel to have but little. I need not, therefore, be above acknowledging the receipt of yours this morning, or of replying to every part of it which is capable of an answer, and you may accordingly prepare for my ringing the changes of the glads and sorrys for the rest of the page.

Unluckily, however, I see nothing to be glad of, unless I make it a matter of joy that Mrs. Wylmot has another son, and that Lord Lucan has taken a mistress, both of which events are, of course, joyful to the actors; but to be sorry I find many occasions. The first is, that your return is to be delayed, and whether I ever get beyond the first is doubtful. It is no use to lament. I never heard that even Queen Mary's lamentation did her any good, and I could not, therefore, expect benefit from mine. We are all sorry, and now that subject is exhausted.

I heard from Martha yesterday. She spends this week with the Harwoods, goes afterwards with James and

Mary for a few days to see Peter Debary and two of his sisters at Eversley, the living of which he has gained on the death of Sir R. Cope, and means to be here on the 24th, which will be Tuesday fortnight. I shall be truly glad if she can keep to her day, but dare not depend on it, and am so apprehensive of farther detention, that, if nothing else occurs to create it, I cannot help thinking she will marry Peter Debary.

It vexed me that I could not get any fish for Kintbury while their family was large, but so it was; and till last Tuesday I could procure none. I then sent them four pair of small soles, and should be glad to be certain of their arriving in good time, but I have heard nothing about them since, and had rather hear nothing than evil. They cost six shillings, and as they travelled in a basket which came from Kintbury a few days before with poultry, &c., I insist upon treating you with the booking, *whatever it may be.* You are only eighteen pence in my debt.

Mrs. E. Leigh did not make the slightest allusion to my uncle's business, as I remember telling you at the time, but you shall have it as often as you like. My mother wrote to her a week ago.

Martha's rug is just finished, and looks well, though not quite so well as I had hoped. I see no fault in the border, but the middle is dingy. My mother desires me to say that she will knit one for you as soon as you return to choose the colours and pattern.

I am sorry I have affronted you on the subject of Mr. Moore, but I do not mean ever to like him; and as to pitying a young woman merely because she cannot live in two places at the same time, and at once enjoy the comforts of being married and single, I shall not attempt it, even for Harriet. You see I have a spirit as well as yourself.

Frank and Mary cannot at all approve of your not being at home in time to help them in their finishing purchases, and desire me to say that, if you are not, they will be as spiteful as possible, and choose everything in the style most likely to vex you – knives that will not cut, glasses that will not hold, a sofa without a seat, and a book-case without shelves.

Our garden is putting in order by a man who bears a remarkably good character, has a very fine com-plexion, and asks something less than the first. The shrubs which border the gravel walk, he says, are only sweetbriar and roses, and the latter of an indifferent sort; we mean to get a few of a better kind, therefore, and at my own particular desire he procures us some syringas. I could not do without a syringa, for the sake of Cowper's line. We talk also of a laburnum. The border under the terrace wall is clearing away to receive currants and gooseberry bushes, and a spot is found very proper for rasp-berries.

The alterations and improvements within doors, too, advance very properly, and the offices will be made very convenient indeed. Our dressing table is constructing on the spot, out of a large kitchen table belonging to the house, for doing which we have the permission of Mr. Husket, Lord Lansdown's painter – domestic painter, I should call him, for he lives in the castle. Domestic chaplains have given way to this more necessary office, and I suppose whenever the walls want no touching up he is employed about my lady's face.

The morning was so wet that I was afraid we should not be able to see our little visitor, but Frank, who alone could go to church, called for her after service, and she is now talking away at my side and examining the treasures of my writing-desk drawers – very happy, I believe. Not at all shy, of course. Her name is Catherine, and her sister's Caroline. She is something like her brother, and as short for her age, but not so well-looking.

What is become of all the shyness in the world? Moral as well as natural diseases disappear in the progress of time, and new ones take their place. Shyness and the sweating sickness have given way to confidence and paralytic complaints.

I am sorry to hear of Mrs. Whitfield's increasing illness, and of poor Marianne Bridges having suffered so much; these are some of my sorrows; and that Mrs. Deedes is to have another child I suppose I may lament.

The death of Mrs. W. K. we had seen. I had no idea that anybody liked her, and therefore felt nothing for any survivor, but I am now feeling away on her husband's account, and think he had better marry Miss Sharpe.

I have this instant made my present, and have the pleasure of seeing it smiled over with genuine satisfaction. I am sure I may, on this occasion, call Kitty Foote, as Hastings did H. Egerton, my "very valuable friend."

Evening. – Our little visitor has just left us, and left us highly pleased with her; she is a nice, natural, open-hearted, affectionate girl, with all the ready civility which one sees in the best children in the present day; so unlike anything that I was myself at her age, that I am often all astonishment and shame. Half her time was spent at spillikins, which I consider as a very valuable part of our household furniture, and as not the least important benefaction from the family of Knight to that of Austen.

But I must tell you a story. Mary has for some time had notice from Mrs. Dickson of the intended arrival of a certain Miss Fowler in this place. Miss F. is an intimate friend of Mrs. D., and a good deal known as such to Mary. On Thursday last she called here while we were out. Mary found, on our return, her card with only her name on it, and she had left word that she would call again. The particularity of this made us talk, and, among other conjectures, Frank said in joke, "I dare say she is staying with the Pearsons." The connection of the names struck Mary, and she immediately recollected Miss Fowler's having been very intimate with persons so called, and, upon putting everything together, we have scarcely a doubt of her being actually staying with the only family in the place whom we cannot visit.

What a *contretemps!* in the language of France. What an unluckiness! in that of Madame Duval. The black gentleman has certainly employed one of his menial imps to bring about this complete, though trifling, mischief. Miss F. has never called again, but we are in daily expectation of it. Miss P. has, of course, given her a proper understanding of the business. It is evident that Miss F. did not expect or wish to have the visit returned, and Frank is quite as much on his guard for his wife as we could desire for her sake or our own.

We shall rejoice in being so near Winchester when Edward belongs to it, and can never have our spare bed filled more to our satisfaction than by him. Does he leave Eltham at Easter?

We are reading *"Clarentine,"* and are surprised to find how foolish it is. I remember liking it much less on a second reading than at the first, and it does not bear a third at all. It is full of unnatural conduct and forced difficulties, without striking merit of any kind.

Miss Harrison is going into Devonshire, to attend Mrs. Dusantoy, as usual. Miss J. is married to young Mr. G., and is to be very unhappy. He swears, drinks, is cross, jealous, selfish, and brutal. The match makes her family miserable, and has occasioned *his* being disinherited.

The Browns are added to our list of acquaintance. He commands the Sea Fencibles here, under Sir Thomas, and was introduced at his own desire by the latter when we saw him last week. As yet the gentlemen only have visited, as Mrs. B. is ill, but she is a nice-looking woman, and wears one of the prettiest straw bonnets in the place.

Monday. – The garret beds are made, and ours will be finished to-day. I had hoped it would be finished on Saturday, but neither Mrs. Hall nor Jenny was able to give help enough for that, and I have as yet done very little, and Mary nothing at all. This week we shall do more, and I should like to have all the five beds completed by the end of it. There will then be the window curtains, sofa-cover, and a carpet to be altered.

I should not be surprised if we were to be visited by James again this week; he gave us reason to expect him soon, and if they go to Eversley he cannot come next week.

There, I flatter myself I have constructed you a smartish letter, considering my want of materials, but, like my dear Dr. Johnson, I believe I have dealt more in notions than facts.

I hope your cough is gone and that you are otherwise well, and remain, with love,

Yours affectionately,

J. A.

Letter XXXVIII – 1807

Southampton: Friday (February 20).

MY DEAR CASSANDRA,

We have at last heard something of Mr. Austen's will. It is believed at Tunbridge that he has left everything after the death of his widow to Mr. M. Austen's third son John; and, as the said John was the only one of the family who attended the funeral, it seems likely to be true. Such ill-gotten wealth can never prosper.

I really have very little to say *this* week, and do not feel as if I should spread that little into the show of much. I am inclined for short sentences.

Mary will be obliged to you to take notice how often Elizabeth nurses her baby in the course of twenty-four hours, how often it is fed, and with what; you need not trouble yourself to *write* the result of your observations, your return will be early enough for the communication of them. You are recommended to bring away some flower seeds from Godmersham, particularly mignonette seed.

My mother has heard this morning from Paragon. My aunt talks much of the violent colds prevailing in Bath, from which my uncle has suffered ever since their return, and she has herself a cough much worse than any she ever had before, subject as she has always been to bad ones. She writes in good humour and cheerful spirits, however. The negotiation between them and Adlestrop so happily over, indeed, what can have power to vex her materially?

Elliston, she tells us, has just succeeded to a considerable fortune on the death of an uncle. I would not have it enough to take *him* from the stage; *she* should quit her business, and live with him in London.

We could not pay our visit on Monday; the weather altered just too soon, and we have since had a touch of almost everything in the weather way; two of the severest frosts since the winter began, preceded by rain, hail, and snow. Now we are smiling again.

Saturday. – I have received your letter, but I suppose you do not expect me to be gratified by its contents. I confess myself much disappointed by this repeated delay of your return, for though I had pretty well given up all idea of your being with us before our removal, I felt sure that March would not pass quite away without bringing you. Before April comes, of course, something else will occur to detain you. But as *you* are happy, all this is selfishness, of which here is enough for one page.

Pray tell Lizzy that if I had imagined her teeth to be really out, I should have said before what I say now, that it was a very unlucky fall indeed, that I am afraid it must have given her a great deal of pain, and that I dare say her mouth looks very comical.

I am obliged to Fanny for the list of Mrs. Coleman's children, whose names I had not, however, quite forgot; the new one I am sure will be Caroline. I have got Mr. Bowen's recipe for you; it came in my aunt's letter.

You must have had more snow at Godmersham than we had here; on Wednesday morning there was a thin covering of it over the fields and roofs of the houses, but I do not think there was any left the next day. Everybody used to Southampton says that snow never lies more than twenty-four hours near it, and, from what we have observed ourselves, it is very true.

Frank's going into Kent depends, of course, upon his being unemployed; but as the First Lord, after promising Lord Moira that Captain A. should have the first good frigate that was vacant, has since given away two or three fine ones, he has no particular reason to expect an appointment now. *He,* however, has scarcely spoken about the Kentish journey. I have my information chiefly from her, and she considers her own going thither as more certain if he should be at sea than if not.

Frank has got a very bad cough, for an Austen; but it does not disable him from making very nice fringe for the drawing-room curtains.

Mrs. Day has now got the carpet in hand, and Monday I hope will be the last day of her employment here. A fortnight afterwards she is to be called again from the shades of her red-checked bed in an alley near the end of the High Street, to clean the new house and air the bedding.

We hear that we are envied our house by many people, and that the garden is the best in the town. There will be green baize enough for Martha's room and ours, not to cover them, but to lie over the part where it is most wanted, under the dressing table. Mary is to have a piece of carpeting for the same purpose; my mother says *she* does not want any, and it may certainly be better done without in her rooms than in Martha's and ours, from the difference of their aspect.

I recommend Mrs. Grant's letters, as a present to the latter; what they are about, and how many volumes they form, I do not know, having never heard of them but from Miss Irvine, who speaks of them as a new and much-admired work, and as one which has pleased her highly. I have inquired for the book here, but find it quite unknown.

I believe *I* put five breadths of linsey also into my flounce; I know I found it wanted more than I had expected, and that I should have been distressed if I had not bought more than I believed myself to need for the sake of the even measure, on which we think so differently. A light morning gown will be a very necessary purchase for you, and I wish you a pretty one. I shall buy such things whenever I am tempted, but as yet there is nothing of the sort to be seen.

We are reading Barretti's other book, and find him dreadfully abusive of poor Mr. Sharpe. I can no longer take his part against you, as I did nine years ago.

Sunday. – This post has brought our Martha's own assurance of her coming on Tuesday evening, which nothing is now to prevent except William should send her word that there is no *remedy* on that day. Her letter was put into the post at Basingstoke on their return from Eversley, where she says they have spent their time very pleasantly. She does not own herself in any danger of being tempted back again, however, and as she signs by her maiden name, we are at least to suppose her not married yet.

They must have had a cold visit, but as she found it agreeable I suppose there was no want of blankets, and we may trust to her sister's taking care that her love of many should be known. She sends me no particulars, having time only to write the needful.

I wish you a pleasant party to-morrow, and not more than you like of Miss Hatton's neck. Lady B. must have been a shameless woman if she named H. Hales as within her husband's reach. It is a piece of impertinence, indeed, in a woman to pretend to fix on anyone, as if she supposed it could be only ask and have. A widower with three children has no right to look higher than his daughter's governess.

I am forced to be abusive for want of subject, having really nothing to say. When Martha comes she will supply me with matter; I shall have to tell you how she likes the house, and what she thinks of Mary.

You must be very cold to-day at Godmersham. We are cold here. I expect a severe March, a wet April, and a sharp May. And with this prophecy I must conclude.

My love to everybody.

Yours affectionately,

J. AUSTEN.

Letter XXXIX – 1808

Godmersham: Wednesday (June 15).

MY DEAR CASSANDRA,

Where shall I begin? Which of all my important nothings shall I tell you first? At half after seven yesterday morning Henry saw us into our own carriage, and we drove away from the Bath Hotel; which, by-the-bye, had been found most uncomfortable quarters – very dirty, very noisy, and very ill-provided. James began his journey by the coach at five. Our first eight miles were hot; Deptford Hill brought to my mind our hot journey into Kent fourteen years ago; but after Blackheath we suffered nothing, and as the day advanced it grew quite cool. At Dartford, which we reached within the two hours and three-quarters, we went to the Bull, the same inn at which we breakfasted in that said journey, and on the present occasion had about the same bad butter.

At half-past ten we were again off, and, travelling on without any adventure reached Sittingbourne by three. Daniel was watching for us at the door of the George, and I was acknowledged very kindly by Mr. and Mrs. Marshall, to the latter of whom I devoted my conversation, while Mary went out to buy some gloves. A few minutes, of course, did for Sittingbourne; and so off we drove, drove, drove, and by six o'clock were at Godmersham.

Our two brothers were walking before the house as we approached, as natural as life. Fanny and Lizzy met us in the Hall with a great deal of pleasant joy; we went for a few minutes into the breakfast parlour, and then proceeded to our rooms. Mary has the Hall chamber. I am in the Yellow room – very literally – for I am writing in it at this moment. It seems odd to me to have such a great place all to myself, and to be at Godmersham without you is also odd.

You are wished for, I assure you: Fanny, who came to me as soon as she had seen her Aunt James to her room, and stayed while I dressed, was as energetic as usual in her longings for you. She is grown both in height and size since last year, but not immoderately, looks very well, and seems as to conduct and manner just what she was and what one could wish her to continue.

Elizabeth, who was dressing when we arrived, came to me for a minute attended by Marianne, Charles, and Louisa, and, you will not doubt, gave me a very affectionate welcome. That I had received such from Edward also I need not mention; but I do, you see, because it is a pleasure. I never saw him look in better health, and Fanny says he is perfectly well.

I cannot praise Elizabeth's looks, but they are probably affected by a cold. Her little namesake has gained in beauty in the last three years, though not all that Marianne has lost. Charles is not quite so lovely as he was. Louisa is much as I expected, and Cassandra I find handsomer than I expected, though at present disguised by such a violent breaking-out that she does not come down after dinner. She has charming eyes and a nice open countenance, and seems likely to be very lovable. Her size is magnificent.

I was agreeably surprised to find Louisa Bridges still here. She looks remarkably well (legacies are very wholesome diet), and is just what she always was. John is at Sandling. You may fancy our dinner party therefore; Fanny, of course, belonging to it, and little Edward, for that day. He was almost too happy, his happiness at least made him too talkative.

It has struck ten; I must go to breakfast.

Since breakfast I have had a *tête-à-tête* with Edward in his room; he wanted to know James's plans and mine, and from what his own now are I think it already nearly certain that I shall return when they do, though not with them. Edward will be going about the same time to Alton, where he has business with Mr. Trimmer, and where he means his son should join him; and I shall probably be his companion to that place, and get on afterwards somehow or other.

I should have preferred a rather longer stay here certainly, but there is no prospect of any later conveyance for me, as he does not mean to accompany Edward on his return to Winchester, from a very natural unwillingness to leave Elizabeth at that time. I shall at any rate be glad not to be obliged to be an incumbrance on those who have brought me here, for, as James has no horse, I must feel in their carriage that I am taking his place. We were rather crowded yesterday, though it does not become me to say so, as I and my boa were of the party, and it is not to be supposed but that a child of three years of age was fidgety.

I need scarcely beg you to keep all this to yourself, lest it should get round by Anna's means. She is very kindly inquired after by her friends here, who all regret her not coming with her father and mother.

I left Henry, I hope, free from his tiresome complaint, in other respects well, and thinking with great pleasure of Cheltenham and Stoneleigh.

The brewery scheme is quite at an end: at a meeting of the subscribers last week it was by general, and I believe very hearty, consent dissolved.

The country is very beautiful. I saw as much as ever to admire in my yesterday's journey.

Thursday. – I am glad to find that Anna was pleased with going to Southampton, and hope with all my heart that the visit may be satisfactory to everybody. Tell her that she will hear in a few days from her mamma, who would have written to her now but for this letter.

Yesterday passed quite *à la* Godmersham: the gentlemen rode about Edward's farm, and returned in time to saunter along Bentigh with us; and after dinner we visited the Temple Plantations, which, to be sure, is a Chevalier Bayard of a plantation. James and Mary are much struck with the beauty of the place. To-day the spirit of the thing is kept up by the two brothers being gone to Canterbury in the chair.

I cannot discover, even through Fanny, that her mother is fatigued by her attendance on the children. I have, of course, tendered my services, and when Louisa is gone, who sometimes hears the little girls read, will try to be accepted in her stead. She will not be here many days longer. The Moores are partly expected to dine here to-morrow or Saturday.

I feel rather languid and solitary – perhaps because I have a cold; but three years ago we were more animated with you and Harriot and Miss Sharpe. We shall improve, I dare say, as we go on.

I have not yet told you how the new carriage is liked – very well, very much indeed, except the lining, which does look rather shabby.

I hear a very bad account of Mrs. Whitefield; a very good one of Mrs. Knight, who goes to Broadstairs next month. Miss Sharpe is going with Miss Bailey to Tenby. The Widow Kennet succeeds to the post of laundress.

Would you believe it my trunk is come already; and, what completes the wondrous happiness, nothing is damaged. I unpacked it all before I went to bed last night, and when I went down to breakfast this morning presented the rug, which was received most gratefully, and met with universal admiration. My frock is also given, and kindly accepted.

Friday. – I have received your letter, and I think it gives me nothing to be sorry for but Mary's cold, which I hope is by this time better. Her approbation of her child's hat makes me very happy. Mrs. J. A. bought one at Gayleard's for Caroline, of the same shape, but brown and with a feather.

I hope Huxham is a comfort to you; I am glad you are taking it. I shall probably have an opportunity of giving Harriot your message tomorrow; she does not come here, they have not a day to spare, but Louisa and I are to go to her in the morning. I send your thanks to Eliza by this post in a letter to Henry.

Lady Catherine is Lord Portmore's daughter. I have read Mr. Jefferson's case to Edward, and he desires to have his name set down for a guinea and his wife's for another; but does not wish for more than one copy of the work. Your account of Anna gives me pleasure. Tell her, with my love, that I like her for liking the quay. Mrs. J. A. seems rather surprised at the Maitlands drinking tea with you, but that does not prevent my approving it. I hope you had not a disagreeable evening with Miss Austen and her niece. You know how interesting the purchase of a sponge-cake is to me.

I am now just returned from Eggerton; Louisa and I walked together and found Miss Maria at home. Her sister we met on our way back. *She* had been to pay her compliments to Mrs. Inman, whose chaise was seen to cross the park while we were at dinner yesterday.

I told Sackree that you desired to be remembered to her, which pleased her; and she sends her duty, and wishes you to know that she has been into the great world. She went on to town after taking William to Eltham, and, as well as myself, saw the ladies go to

Court on the 4th. She had the advantage indeed of me in being in the Palace.

Louisa is not so handsome as I expected, but she is not quite well. Edward and Caroline seem very happy here; he has nice playfellows in Lizzy and Charles. They and their attendant have the boys' attic. Anna will not be surprised that the cutting off her hair is very much regretted by several of the party in this house; I am tolerably reconciled to it by considering that two or three years may restore it again.

You are very important with your Captain Bulmore and Hotel Master, and I trust, if your trouble overbalances your dignity on the occasion, it will be amply repaid by Mrs. Craven's approbation, and a pleasant scheme to see her.

Mrs. Cooke has written to my brother James to invite him and his wife to Bookham in their way back, which, as I learn through Edward's means, they are not disinclined to accept, but that my being with them would render it impracticable, the nature of the road affording no conveyance to James. I shall therefore make them easy on that head as soon as I can.

I have a great deal of love to give from everybody.

Yours most affectionately,

JANE.

My mother will be glad to be assured that the size of the rug does perfectly well. It is not to be used till winter.

Letter XL – 1808

Godmersham: Thursday (June 20).

MY DEAR CASSANDRA,

I will first talk of my visit to Canterbury, as Mr. J. A.'s letter to Anna cannot have given you every particular of it which you are likely to wish for. I had a most affectionate welcome from Harriot, and was happy to see her looking almost as well as ever. She walked with me to call on Mrs. Brydges, when Elizabeth and Louisa went to Mrs. Milles'. Mrs. B. was dressing, and could not see us, and we proceeded to the White Friars, where Mrs. B. was alone in her drawing room, as gentle, and kind, and friendly as usual. She inquired after everybody, especially my mother and yourself. We were with her a quarter of an hour before Elizabeth and Louisa, hot from Mrs. Baskerville's shop, walked in; they were soon followed by the carriage, and another five minutes brought Mr. Moore himself, just returned from his morning ride.

Well, and what do I think of Mr. Moore? will not pretend in one meeting to *dislike* him, whatever Mary may say, but I can honestly assure her that I saw nothing in him to admire. His manners, as you have always said, are gentleman-like, but by no means winning. He made one formal inquiry after you.

I saw their little girl, and very small and very pretty she is. Her features are as delicate as Mary Jane's, with nice dark eyes; and if she had Mary Jane's fine colour she would be quite complete. Harriot's fondness for her seems just what is amiable and natural, and not foolish. I saw Caroline also, and thought her very plain.

Edward's plan for Hampshire does not vary; he only improves it with the kind intention of taking me on to Southampton, and spending one whole day with you; and, if it is found practicable, Edward, jun., will be added to our party for that one day also, which is to be Sunday, the 10th of July. I hope you may have beds for them. We are to begin our journey on the 8th, and reach you late on the 9th.

This morning brought me a letter from Mrs. Knight, containing the usual fee, and all the usual kindness. She asks me to spend a day or two with her this week, to meet Mrs. C. Knatchbull, who, with her husband, comes to the White Friars to-day, and I believe I shall go. I have consulted Edward, and think it will be arranged for Mrs. J. A.'s going with me one morning, my staying the night, and Edward's driving me home the next evening. Her very agreeable present will make my circumstances quite easy. I shall reserve half for my pelisse. I hope by this early return I am sure of seeing Catherine and Alethea; and I propose that, either with or without them, you and I and Martha shall have a snug fortnight while my mother is at Steventon.

We go on very well here. Mary finds the children less troublesome than she expected, and, independent of them, there is certainly not much to try the patience or hurt the spirits at Godmersham. I initiated her yesterday into the mysteries of Inmanism. The poor old lady is as thin and cheerful as ever, and very thankful for a new acquaintance. I had called on her before with Elizabeth and Louisa.

I find John Bridges grown very old and black, but his manners are not altered; he is very pleasing, and talks of Hampshire with great admiration.

Pray let Anna have the pleasure of knowing that she is remembered with kindness, both by Mrs. Cooke and Miss Sharpe. Her manners must be very much worsted by your description of them, but I hope they will improve by this visit.

Mrs. Knight finished her letter with,

> "Give my best love to Cassandra when you write to her."

I shall like spending a day at the White Friars very much.

We breakfasted in the library this morning for the first time, and most of the party have been complaining all day of the heat; but Louisa and I feel alike as to weather, and are cool and comfortable.

Wednesday. – The Moores came yesterday in their curricle, between one and two o'clock, and immediately after the noonshine which succeeded their arrival a party set off for Buckwell, to see the pond dragged – Mr. Moore, James, Edward, and James; Edward on horseback, John Bridges driving Mary in his gig. The rest of us remained quietly and comfortably at home.

We had a very pleasant dinner, at the lower end of the table at least; the merriment was chiefly between Edward, Louisa, Harriot, and myself. Mr. Moore did not talk so much as I expected, and I understand from Fanny that I did not see him at all as he is in general. Our being strangers made him so much more silent and quiet. Had I had no reason for observing what he said and did, I should scarcely have thought about him. His manners to her want tenderness, and he was a little violent at last about the impossibility of her going to Eastwell. I cannot see any unhappiness in her, however, and as to kind-heartedness, &c., she is quite unaltered. Mary was disappointed in *her* beauty, and thought *him* very disagreeable; James admires *her,* and finds *him* conversable and pleasant.

I sent my answer by them to Mrs. Knight, my double acceptance of her note and her invitation, which I wrote without much effort, for I was rich, and the rich are always respectable, whatever be their style of writing.

I am to meet Harriot at dinner to-morrow. It is one of the audit days, and Mr. M. dines with the Dean, who is just come to Canterbury. On Tuesday there is to be a family meeting at Mrs. C. Milles's: Lady Bridges and Louisa from Goodnestone, the Moores, and a party from this house – Elizabeth, John Bridges, and myself. It will give me pleasure to see Lady B.; she is now quite well. Louisa goes home on Friday, and John with her, but he returns the next day. These are our engagements; make the most of them.

Mr. Waller is dead, I see. I cannot grieve about it, nor, perhaps, can his widow very much. Edward began cutting sanfoin on Saturday, and, I hope, is likely to have favourable weather. The crop is good.

There has been a cold and sore-throat prevailing very much in this house lately; the children have almost all been ill with it, and we were afraid Lizzy was going to be very ill one day. She had specks and a great deal of fever. It went off, however, and they are all pretty well now.

I want to hear of your gathering strawberries; we have had them three times here. I suppose you have been obliged to have in some white wine, and must visit the store closet a little oftener than when you were quite by yourselves.

One begins really to expect the St. Albans now, and I wish she may come before Henry goes to Cheltenham, it will be so much more convenient to him. He will be very glad if Frank can come to him in London, as his own time is likely to be very precious, but does not depend on it. I shall not forget Charles next week.

So much did I write before breakfast, and now, to my agreeable surprise, I have to acknowledge another letter from you. I had not the least notion of hearing before to-morrow, and heard of Russell's being about to pass the windows without any anxiety. You are very amiable and very clever to write such long letters; every page of yours has more lines than this, and every line more words than the average of mine. I am quite ashamed; but you have certainly more little events than we have. Mr. Lyford supplies you with a great deal of interesting matter (matter intellectual, not physical), but I have nothing to say of Mr. Scudamore.[6]

---

6 The doctor who attended the Godmersham family. He lived at Wye.

And now, that is such a sad, stupid attempt at wit about matter that nobody can smile at it, and I am quite out of heart. I am sick of myself and my bad pens. I have no other complaint, however; my languor is entirely removed.

Ought I to be very much pleased with *"Marmion"*? As yet I am not. James reads it aloud in the evening – the short evening, beginning at about 10, and broken by supper.

Happy Mrs. Harrison and Miss Austen! You seem to be always calling on them. I am glad your various civilities have turned out so well, and most heartily wish you success and pleasure in your present engagement. I shall think of you to-night as at Netley, and to-morrow too, that I may be quite sure of being right, and therefore I guess you will not go to Netley at all.

This is a sad story about Mrs. P. I should not have suspected such a thing. She stayed the Sacrament, I remember, the last time that you and I did. A hint of it, with initials, was in yesterday's "Courier," and Mr. Moore guessed it to be Lord S., believing there was no other Viscount S. in the peerage, and so it proved, Lord Viscount S. not being there.

Yes, I enjoy my apartment very much, and always spend two or three hours in it after breakfast. The change from Brompton quarters to these is material as to space. I catch myself going on to the hall chamber now and then.

Little Caroline looks very plain among her cousins; and though she is not so headstrong or humoursome as they are, I do not think her at all more engaging. Her brother is to go with us to Canterbury to-morrow, and Fanny completes the party. I fancy Mrs. K. feels less interest in that branch of the family than any other. I dare say she will do her *duty,* however, by the boy. His Uncle Edward talks nonsense to him delightfully; more than he can always understand. The two Morrises are come to dine and spend the day with him.

Mary wishes my mother to buy whatever she thinks necessary for Anna's shifts, and hopes to see her at Steventon soon after the 9th of July, if that time is as convenient to my mother as any other. I have hardly done justice to what she means on the subject, as her intention is that my mother should come at whatever time she likes best. They will be at home on the 9th.

I always come in for a morning visit from Crundale, and Mr. and Mrs. Filmer have just given me my due. He and I talked away gaily of Southampton, the Harrisons, Wallers, &c.

Fanny sends her best love to you all, and will write to Anna very soon.

Yours very affectionately,

JANE.

I want some news from Paragon.

I am almost sorry that Rose Hill Cottage should be so near suiting us, as it does not quite.

Letter XLI – 1808

Godmersham: Sunday (June 26).

MY DEAR CASSANDRA,

I am very much obliged to you for writing to me on Thursday, and very glad that I owe the pleasure of hearing from you again so soon to such an agreeable cause; but you will not be surprised, nor perhaps so angry as I should be, to find that Frank's history has reached me before in a letter from Henry. We are all very happy to hear of his health and safety; he wants nothing but a good prize to be a perfect character.

This scheme to the island is an admirable thing for his wife; she will not feel the delay of his return in such variety. How very kind of Mrs. Craven to ask her! I think I quite understand the whole island arrangements, and shall be very ready to perform my part in them. I hope my mother will go, and I trust it is certain that there will be Martha's bed for Edward when he brings me home. What can you do with Anna? for her bed will probably be wanted for young Edward. His father writes to Dr. Goddard to-day to ask leave, and we have the pupil's authority for thinking it will be granted.

I have been so kindly pressed to stay longer here, in consequence of an offer of Henry's to take me back some time in September, that, not being able to detail all my objections to such a plan, I have felt myself obliged to give Edward and Elizabeth one private reason for my wishing to be at home in July. They feel the strength of it and say no more, and one can rely on their secrecy. After this I hope we shall not be disappointed of our friend's visit; my honour as well as my affection will be concerned in it.

Elizabeth has a very sweet scheme of our accompanying Edward into Kent next Christmas. A legacy might make it very feasible – a legacy is our sovereign good. In the meanwhile, let me remember that I have now some money to spare, and that I wish to have my name put down as a subscriber to Mr. Jefferson's works. My last letter was closed before it occurred to me how possible, how right, and how gratifying such a measure would be.

Your account of your visitors' good journey, voyage, and satisfaction in everything gave me the greatest pleasure. They have nice weather for their introduction to the island, and I hope, with such a disposition to be pleased, their general enjoyment is as certain as it will be just. Anna's being interested in the embarkation shows a taste that one values. Mary Jane's delight in the water is quite ridiculous. Elizabeth supposes Mrs. Hall will account for it by the child's knowledge of her father's being at sea.

And now I believe I have made all the needful replies and communications, and may disport myself as I can on my Canterbury visit.

It was a very agreeable visit. There was everything to make it so – kindness, conversation, variety, without care or cost. Mr. Knatchbull, from Provender, was at the W. Friars when we arrived, and stayed dinner, which, with Harriot, who came, as you may suppose, in a great hurry, ten minutes after the time, made our number six. Mr. K. went away early; Mr. Moore succeeded him, and we sat quietly working and talking till 10, when he ordered his wife away, and we adjourned to the dressing-room to eat our tart and jelly. Mr. M. was not unagreeable, though nothing seemed to go right with him. He is a sensible man and tells a story well.

Mrs. C. Knatchbull and I breakfasted *tête-à-tête* the next day, for her husband was gone to Mr. Toke's, and Mrs. Knight had a sad headache which kept her in bed. She had had too much company the day before. After my coming, which was not till past two, she had Mrs. Milles, of Nackington, a Mrs. and Miss Gregory, and Charles Graham; and she told me it had been so all the morning.

Very soon after breakfast on Friday, Mrs. C. K., who is just what we have always seen her, went with me to Mrs. Brydges, and Mrs. Moore's, paid some other visits while I remained with the latter, and we finished with Mrs. C. Milles, who luckily was not at home, and whose new house is a very convenient short cut from the Oaks to the W. Friars.

We found Mrs. Knight up and better; but early as it was – only 12 o'clock – we had scarcely taken off our bonnets before company came – Ly. Knatchbull and her mother; and after them succeeded Mrs. White, Mrs. Hughes and her two children, Mr. Moore, Harriot and Louisa, and John Bridges, with such short intervals between any as to make it a matter of wonder to me that Mrs. K. and I should ever have been ten minutes alone or have had any leisure for comfortable talk, yet we had time to say a little of everything. Edward came to dinner, and at 8 o'clock he and I got into the chair, and the pleasures of my visit concluded with a delightful drive home.

Mrs. and Miss Brydges seemed very glad to see me. The poor old lady looks much as she did three years ago, and was very particular in her inquiries after my mother. And from her and from the Knatchbulls I have all manner of kind compliments to give you both.

As Fanny writes to Anna by this post I had intended to keep my letter for another day, but, recollecting that I must keep it two, I have resolved rather to finish and send it now. The two letters will not interfere, I dare say; on the contrary, they may throw light on each other.

Mary begins to fancy, because she has received no message on the subject, that Anna does not mean to answer her letter, but it must be for the pleasure of fancying it. I think Elizabeth better and looking better than when we came.

Yesterday I introduced James to Mrs. Inman; in the evening John Bridges returned from Goodnestone, and this morning, before we had left the breakfast table, we had a visit from Mr. Whitfield, whose object, I imagine, was principally to thank my eldest brother for his assistance. Poor man! he has now a little intermission of his excessive solicitude on his wife's account, as she is rather better. James does duty at Godmersham to-day.

The Knatchbulls had intended coming here next week, but the rent-day makes it impossible for them to be received, and I do not think there will be any spare time afterwards. They return into Somersetshire by way of Sussex and Hants, and are to be at Fareham and, perhaps, may be in Southampton, on which possibility I said all that I thought right, and, if they are in the place, Mrs. K. has promised to call in Castle Square; it will be about the end of July. She seems to have a prospect, however, of being in that county again in the spring for a longer period, and will spend a day with us if she is.

You and I need not tell each other how glad we shall be to receive attention from, or pay it to anyone connected with, Mrs. Knight. I cannot help regretting that now, when I feel enough her equal to relish her society, I see so little of the latter.

The Milles of Nackington dine here on Friday, and perhaps the Hattons. It is a compliment as much due to me as a call from the Filmers.

When you write to the island, Mary will be glad to have Mrs. Craven informed, with her love, that she is now sure it will not be in her power to visit Mrs. Craven during her stay there, but that if Mrs. Craven can take Steventon in her way back it will be giving my brother and herself great pleasure. She also congratulates her namesake on hearing from her husband. That said namesake is rising in the world; she was thought excessively improved in her late visit. Mrs. Knight thought her so last year. Henry sends us the welcome information of his having had no face-ache since I left them.

You are very kind in mentioning old Mrs. Williams so often. Poor creature! I cannot help hoping that each letter may tell of her sufferings being over. If she wants sugar I should like to supply her with it.

The Moores went yesterday to Goodnestone, but return to-morrow. After Tuesday we shall see them no more, though Harriot is very earnest with Edward to take Wrotham in his journey, but we shall be in too great a hurry to get nearer to it than Wrotham Gate. He wishes to reach Guildford on Friday night, that we may have a couple of hours to spare for Alton. I shall be sorry to pass the door at Seale without calling, but it must be so; and I shall be nearer to Bookham than I could wish in going from Dorking to Guildford; but till I have a travelling purse of my own I must submit to such things.

The Moores leave Canterbury on Friday, and go for a day or two to Sandling. I really hope Harriot is altogether very happy, but she cannot feel quite so much at her ease with her husband as the wives she has been used to.

Good-bye. I hope you have been long recovered from your worry on Thursday morning, and that you do not much mind not going to the Newbury races. I am withstanding those of Canterbury. Let that strengthen you.

Yours very sincerely,

JANE.

Letter XLII – 1808

Godmersham: Thursday (June 20).

MY DEAR CASSANDRA,

I give you all joy of Frank's return, which happens in the true sailor way, just after our being told not to expect him for some weeks. The wind has been very much against him, but I suppose he must be in our neighbourhood by this time. Fanny is in hourly expectation of him here. Mary's visit in the island is probably shortened by this event. Make our kind love and congratulations to her.

What cold disagreeable weather, ever since Sunday! I dare say you have fires every day. My kerseymere spencer is quite the comfort of our evening walks.

Mary thanks Anna for her letter, and wishes her to buy enough of her new coloured frock to make a shirt handkerchief. I am glad to hear of her Aunt Maitland's kind present. We want you to send us Anna's height, that we may know whether she is as tall as Fanny; and pray can you tell me of any little thing that would be probably acceptable to Mrs. F. A.? I wish to bring her something: has she a silver knife, or would you recommend a brooch? I shall not spend more than half a guinea about it. Our Tuesday's engagement went off very pleasantly; we called first on Mrs. Knight, and found her very well; and at dinner had only the Milles' of Nackington, in addition to Goodnestone and Godmersham, and Mrs. Moore. Lady Bridges looked very well, and would have been very agreeable, I am sure, had there been time enough for her to talk to me; but as it was, she could only be kind and amiable, give one good-humoured smiles, and make friendly inquiries. Her son Edward was also looking very well, and with manners as unaltered as hers. In the evening came Mr. Moore, Mr. Toke, Dr. and Mrs. Walsby, and others. One card-table was formed, the rest of us sat and talked, and at half after nine we came away.

Yesterday my two brothers went to Canterbury, and J. Bridges left us for London in his way to Cambridge, where he is to take his master's degree.

Edward and Caroline and their mamma have all had the Godmersham cold, the former with sore-throat and fever, which his looks are still suffering from. *He* is very happy here, however, but I believe the little girl will be glad to go home; her cousins are too much for her. We are to have Edward, I find, at Southampton, while his mother is in Berkshire for the races, and are very likely to have his father too. If circumstances are favourable, that will be a good time for our scheme to Beaulieu.

Lady E. Hatton called here a few mornings ago, her daughter Elizth. with her, who says as little as ever, but holds up her head and smiles, and is to be at the races. Annamaria was there with Mrs. Hope, but we are to see her here to-morrow.

So much was written before breakfast; it is now half-past twelve, and, having heard Lizzy read, I am moved down into the library for the sake of fire, which agreeably surprised us when we assembled at ten, and here in warm and happy solitude proceed to acknowledge this day's letter.

We give you credit for your spirited voyage, and are very glad it was accomplished so pleasantly, and that Anna enjoyed it so much. I hope you are not the worse for the fatigue; but to embark at four you must have got up at three, and most likely had no sleep at all. Mary's not choosing to be at home occasions a general small surprise. As to Martha, she has not the least chance in the world of hearing from me again, and I wonder at her impudence in proposing it. I assure you I am as tired of writing long letters as you can be. What a pity that one should still be so fond of receiving them!

Fanny Austen's match is quite news, and I am sorry she has behaved so ill. There is some comfort to us in her misconduct, that we have not a congratulatory letter to write.

James and Edward are gone to Sandling to-day – a nice scheme for James, as it will show him a new and fine country. Edward certainly excels in doing the honours to his visitors, and providing for their amusement. They come back this evening.

Elizabeth talks of going with her three girls to Wrotham while her husband is in Hampshire; she is improved in looks since we first came, and, excepting a cold, does not seem at all unwell. She is considered, indeed, as more than usually active for her situation and size. I have tried to give James pleasure by telling him of his daughter's taste, but if he felt he did not express it. I rejoice in it very sincerely.

Henry talks, or rather writes, of going to the Downes, if the "St. Albans" continues there, but I hope it will be settled otherwise. I had everybody's congratulations on her arrival at Canterbury. It is pleasant to be among people who know one's connections and care about them, and it amuses me to hear John Bridges talk of "Frank." I have thought a little of writing to the Downs, but I shall not, it is so very certain that he would be somewhere else when my letter got there.

Mr. Tho. Leigh is again in town, or was very lately. Henry met with him last Sunday in St. James's Church. He owned being come up unexpectedly on business, which we of course think can be only *one* business, and he came post from Adlestrop in one day, whichs if it could be doubted before, convinces Henry that he will live or ever.

Mrs. Knight is kindly anxious for our good, and thinks Mr. L. P.[7] *must* be desirous for *his family's* sake to have everything settled. Indeed I do not know where we are to get our legacy, but we will keep a sharp look-out. Lady B. was all in prosperous black the other day.

A letter from Jenny Smalbone to her daughter brings intelligence which is to be forwarded to my mother – the calving of a cow at Steventon. I am also to give her mamma's love to Anna, and say that as her papa talks of writing her a letter of comfort she will *not* write, because she knows it would certainly prevent his doing so.

When are calculations ever right? I could have sworn that Mary must have heard of the "St. Albans'" return, and would have been wild to come home or to be doing something. Nobody ever feels or acts, suffers or enjoys, as one expects.

I do not at all regard Martha's disappointment in the island; she will like it the better in the end. I cannot help thinking and re-thinking of your going to the

---

7   Leigh Perrot.

island so heroically. It puts me in mind of Mrs. Hastings' voyage down the Ganges, and, if we had but a room to retire into to eat our fruit, we would have a picture of it hung there.

Friday, July 1. – The weather is mended, which I attribute to my writing about it; and I am in hopes, as you make no complaint, though on the water and at four in the morning, that it has not been so cold with you.

It will be two years to-morrow since we left Bath for Clifton, with what happy feelings of escape!

This post has brought me a few lines from the amiable Frank, but he gives us no hope of seeing him here. We are not unlikely to have a peep at Henry, who, unless the "St. Albans" moves quickly, will be going to the Downs, and who will not be able to be in Kent without giving a day or two to Godmersham.

James has heard this morning from Mrs. Cooke, in reply to his offer of taking Bookham in his way home, which is kindly accepted; and Edwd. has had a less agreeable answer from Dr. Goddard, who actually refuses the petition. Being once fool enough to make a rule of never letting a boy go away an hour before the breaking-up hour, he is now fool enough to keep it. We are all disappointed. His letter brings a double disappointment, for he has no room for George this summer. My brothers returned last night at ten, having spent a very agreeable day in the usual routine. They found Mrs. D.[8] at home, and Mr. D. returned from business abroad to dinner. James admires the place very much, and thinks the two eldest girls handsome, but Mary's beauty has the preference. The number of children struck him a good deal, for not only are their own eleven all at home, but the three little Bridgeses are also with them.

James means to go once more to Canty. to see his friend Dr. Marlowe, who is coming about this time. *I* shall hardly have another opportunity of going there. In another week I shall be at home, and there, my having been at Godmersham will seem like a dream, as my visit at Brompton seems already.

The orange wine will want our care soon. But in the meantime, for elegance and ease and luxury, the Hattons and Milles' dine here to-day, and I shall eat ice and drink French wine, and be above vulgar economy. Luckily the pleasures of friendship, of unreserved conversation, of similarity of taste and opinions, will make good amends for orange wine.

Little Edwd. is quite well again.

Yours affectionately, with love from all,

---

8 Deedes.

J. A.

Letter XLIII – 1808

Castle Square: Saturday (October 1).

MY DEAR CASSANDRA,

Your letter this morning was quite unexpected, and it is well that it brings such good news to counterbalance the disappointment to me of losing my first sentence, which I had arranged full of proper hopes about your journey, intending to commit them to paper to-day, and not looking for certainty till to-morrow.

We are extremely glad to hear of the birth of the child, and trust everything will proceed as well as it begins. His mamma has our best wishes, and he our second best for health and comfort – though I suppose, unless he has our best too, we do nothing for *her.* We are glad it was all over before your arrival, and I am most happy to find who the godmother is to be. My mother was some time guessing the names.

Henry's present to you gives me great pleasure, and I shall watch the weather for him at this time with redoubled interest.

We have had four brace of birds lately, in equal lots, from Shalden and Neatham.

Our party at Mrs. Duer's produced the novelties of two old Mrs. Pollens and Mrs. Heywood, with whom my mother made a quadrille table; and of Mrs. Maitland and Caroline, and Mr. Booth without his sisters, at commerce. I have got a husband for each of the Miss Maitlands; Colonel Powlett and his brother have taken Argyle's inner house, and the consequence is so natural that I have no ingenuity in planning it. If the brother should luckily be a little sillier than the Colonel, what a treasure for Eliza!

Mr. Lyford called on Tuesday to say that he was disappointed of his son and daughter's coming, and must go home himself the following morning; and as I was determined that he should not lose every pleasure, I consulted him on my complaint. He recommended cotton, moistened with oil of sweet almonds, and it has done me good. I hope, therefore, to have nothing more to do with Eliza's receipt than to feel obliged to her for giving it, as I very sincerely do.

Mrs. Tilson's remembrance gratifies me, and I will use her patterns if I can.

I have just finished a handkerchief for Mrs. James Austen, which I expect her husband to give me an opportunity of sending to her ere long. Some fine day in October will certainly bring him to us in the garden, between three and four o'clock. *She* hears that Miss Bigg is to be married in a fortnight. I wish it may be so.

About an hour and a-half after your toils on Wednesday ended, ours began. At seven o'clock Mrs. Harrison, her two daughters and two visitors, with Mr. Debary and his eldest sister, walked in.

A second pool of commerce, and all the longer by the addition of the two girls, who during the first had one corner of the table and spillikens to themselves, was the ruin of us; it completed the prosperity of Mr. Debary, however, for he won them both.

Mr. Harrison came in late, and sat by the fire, for which I envied him, as we had our usual luck of having a very cold evening. It rained when our company came, but was dry again before they left us.

The Miss Ballards are said to be remarkably well-informed; their manners are unaffected and pleasing, but they do not talk quite freely enough to be agreeable, nor can I discover any right they had by taste or feeling to go their late tour.

Miss Austen and her nephew are returned, but Mr. Choles is still absent. "Still absent," say you. "I did not know that he was gone anywhere;" neither did I know that Lady Bridges was at Godmersham at all, till I was told of her being *still* there, which I take, therefore, to be the most approved method of announcing arrivals and departures.

Mr. Choles is gone to drive a cow to Brentford, and his place is supplied to us by a man who lives in the same sort of way by odd jobs, and among other capabilities has that of working in a garden, which my mother will not forget if we ever have another garden here. In general, however, she thinks much more of Alton, and really expects to move there.

Mrs. Lyell's 130 guineas rent have made a great impression. To the purchase of furniture, whether here or there, she is quite reconciled, and talks of the *trouble* as the only evil. I depended upon Henry's liking the Alton plan, and expect to hear of something perfectly unexceptionable there, through him.

Our Yarmouth division seem to have got nice lodgings; and, with fish almost for nothing and plenty of engagements and plenty of each other, must be very happy.

My mother has undertaken to cure six hams for Frank; at first it was a distress, but now it is a pleasure. She desires me to say that she does not doubt your making out the star pattern very well, as you have the breakfast-room rug to look at.

We have got the second volume of *"Espriella's Letters,"* and I read it aloud by candle-light. The man describes well, but is horribly anti-English. He deserves to be the foreigner he assumes.

Mr. Debary went away yesterday, and I, being gone with some partridges to St. Maries, lost his parting visit.

I have heard to-day from Miss Sharpe, and find that she returns with Miss B. to Hinckley, and will continue there at least till about Christmas, when she thinks they may both travel southward. Miss B., however, is probably to make only a temporary absence from Mr. Chessyre, and I should not wonder if Miss Sharpe were to continue with her; unless anything more eligible offer she certainly will. She describes Miss B as very anxious that she should do so.

Sunday. – I had not expected to hear from you again so soon, and am much obliged to you for writing as you did; but now, as you must have a great deal of the business upon your hands, do not trouble yourself with me for the present; I shall consider silence as good news, and not expect another letter from you till Friday or Saturday.

You must have had a great deal more rain than has fallen here; cold enough it has been, but not wet, except for a few hours on Wednesday evening, and I could have found nothing more plastic than dust to stick in; now, indeed, we are likely to have a wet day, and, though Sunday, my mother begins it without any ailment.

Your plants were taken in one very cold, blustering day, and placed in the dining-room, and there was a frost the very same night. If we have warm weather again they are to be put out of doors; if not, my mother will have them conveyed to their winter quarters. I gather some currants every now and then, when I want either fruit or employment.

Pray tell my little goddaughter that I am delighted to hear of her saying her lesson so well.

You have used me ill: you have been writing to Martha without telling me of it, and a letter which I sent her on Wednesday to give her information of you must have been good for nothing. I do not know how to think that something will not happen to prevent her returning by the 10th; and if it does, I shall not much regard it on my own account, for I am now got into such a way of being alone that I do not wish even for her.

The Marquis has put off being cured for an-other year; after waiting some weeks in vain for the return of the vessel he had agreed for, he is gone into Cornwall to order a vessel built for himself by a famous man in that country, in which he means to go abroad a twelvemonth hence.

Everybody who comes to Southampton finds it either their duty or pleasure to call upon us; yesterday we were visited by the eldest Miss Cotterel, just arrived from Waltham. Adieu! With love to all,

Yours affectionately,

J. A.

We had two pheasants last night from Neatham. To-morrow evening is to be given to the Maitlands. We are just asked to meet Mrs. Heywood and Mrs. Duer.

Letter XLIV – 1808

Castle Square: Friday (October 7).

MY DEAR CASSANDRA,

Your letter on Tuesday gave us great pleasure, and we congratulate you all upon Elizabeth's hitherto happy recovery; tomorrow, or Sunday, I hope to hear of its advancing in the same style. We are also very glad to know that you are so well yourself, and pray you to continue so.

I was rather surprised on Monday by the arrival of a letter for you, from your Winchester correspondent, who seemed perfectly unsuspicious of your being likely to be at Godmersham. I took complete possession of the letter by reading, paying for, and answering it; and he will have the biscuits to-day – a very proper day for the purpose, though I did not think of it at the time. I wish my brother joy of completing his thirtieth year, and hope the day will be remembered better than it was six years ago.

The masons are now repairing the chimney, which they found in such a state as to make it wonderful that it should have stood so long, and next to impossible that another violent wind should not blow it down. We may, therefore, thank *you* perhaps for saving us from being thumped with old bricks. You are also to be thanked by Eliza's desire for your present to her of dyed satin, which is made into a bonnet, and I fancy surprises her by its good appearance.

My mother is preparing mourning for Mrs. E. K.; she has picked her old silk pelisse to pieces, and means to have it dyed black for a gown – a very interesting scheme, though just now a little injured by finding that it must be placed in Mr. Wren's hands, for Mr. Chambers is gone. As for Mr. Floor, he is at present rather low in our estimation. How is your blue gown? Mine is all to pieces. I think there must have been something wrong in the dye, for in places it divided with a touch. There was four shillings thrown away, to be added to my subjects of never-failing regret.

We found ourselves tricked into a thorough party at Mrs. Maitland's, a quadrille and a commerce table, and music in the other room. There were two pools at commerce, but I would not play more than one, for the stake was three shillings, and I cannot afford to lose that twice in an evening. The Miss M.'s were as civil and as silly as usual.

You know of course that Martha comes to-day, yesterday brought us notice of it, and the spruce beer is brewed in consequence.

On Wednesday I had a letter from Yarmouth, to desire me to send Mary's flannels and furs, &c.; and, as there was a packing case at hand, I could do it without any trouble.

On Tuesday evening Southampton was in a good deal of alarm for about an hour: a fire broke out soon after nine at Webb's, the pastry-cook, and burnt for some time with great fury. I cannot learn exactly how it originated; at the time it was said to be their bakehouse, but now I hear it was in the back of their dwelling-house, and that one room was consumed.

The flames were considerable: they seemed about as near to us as those at Lyme, and to reach higher. One could not but feel uncomfortable, and I began to think of what I should do if it came to the worst; happily, however, the night was perfectly still, the engines were immediately in use, and before ten the fire was nearly extinguished, though it was twelve before everything was considered safe, and a guard was kept the whole night. Our friends the Duers were alarmed, but not out of their good sense or benevolence.

I am afraid the Webbes have lost a great deal, more perhaps from ignorance or plunder than the fire; they had a large stock of valuable china, and, in order to save it, it was taken from the house and thrown down anywhere.

The adjoining house, a toyshop, was almost equally injured, and Hibbs, whose house comes next, was so scared from his senses that he was giving away all his goods, valuable laces, &c., to anybody who would take them.

The crowd in the High Street, I understand, was immense; Mrs. Harrison, who was drinking tea with a lady at Millar's, could not leave at twelve o'clock. Such are the prominent features of our fire. Thank God they were not worse!

Saturday. – Thank you for your letter, which found me at the breakfast table with my two companions.

I am greatly pleased with your account of Fanny; I found her in the summer just what you describe, almost another sister; and could not have supposed that a niece would ever have been so much to me. She is quite after one's own heart; give her my best love, and tell her that I always think of her with pleasure.

I am much obliged to you for inquiring about my ear, and am happy to say that Mr. Lyford's prescription has entirely cured me. I feel it a great blessing to hear again.

Your gown shall be unpicked, but I do not remember its being settled so before.

Martha was here by half-past six, attended by Lyddy; they had some rain at last, but a very good journey on the whole; and if looks and words may be trusted Martha is very happy to be returned. We receive her with Castle Square weather; it has blown a gale from the N.W. ever since she came, and we feel ourselves in luck that the chimney was mended yesterday.

She brings several good things for the larder, which is now very rich; we had a pheasant and hare the other day from the Mr. Grays of Alton. Is this to entice us to Alton, or to keep us away? Henry had probably some share in the two last baskets from that neighbourhood, but we have not seen so much of his handwriting, even as a direction to either.

Martha was an hour and half in Winchester, walking about with the three boys and at the pastry cook's. She thought Edward grown, and speaks with the same admiration as before of his manners; she saw in George a little likeness to his Uncle Henry.

I am glad you are to see Harriot; give my love to her. I wish you may be able to accept Lady Bridges' invitation, though *I* could not her son Edward's; she is a nice woman and honours me by her remembrance.

Do you recollect whether the Manydown family sent about their wedding cake? Mrs. Dundas has set her heart upon having a piece from her friend Catherine, and Martha, who knows what importance she attaches to this sort of thing, is anxious for the sake of both that there should not be a disappointment.

Our weather, I fancy, has been just like yours; we have had *some* very delightful days, our 5th and 6th were what the 5th and 6th of October should always be, but we have always wanted a fire *within* doors, at least except for just the middle of the day.

Martha does not find the key which you left in my charge for her suit the keyhole, and wants to know whether you think you can have mistaken it. It should open the interior of her high drawers, but she is in no hurry about it.

Sunday. – It is cold enough now for us to prefer dining upstairs to dining below without a fire, and being only three we manage it very well, and to-day with two more we shall do just as well, I dare say. Miss Foote and Miss Wethered are coming.

My mother is much pleased with Elizabeth's admiration of the rug; and pray tell Elizabeth that the new mourning gown is to be made double *only* in the body and sleeves.

Martha thanks you for your message, and desires you may be told, with her best love, that your wishes are answered, and that she is full of peace and comfort here. I do not think, however, that here she will remain a great while; she does not herself expect that Mrs. Dundas will be able to do with her long. She *wishes* to stay with us till Christmas, if possible. Lyddy goes home to-morrow: she seems well, but does not mean to to to service at present.

The Wallops are returned. Mr. John Harrison has paid his visit of duty and is gone. We have got a new physician, a Dr. Percival, the son of a famous Dr. Percival, of Manchester, who wrote moral tales for Edward to give to me.

When you write again to Catherine, thank her on my part for her very kind and welcome mark of friendship; I shall value such a brooch very much. Good-bye, my dearest Cassandra.

Yours very affectionately,

J. A.

Have you written to Mrs. E. Leigh? Martha will be glad to find Anne in work at present, and I am as glad to have her so found. We must turn our black pelisses into new, for velvet is to be very much worn this winter.

Letter XLV – 1808

Castle Square (October 13).

MY DEAREST CASSANDRA,

I have received your letter, and with most melancholy anxiety was it expected, for the sad news reached us last night, but without any particulars. It came in a short letter to Martha from her sister, begun at Steventon and finished in Winchester.

We have felt – we do feel – for you all, as you will not need to be told: for you, for Fanny, for Henry, for Lady Bridges, and for dearest Edward, whose loss and whose sufferings seem to make those of every other person nothing. God be praised that you can say what you do of him: that he has a religious mind to bear him up, and a disposition that will gradually lead him to comfort.

My dear, dear Fanny, I am so thankful that she has you with her! You will be everything to her; you will give her all the consolation that human aid can give. May the Almighty sustain you all, and keep you, my dearest Cassandra, well; but for the present I dare say you are equal to everything.

You will know that the poor boys are at Steventon. Perhaps it is best for them, as they will have more means of exercise and amusement there than they could have with us, but I own myself disappointed by the arrangement. I should have loved to have them with me at such a time. I shall write to Edward by this post.

We shall, of course, hear from you again very soon, and as often as you can write. We will write as you desire, and I shall add Bookham. Hamstall, I suppose, you write to yourselves, as you do not mention it.

What a comfort that Mrs. Deedes is saved from present misery and alarm! But it will fall heavy upon poor Harriot; and as for Lady B., but that her fortitude does seem truly great, I should fear the effect of such a blow, and so unlooked for. I long to hear more of you all. Of Henry's anguish I think with grief and solicitude; but he will exert himself to be of use and comfort.

With what true sympathy our feelings are shared by Martha you need not be told; she is the friend and sister under every circumstance.

We need not enter into a panegyric on the departed, but it is sweet to think of her great worth, of her solid principles, of her true devotion, her excellence in every relation of life. It is also consolatory to reflect on the shortness of the sufferings which led her from this world to a better.

Farewell for the present, my dearest sister. Tell Edward that we feel for him and pray for him.

Yours affectionately,

J. AUSTEN.

I will write to Catherine.

Perhaps you can give me some directions about mourning.

Letter XLVI – 1808

Castle Square: Saturday night (October 15).

MY DEAR CASSANDRA,

Your accounts make us as comfortable as we can expect to be at such a time. Edward's loss is terrible, and must be felt as such, and these are too early days indeed to think of moderation in grief, either in him or his afflicted daughter, but soon we may hope that our dear Fanny's sense of duty to that beloved father will rouse her to exertion. For his sake, and as the most acceptable proof of love to the spirit of her departed mother, she will try to be tranquil and resigned. Does she feel you to be a comfort to her, or is she too much overpowered for anything but solitude?

Your account of Lizzy is very interesting. Poor child! One must hope the impression *will* be strong, and yet one's heart aches for a dejected mind of eight years old.

I suppose you see the corpse? How does it appear? We are anxious to be assured that Edward will not attend the funeral, but when it comes to the point I think he must feel it impossible.

Your parcel shall set off on Monday, and I hope the shoes will fit; Martha and I both tried them on. I shall send you such of your mourning as I think most likely to be useful, reserving for myself your stockings and half the velvet, in which selfish arrangement I know I am doing what you wish.

I am to be in bombazeen and crape, according to what we are told is universal *here,* and which agrees with Martha's previous observation. My mourning, however, will not impoverish me, for by having my velvet pelisse fresh lined and made up, I am sure I shall have no occasion *this winter* for anything new of that sort. I take my cloak for the lining, and shall send yours on the chance of its doing something of the same for you, though I believe your pelisse is in better repair than mine. *One* Miss Baker makes my gown and the other my bonnet, which is to be silk covered with crape.

I have written to Edward Cooper, and hope he will not send one of his letters of cruel comfort to my poor brother; and yesterday I wrote to Alethea Bigg, in reply to a letter from her. She tells us in confidence that Catherine is to be married on Tuesday se'nnight. Mr. Hill is expected at Manydown in the course of the ensuing week.

We are desired by Mrs. Harrison and Miss Austen to say everything proper for them to yourself and Edward on this sad occasion, especially that nothing but a wish of not giving additional trouble where so much is inevitable prevents their writing themselves to express their concern. They seem truly to feel concern.

I am glad you can say what you do of Mrs. Knight and of Goodnestone in general; it is a great relief to me to know that the shock did not make any of them ill. But what a task was yours to announce it! *Now* I hope you are not overpowered with letter-writing, as Henry and John can ease you of many of your correspondents.

Was Mr. Scudmore in the house at the time, was any application attempted, and is the seizure at all accounted for?

Sunday. – As Edward's letter to his son is not come here, we know that you must have been informed as early as Friday of the boys being at Steventon, which I am glad of.

Upon your letter to Dr. Goddard's being forwarded to them, Mary wrote to ask whether my mother wished to have her grandsons sent to her. We decided on their remaining where they were, which I hope my brother will approve of. I am sure he will do us the justice of believing that in such a decision we sacrificed inclination to what we thought best.

I shall write by the coach to-morrow to Mrs. J. A., and to Edward, about their mourning, though this day's post will probably bring directions to them on that subject from yourselves. I shall certainly make use of the opportunity of addressing our nephew on the most serious of all concerns, as I naturally did in my letter to him before. The poor boys are, perhaps, more comfortable at Steventon than they could be here, but you will understand *my feelings* with respect to it.

To-morrow will be a dreadful day for you all. Mr. Whitfield's will be a severe duty.[9] Glad shall I be to hear that it is over.

That you are forever in our thoughts you will not doubt. I see your mournful party in my mind's eye under every varying circumstance of the day; and in the evening especially figure to myself its sad gloom: the efforts to talk, the frequent summons to melancholy orders and cares, and poor Edward, restless in misery, going from one room to another, and perhaps not seldom upstairs, to see all that remains of his Elizabeth. Dearest Fanny must now look upon herself as his prime source of comfort, his dearest friend; as the being who is gradually to supply to him, to the

---

9   Mr. Whitfield was the Rector of Godmersham at this time, having come there in 1778.

extent that is possible, what he has lost. This consideration will elevate and cheer her.

Adieu. You cannot write too often, as I said before. We are heartily rejoiced that the poor baby gives you no particular anxiety. Kiss dear Lizzy for us. Tell Fanny that I shall write in a day or two to Miss Sharpe.

My mother is not ill.

Yours most truly,

J. AUSTEN.

Tell Henry that a hamper of apples is gone to him from Kintbury, and that Mr. Fowle intended writing on Friday (supposing him in London) to beg that the charts, &c. may be consigned to the care of the Palmers. Mrs. Fowle has also written to Miss Palmer to beg she will send for them.

Letter XLVII – 1808

Castle Square: Monday (October 24).

MY DEAR CASSANDRA,

Edward and George came to us soon after seven on Saturday, very well, but very cold, having by choice travelled on the outside, and with no great coat but what Mr. Wise, the coachman, good-naturedly spared them of his, as they sat by his side. They were so much chilled when they arrived, that I was afraid they must have taken cold; but it does not seem at all the case; I never saw them looking better.

They behave extremely well in every respect, showing quite as much feeling as one wishes to see, and on every occasion speaking of their father with the liveliest affection. His letter was read over by each of them yesterday, and with many tears; George sobbed aloud, Edward's tears do not flow so easily; but as far as I can judge they are both very properly impressed by what has happened. Miss Lloyd, who is a more impartial judge than I can be, is exceedingly pleased with them.

George is almost a new acquaintance to me, and I find him in a different way as *engaging as Edward.*

We do not want amusement: bilbocatch, at which George is indefatigable; spillikins, paper ships, riddles, conundrums, and cards, with watching the flow and ebb of the river, and now and then a stroll out, keep us well employed; and we mean to avail ourselves of our kind papa's consideration, by not returning to Winchester till quite the evening of Wednesday.

Mrs. J. A. had not time to get them more than one suit of clothes; their others are making here, and though I do not believe Southampton is famous for tailoring, I hope it will prove itself better than Basingstoke. Edward has an old black coat, which will save *his* having a second new one; but I find that black pantaloons are considered by them as necessary, and of course one would not have them made uncomfortable by the want of what is usual on such occasions.

Fanny's letter was received with great pleasure yesterday, and her brother sends his thanks and will answer it soon. We all saw what she wrote, and were very much pleased with it.

To-morrow I hope to hear from you, and to-morrow we must think of poor Catherine. To-day Lady Bridges is the heroine of our thoughts, and glad shall we be when we can fancy the meeting over. There will then be nothing so very bad for Edward to undergo.

The "St. Albans," I find, sailed on the very day of my letters reaching Yarmouth, so that we must not expect an answer at present; we scarcely feel, however, to be in suspense, or only enough to keep our plans to ourselves. We have been obliged to explain them to our young visitors, in consequence of Fanny's letter, but we have not yet mentioned them to Steventon. We are all quite familiarised to the idea ourselves; my mother only wants Mrs. Seward to go out at Midsummer.

What sort of a kitchen garden is there? Mrs. J. A. expresses her fear of our settling in Kent, and, till this proposal was made, we began to look forward to it here; my mother was actually talking of a house at Wye. It will be best, however, as it is.

Anne has just given her mistress warning; she is going to be married; I wish she would stay her year.

On the subject of matrimony, I must notice a wedding in the Salisbury paper, which has amused me very much, Dr. Phillot to Lady Frances St. Lawrence. *She* wanted to have a husband I suppose, once in her life, and *he* a Lady Frances.

I hope your sorrowing party were at church yesterday, and have no longer *that* to dread. Martha was kept at home by a *cold, but I went with my two nephews, and I saw Edward was much affected by the sermon, which, indeed, I could have supposed purposely addressed* to the afflicted, if the text had not naturally come in the course of Dr. Mant's observations on the Litany: "All that are in danger, necessity, or tribulation," was the subject of it. The weather did not allow us afterwards to get farther than the quay, where George was very happy as long as we could stay, flying about from one side to the other, and skipping on board a collier immediately.

In the evening we had the Psalms and Lessons, and a sermon at home, to which they were very attentive; but you will not expect to hear that they did not return to conundrums the moment it *was over.* Their aunt has written pleasantly of them, which was more than I hoped.

While I write now, George is most industriously making and naming paper ships, at which he afterwards shoots with horse-chestnuts brought from Steventon on purpose; and Edward equally intent over the "Lake of Killarney," twisting himself about in one of our great chairs.

Tuesday. – Your close-written letter makes me quite ashamed of my wide lines; you have sent me a great deal of matter, most of it very welcome. As to your lengthened stay, it is no more than I expected, and what must be, but you cannot suppose I like it.

All that you say of Edward is truly comfortable; I began to fear that when the bustle of the first week was over, his spirits might for a time be more depressed; and perhaps one must still expect something of the kind. If you escape a bilious attack, I shall wonder almost as much as rejoice. I am glad you mentioned where Catherine goes to-day; it is a good plan, but sensible people may generally be trusted to form such.

The day began cheerfully, but it is not likely to continue what it should, for them or for us. *We had a little water party* yesterday; I and my two nephews went from the Itchen Ferry up to Northam, where we landed, looked into the 74, and walked home, and it was so much enjoyed that I had intended to take them to Netley to-day; the tide is just right for our going immediately after moonshine, but I am afraid there will be rain; if we cannot get so far, however, we may perhaps go round from the ferry to the quay.

I had not proposed doing more than cross the Itchen yesterday, but it proved so pleasant, and so much to the satisfaction of all, that when we reached the middle of the stream we agreed to be rowed up the river; both the boys rowed great part of the way, and their questions and remarks, as well as their enjoyment, were very amusing; George's inquiries were endless, and his eagerness in everything reminds me often *of his Uncle Henry.*

Our evening was equally agreeable in its way: I introduced *speculation,* and it was so much approved that we hardly knew how to leave off.

Your idea of an early dinner to-morrow is exactly what we propose, for, after writing the first part of this letter, it came into my head that at this time of year we have not summer evenings. We shall watch the light to-day, that we may not give them a dark drive to-morrow.

They send their best love to papa and everybody, with George's thanks for the letter brought by this post. Martha begs my brother may be assured of her interest in everything relating to him and his family, and of her sincerely partaking our pleasure in the receipt of every good account from Godmersham.

Of Chawton I think I can have nothing more to say, but that everything you say about it in the letter now before me will, I am sure, as soon as I am able to read it to her, make my mother consider the plan with more and more pleasure. We had formed the same views on H. Digweed's farm.

A very kind and feeling letter is arrived to-day from Kintbury. Mrs. Fowle's sympathy and solicitude on such an occasion you will be able to do justice to, and to express it as she wishes to my brother. Concerning *you,* she says: "Cassandra will, I know, excuse my writing to her; it is not to save myself but *her* that I omit so doing. Give my best, my kindest love to her, and tell her I feel for her as I know she would for me on the same occasion, and that I most sincerely hope her health will not suffer."

We have just had two hampers of apples from Kintbury, and the floor of our little garret is almost covered. Love to all.

Yours very affectionately,

J. A.

Letter XLVIII − 1808

Castle Square: Sunday (November 21).

Your letter, my dear Cassandra, obliges me to write immediately, that you may have the earliest notice of Frank's intending, if possible, to go to Godmersham exactly at the time now fixed for your visit to Goodnestone.

He resolved, almost directly on the receipt of your former letter, to try for an extension of his leave of absence, that he might be able to go down to you for two days, but charged me not to give you any notice of it, on account of the uncertainty of success. Now, however, I must give it, and now perhaps he may be giving it himself; for I am just in the hateful predicament of being obliged to write what I know will somehow or other be of no use.

He meant to ask for five days more, and if they were granted, to go down by Thursday night's mail, and spend Friday and Saturday with you; and he considered his chance of succeeding by no means bad. I hope it will take place as he planned, and that your arrangements with Goodnestone may admit of suitable alteration.

Your news of Edward Bridges was *quite* news, for I have had no letter from Wrotham. I wish him happy with all my heart, and hope his choice may turn out according to his own expectations, and beyond those of his family; and I dare say it will. Marriage is a great improver, and in a similar situation Harriet may be as amiable as Eleanor. As to money, that will come, you may be sure, because they cannot do without it. When you see him again, pray give him our congratulations and best wishes. This match will certainly set John and Lucy going.

There are six bedchambers at Chawton; Henry wrote to my mother the other day, and luckily mentioned the number, which is just what we wanted to be assured of. He speaks also of garrets for store places, one of which she immediately planned fitting up for Edward's man-servant; and now perhaps it must be for our own; for she is already quite reconciled to our keeping one. The difficulty of doing without one had been thought of before. His name shall be Robert, if you please.

Before I can tell you of it, you will have heard that Miss Sawbridge is married. It took place, I believe, on Thursday. Mrs. Fowle has for some time been in the secret, but the neighbourhood in general were quite unsuspicious. Mr. Maxwell *was* tutor to the young Gregorys – consequently, they must be one of the happiest couples in the world, and either of them worthy of envy, for *she* must be excessively in love, and he mounts from nothing to a comfortable home. Martha has heard him very highly spoken of. They continue for the present at Speen Hill.

I have a Southampton match to return for your Kentish one, Captain G. Heathcote and Miss A. Lyell. I have it from Alethea, and like it, because I had made it before.

Yes, the Stoneleigh business is concluded, but it was not till yesterday that my mother was regularly informed of it, though the news had reached us on Monday evening by way of Steventon. My aunt says as little as may be on the subject by way of information, and nothing at all by way of satisfaction. She reflects on Mr. T. Leigh's dilatoriness, and looks about with great diligence and success for inconvenience and evil, among which she ingeniously places the danger of her new housemaids catching cold on the outside of the coach, when she goes down to Bath, for a carriage makes her sick.

John Binns has been offered their place, but declines it; as she supposes, because he will not wear a livery. Whatever be the cause, I like the effect.

In spite of all my mother's long and intimate knowledge of the writer, she was not up to the expectation of such a letter as this; the discontentedness of it shocked and surprised her – but *I* see nothing in it out of nature, though a sad nature.

She does not forget to wish for Chambers, you may be sure. No particulars are given, not a word of arrears mentioned, though in her letter to James they were in a *general way* spoken of. The amount of them is a matter of conjecture, and to my mother a most interesting one; she cannot fix any time for their beginning with any satisfaction to herself but Mrs. Leigh's death, and Henry's two thousand pounds neither agrees with that period nor any other. I did not like to own our previous information of what was intended last July, and have therefore only said that if we could see Henry we might hear many particulars, as I had understood that some confidential conversation had passed between him and Mr. T. L. at Stoneleigh.

We have been as quiet as usual since Frank and Mary left us; Mr. Criswick called on Martha that very morning on his way home again from Portsmouth, and we have had no visitor since.

We called on the Miss Lyells one day, and heard a good account of Mr. Heathcote's canvass, the success of which, of course, exceeds his expectations. Alethea in her letter hopes for *my interest,* which I conclude means Edwards's, and I take this opportunity, therefore, of requesting that he will bring in Mr. Heathcote. Mr. Lane told us yesterday that Mr. H. had behaved very handsomely, and waited on Mr. Thistlethwaite, to say that if *he* (Mr. T.) would stand, *he* (Mr. H.) would not oppose him; but Mr. T. declined it, acknowledging himself still smarting under the payment of late electioneering costs.

The Mrs. Hulberts, we learn from Kintbury, come to Steventon this week, and bring Mary Jane Fowle with them on her way to Mrs. Nunes; she returns at Christmas with her brother.

Our brother we may perhaps see in the course of a few days, and we mean to take the opportunity of his help to go one night to the play. Martha ought to see the inside of the theatre once while she lives in Southampton, and I think she will hardly wish to take a second view.

The furniture of Bellevue is to be sold to-morrow, and we shall take it in our usual walk, if the weather be favourable.

How could you have a wet day on Thursday? With us it was a prince of days, the most delightful we have had for weeks; soft, bright, with a brisk wind from the southwest; everybody was out and talking of spring, and Martha and I did not know how to turn back. On Friday evening we had some very blowing weather – from 6 to 9, I think we never heard it worse, even here. And one night we had so much rain that it forced its way again into the store closet, and though the evil was comparatively slight and the mischief nothing, I had some employment the next day in drying parcels, &c. I have now moved still more out of the way.

Martha sends her best love, and thanks you for admitting her to the knowledge of the pros and cons about Harriet Foote; she has an interest in all such matters. I am also to say that she wants to see you. Mary Jane missed her papa and mama a good deal at first, but now does very well without them. I am glad to hear of little John's being better; and hope your accounts of Mrs. Knight will also improve. Adieu! remember me affectionately to everybody, and believe me,

Ever yours,

J. A.

Letter XLIX – 1808

Castle Square: Friday (December 9).

Many thanks, my dear Cassandra, to you and Mr. Deedes for your joint and agreeable composition, which took me by surprise this morning. He has certainly great merit as a writer; he does ample justice to his subject, and, without being diffuse, is clear and correct; and though I do not mean to compare his epistolary powers with yours, or to give him the same portion of my gratitude, he certainly has a very pleasing way of winding up a whole, and speeding truth into the world.

"But all this," as my dear Mrs. Piozzi says, "is flight and fancy, and nonsense, for my master has his great casks to mind and I have my little children." It is *you,* however, in this instance, that have the little children, and *I* that have the great cask, for we are brewing spruce beer again; but my meaning really is, that I am extremely foolish in writing all this unnecessary stuff when I have so many matters to write about that my paper will hardly hold it all. Little matters they are, to be sure, but highly important.

In the first place, Miss Curling is actually at Portsmouth, which I was always in hopes would not happen. I wish her no worse, however, than a long and happy abode there. *Here* she would probably be dull, and I am sure she would be troublesome.

The bracelets are in my possession, and everything I could wish them to be. They came with Martha's pelisse, which likewise gives great satisfaction.

Soon after I had closed my last letter to you we were visited by Mrs. Dickens and her sister-in-law, Mrs. Bertie, the wife of a lately-made Admiral. Mrs. F. A.[10] I believe, was their first object, but they put up with us very kindly, and Mrs. D., finding in Miss Lloyd a friend of Mrs. Dundas, had another motive for the acquaintance. She seems a really agreeable woman – that is, her manners are gentle, and she knows a great many of our connections in West Kent. Mrs. Bertie lives in the Polygon, and was out when we returned her visit, which are *her* two virtues.

A larger circle of acquaintance, and an increase of amusement, is quite in character with our approaching removal. Yes, I mean to go to as many balls as possible, that I may have a good bargain. Everybody is very much concerned at our going away, and everybody is acquainted with Chawton, and speaks of it as a remarkably pretty village, and everybody knows the house we describe, but nobody fixes on the right.

---

10   Frank Austen.

I am very much obliged to Mrs. Knight for such a proof of the interest she takes in me, and she may depend upon it that I *will* marry Mr. Papillon, whatever may be his reluctance or my own. I owe her much more than such a trifling sacrifice.

Our ball was rather more amusing than I expected. Martha liked it very much, and I did not gape till the last quarter of an hour. It was past nine before we were sent for and not twelve when we returned. The room was tolerably full, and there were, perhaps, thirty couple of dancers. The melancholy part was, to see so many dozen young women standing by without partners, and each of them with two ugly naked shoulders.

It was the same room in which we danced fifteen years ago. I thought it all over, and in spite of the shame of being so much older, felt with thankfulness that I was quite as happy now as then. We paid an additional shilling for our tea, which we took as we chose in an adjoining and very comfortable room.

There were only four dances, and it went to my heart that the Miss Lances (one of them, too, named *Emma*) should have partners only for two. You will not expect to hear that I was asked to dance, but I was – by the gentleman whom we met *that Sunday* with Captain D'Auvergne. We have always kept up a bowing acquaintance since, and, being pleased with his black eyes,

I spoke to him at the ball, which brought on me this civility; but I do not know his name, and he seems so little at home in the English language, that I believe his black eyes may be the best of him. Captain D'Auvergne has got a ship.

Martha and I made use of the very favourable state of yesterday for walking, to pay our duty at Chiswell. We found Mrs. Lance at home and alone, and sat out three other ladies who soon came in. We went by the ferry, and returned by the bridge, and were scarcely at all fatigued.

Edward must have enjoyed the last two days. You, I presume, had a cool drive to Canterbury. Kitty Foote came on Wednesday, and her evening visit began early enough for the last part, the apple pie, of our dinner, for we never dine now till five.

Yesterday I – or, rather, you – had a letter from Nanny Hilliard, the object of which is, that she would be very much obliged to us if we would get Hannah a place. I am sorry that I cannot assist her; if you can, let me know, as I shall not answer the letter immediately. Mr. Sloper is married again, not much to Nanny's, or anybody's satisfaction. The lady was governess to Sir Robert's natural children, and seems to have nothing to recommend her. I do not find, however, that Nanny is likely to lose her place in consequence. She says not a word of what service she wishes for Hannah, or what Hannah can do, but a nursery, I suppose, or something of that kind, must be the thing.

Having now cleared away my smaller articles of news, I come to a communication of some weight; no less than that my uncle and aunt[11] are going to allow James 100*l.* a year. We hear of it through Steventon. Mary sent us the other day an extract from my aunt's letter on the subject, in which the donation is made with the greatest kindness, and intended as a compensation for his loss in the conscientious refusal of Hampstead living; 100*l.* a year being all that he had at the time called its worth, as I find it was always intended at Steventon to divide the real income with Kintbury.

Nothing can be more affectionate than my aunt's language in making the present, and like-wise in expressing her hope of their being much more together in future than, to her great regret, they have of late years been. My expectations for my mother do not rise with this event. We will allow a little more time, however, before we fly out.

If not prevented by parish business, James comes to us on Monday. The Mrs. Hulberts and Miss Murden are their guests at present, and likely to continue

---

11 Mr. and Mrs. Leigh Perrot.

such till Christmas. Anna comes home on the 19th. The hundred a year begins next Lady-day.

I am glad you are to have Henry with you again; with him and the boys you cannot but have a cheerful, and at times even a merry, Christmas. Martha is so—[12]

We want to be settled at Chawton in time for Henry to come to us for some shooting in October, at least, or a little earlier, and Edward may visit us after taking his boys back to Winchester. Suppose we name the 4th of September. Will not that do?

I have but one thing more to tell you. Mrs. Hill called on my mother yesterday while we were gone to Chiswell, and in the course of the visit asked her whether she knew anything of a clergyman's family of the name of *Alford*, who had resided in our part of Hampshire. Mrs. Hill had been applied to as likely to give some information of them on account of their probable vicinity to Dr. Hill's living, by a lady, or for a lady, who had known Mrs. and the two Miss Alfords in Bath, whither they had removed, it seems, from Hampshire, and who now wishes to convey to the Miss Alfords some work or trimming which she has been doing for them; but the mother and daughters have left Bath, and the lady cannot learn where they are gone to. While my mother gave us the account, the

---

12 MS. torn

probability of its being ourselves occurred to us, and it had previously struck herself . . . what makes it more likely, and even indispensably to be *us,* is that she mentioned Mr. Hammond as now having the living or curacy which the father had had. I cannot think who our kind lady can be, but I dare say we shall not like the work.

Distribute the affectionate love of a heart not so tired as the right hand belonging to it.

Yours ever sincerely,

J. A.

Letter L – 1809

Castle Square: Tuesday (December 27).

MY DEAR CASSANDRA,

I can now write at leisure and make the most of my subjects, which is lucky, as they are not numerous this week.

Our house was cleared by half-past eleven on Saturday, and we had the satisfaction of hearing yesterday that the party reached home in safety soon after five.

I was very glad of your letter this morning, for, my mother taking medicine, Eliza keeping her bed with a cold, and Choles not coming, made us rather dull and dependent on the post. You tell me much that gives me pleasure, but I think not much to answer. I wish I *could* help you in your needle-work. I have two hands and a new thimble that lead a very easy life.

Lady Sondes' match surprises, but does not offend me; had her first marriage been of affection, or had there been a grown-up single daughter, I should not have forgiven her; but I consider everybody as having a right to marry *once* in their lives for love, if they can, and provided she will now leave off having bad headaches and being pathetic, I can allow her, I can *wish* her, to be happy.

Do not imagine that your picture of your *tête-à-tête* with Sir B. makes any change in our expectations here; he could not be really reading, though he held the newspaper in his hand; he was making up his mind to the deed, and the manner of it. I think you will have a letter from him soon.

I heard from Portsmouth yesterday, and as I am to send them more clothes, they cannot be expecting a very early return to us. Mary's face is pretty well, but she must have suffered a great deal with it; an abscess was formed and opened.

Our evening party on Thursday produced nothing more remarkable than Miss Murden's coming too, though she had declined it absolutely in the morning, and sitting very ungracious and very silent with us from seven o'clock till half after eleven, for so late was it, owing to the chairmen, before we got rid of them.

The last hour, spent in yawning and shivering in a wide circle round the fire, was dull enough, but the tray had admirable success. The widgeon and the preserved ginger were as delicious as one could wish. But as to our black butter, do not decoy anybody to Southampton by such a lure, for it is all gone. The first pot was opened when Frank and Mary were here, and proved not at all what it ought to be; it was neither solid nor entirely sweet, and on seeing it Eliza remembered that Miss Austen had said she did not think it had been boiled enough. It was made, you know, when we were absent. Such being the event of the first pot, I would not save the second, and we therefore ate it in unpretending privacy; and though not what it ought to be, part of it was very good.

James means to keep three horses on this increase of income; at present he has but one. Mary wishes the other two to be fit to carry women, and in the purchase of one Edward will probably be called upon to fulfil his promise to his godson. We have now pretty well ascertained James's income to be eleven hundred pounds, curate paid, which makes us very happy – the ascertainment as well as the income.

Mary does not talk of the garden; it may well be a disagreeable subject to her, but her husband is persuaded that nothing is wanting to make the first new one good but trenching, which is to be done by his own servants and John Bond, by degrees, not at the expense which trenching the other amounted to.

I was happy to hear, chiefly for Anna's sake, that a ball at Manydown was once more in agitation; it is called a child's ball, and given by Mrs. Heathcote to Wm. Such was its beginning at least, but it will probably swell into something more. Edward was invited during his stay at Manydown, and it is to take place between this and Twelfth-day. Mrs. Hulbert has taken Anna a pair of white shoes on the occasion.

I forgot in my last to tell you that we hear, by way of Kintbury and the Palmers, that they were all well at Bermuda in the beginning of Nov.

Wednesday. – Yesterday must have been a day of sad remembrance at Gm. I am glad it is over. We spent Friday evening with our friends at the boarding-house, and our curiosity was gratified by the sight of their fellow-inmates, Mrs. Drew and Miss Hook, Mr. Wynne and Mr. Fitzhugh; the latter is brother to Mrs. Lance, and very much the gentleman. He has lived in that house more than twenty years, and, poor man! is so totally deaf that they say he could not hear a cannon, were it fired close to him; having no cannon at hand to make the experiment, I took it for granted, and talked to him a little with my fingers, which was funny enough. I recommended him to read *Corinna.*

Miss Hook is a well-behaved, genteelish woman; Mrs. Drew well behaved, without being at all genteel. Mr. Wynne seems a chatty and rather familiar young man. Miss Murden was quite a different creature this last evening from what she had been before, owing to her having with Martha's help found a situation in the morning, which bids very fair for comfort. When she leaves Steventon, she comes to board and lodge with Mrs. Hookey, the chemist – for there is no Mr. Hookey. I cannot say that I am in any hurry for the conclusion of her present visit, but I was truly glad to see her comfortable in mind and spirits; at her age, perhaps, one may be as friendless one-self, and in similar circumstances quite as captious.

My mother has been lately adding to her possessions in plate – a whole tablespoon and a whole dessert-spoon, and six whole teaspoons – which makes our sideboard border on the magnificent. They were mostly the produce of old or useless silver. I have turned the 11s. in the list into 12s., and the card looks all the better; a silver tea-ladle is also added, which will at least answer the purpose of making us sometimes think of John Warren.

I have laid Lady Sondes' case before Martha, who does not make the least objection to it, and is particularly pleased with the name of Montresor. I do not agree with her there, but I like his rank very much, and always affix the ideas of strong sense and highly elegant manners to a general.

I must write to Charles next week. You may guess in what extravagant terms of praise Earle Harwood speaks of him. He is looked up to by everybody in all America.

I shall not tell you anything more of Wm. Digweed's china, as your silence on the subject makes you unworthy of it. Mrs. H. Digweed looks forward with great satisfaction to our being her neighbours. I would have her enjoy the idea to the utmost, as I suspect there will not be much in the reality. With equal pleasure we anticipate an intimacy with her husband's bailiff and his wife, who live close by us, and are said to be remarkably good sort of people.

Yes, yes, we *will* have a pianoforte, as good a one as can be got for thirty guineas, and I will practise country dances, that we may have some amusement for our nephews and nieces, when we have the pleasure of their company.

Martha sends her love to Henry, and tells him that he will soon have a bill of Miss Chaplin's, about 14*l.*, to pay on her account; but the bill shall not be sent in till his return to town. I hope he comes to you in good health, and in spirits as good as a first return to Godmersham can allow. With his nephews he will force himself to be cheerful, till he really is so. Send me some intelligence of Eliza; it is a long while since I have heard of her.

We have had snow on the ground here almost a week; it is now going, but Southampton must boast no longer. We all send our love to Edward junior and his brothers, and I hope Speculation is generally liked.

Fare you well.

Yours ever sincerely,

J. AUSTEN.

My mother has not been out of doors this week, but she keeps pretty well. We have received through Bookham an indifferent account of your godmother.

Letter LI – 1809

Castle Square: Tuesday (January 10).

I am not surprised, my dear Cassandra, that you did not find my last letter very full of matter, and I wish this may not have the same deficiency; but we are doing nothing ourselves to write about, and I am therefore quite dependent upon the communications of our friends, or my own wits.

This post brought me two interesting letters, yours and one from Bookham, in answer to an inquiry of mine about your good godmother, of whom we had lately received a very alarming account from Paragon. Miss Arnold was the informant then, and she spoke of Mrs. E. L. having been very dangerously ill, and attended by a physician from Oxford.

Your letter to Adlestrop may perhaps bring you information from the spot, but in case it should not, I must tell you that she is better; though Dr. Bourne cannot yet call her out of danger; such was the case last Wednesday, and Mrs. Cooke's having had no later account is a favourable sign. I am to hear again from the latter *next* week, but not *this,* if everything goes on well.

Her disorder is an inflammation on the lungs, arising from a severe chill, taken in church last Sunday three weeks; her mind all pious composure, as may be supposed. George Cooke was there when her illness began; his brother has now taken his place. Her age and feebleness considered, one's fears cannot but preponderate, though her amendment has already surpassed the expectation of the physician at the beginning. I am sorry to add that *Becky* is laid up with a complaint of the same kind.

I am very glad to have the time of your return at all fixed; we all rejoice in it, and it will not be later than I had expected. I dare not hope that Mary and Miss Curling may be detained at Portsmouth so long or half so long; but it would be worth twopence to have it so.

The "St. Albans" perhaps may soon be off to help bring home what may remain by this time of our poor army, whose state seems dreadfully critical. The "Regency" seems to have been heard of only here; my most political correspondents make no mention of it. Unlucky that I should have wasted so much reflection on the subject.

I can now answer your question to my mother more at large, and likewise more at small – with equal perspicuity and minuteness; for the very day of our leaving Southampton is fixed; and if the knowledge is of no *use* to Edward, I am sure it will give him pleasure. Easter Monday, April 3, is the day; we are to sleep that night at Alton, and be with our friends at Bookham the next, if they are then at home; there we remain till the following Monday, and on Tuesday, April 11, hope to be at Godmersham. If the Cookes are absent, we shall finish our journey on the 5th. These plans depend of course upon the weather, but I hope there will be no settled cold to delay us materially.

To make you amends for being at Bookham, it is in contemplation to spend a few days at Baiton Lodge in our way *out* of Kent. The hint of such a visit is most affectionately welcomed by Mrs. Birch, in one of her odd, pleasant letters lately, in which she speaks of *us* with the usual distinguished kindness, declaring that she shall not be at all satisfied unless a very *handsome* present is made us immediately from one quarter.

Fanny's not coming with you is no more than we expected, and as we have not the hope of a bed for her, and shall see her so soon afterwards at Godmersham, we cannot wish it otherwise.

William will be quite recovered, I trust, by the time you receive this. What a comfort his cross-stitch must have been! Pray tell him that I should like to see his work very much. I hope our answers this morning have given satisfaction; we had great pleasure in Uncle Deedes' packet; and pray let Marianne know, in private, that I think she is quite right to work a rug for Uncle John's coffee urn, and that I am sure it must give great pleasure to herself now, and to him when he receives it.

The preference of Brag over Speculation does not greatly surprise me, I believe, because I feel the same myself; but it mortifies me deeply, because Speculation was under my patronage; and, after all, what is there so delightful in a pair royal of Braggers? It is but three nines or three knaves, or a mixture of them. When one comes to reason upon it, it cannot stand its ground against Speculation – of which I hope Edward is now convinced. Give my love to him if he is.

The letter from Paragon before mentioned was much like those which had preceded it, as to the felicity of its writer. They found their house so dirty and so damp that they were obliged to be a week at an inn. John Binns had behaved most unhandsomely and engaged himself elsewhere. They *have* a man, however, on the same footing, which my aunt does not like, and she finds both him and the new maidservant very, very inferior to Robert and Martha. Whether they mean to have any other domestics does not appear, nor whether they are to have a carriage while they are in Bath.

The Holders are as usual, though I believe it is not very usual for them to be happy, which they now are at a great rate, in Hooper's marriage. The Irvines are not mentioned.

The American lady improved as we went on; but still the same faults in part recurred. We are now in *Margiana,* and like it very well indeed. We are just going to set off for Northumberland to be shut up in Widdrington Tower, where there must be two or three sets of victims already immured under a very fine villain.

Wednesday. – Your report of Eliza's health gives me great pleasure, and the progress of the bank is a constant source of satisfaction. With such increasing profits; tell Henry that I hope he will not work poor High-diddle so hard as he used to do.

Has your newspaper given a sad story of a Mrs. Middleton, wife of a farmer in Yorkshire, her sister, and servant, being almost frozen to death in the late weather, her little child quite so? I hope the sister is not our friend Miss Woodd, and I rather think her brother-in-law had moved into Lincolnshire, but their name and station accord too well. Mrs. M. and the maid are said to be tolerably recovered, but the sister is likely to lose the use of her limbs.

Charles' rug will be finished to-day, and sent to-morrow to Frank, to be consigned by him to Mr. Turner's care; and I am going to send *Marmion* out with it – very generous in me, I think.

As we have no letter from Adlestrop, we may suppose the good woman was alive on Monday, but I cannot help expecting bad news from thence or Bookham in a few days. Do you continue quite well?

Have you nothing to say of your little name-sake? We join in love and many happy returns.

Yours affectionately,

J. AUSTEN.

The Manydown ball was a smaller thing than I expected, but it seems to have made Anna very happy. At *her* age it would not have done for *me.*

Letter LII – 1809

Castle Square: Tuesday (January 17).

MY DEAR CASSANDRA,

I am happy to say that we had no second letter from Bookham last week. Yours has brought its usual measure of satisfaction and amusement, and I beg your acceptance of all the thanks due on the occasion. Your offer of cravats is very kind, and happens to be particularly adapted to my wants, but it was an odd thing to occur to you.

Yes, we have got another fall of snow, and are very dreadful; everything seems to turn to snow this winter.

I hope you have had no more illness among you, and that William will be soon as well as ever. His working a footstool for Chawton is a most agreeable surprise to me, and I am sure his grandmamma will value it very much as a proof of his affection and industry, but we shall never have the heart to put our feet upon it. I believe I must work a muslin cover in satin stitch to keep it from the dirt. I long to know what his colours are. I guess greens and purples.

Edward and Henry have started a difficulty respecting our journey, which, I must own with some confusion, had never been thought of by us; but if the former expected by it to prevent our travelling into Kent entirely he will be disappointed, for we have already determined to go the Croydon road on leaving Bookham and sleep at Dartford. Will not that do? There certainly does seem no convenient resting place on the other road.

Anna went to Clanville last Friday, and I have hopes of her new aunt's being really worth her knowing. Perhaps you may never have heard that James and Mary paid a morning visit there in form some weeks ago, and Mary, though by no means disposed to like her, was very much pleased with her indeed. *Her* praise, to be sure, proves nothing more than Mrs. M.'s being civil and attentive to them, but her being so is in favour of her having good sense. Mary writes of Anna as improved in person, but gives her no other commendation. I am afraid her absence now may deprive her of one pleasure, for that silly Mr. Hammond is actually to give his ball on Friday.

We had some reason to expect a visit from Earle Harwood and James this week, but they do not come. Miss Murden arrived last night at Mrs. Hookey's, as a message and a basket announced to us. You will therefore return to an enlarged and, of course, improved society here, especially as the Miss Williamses are come back.

We were agreeably surprised the other day by a visit from your beauty and mine, each in a new cloth mantle and bonnet; and I dare say you will value yourself much on the modest propriety of Miss W.'s taste, hers being purple and Miss Grace's scarlet.

I can easily suppose that your six weeks here will be fully occupied, were it only in lengthening the waists of your gowns. I have pretty well arranged my spring and summer plans of that kind, and mean to wear out my spotted muslin before I go. You will exclaim at this, but mine really has signs of feebleness, which, with a little care, may come to something.

Martha and Dr. Mant are as bad as ever; he runs after her in the street to apologise for having spoken to a gentleman while *she* was near him the day before. Poor Mrs. Mant can stand it no longer; she is retired to one of her married daughter's.

When William returns to Winchester Mary Jane is to go to Mrs. Nune's for a month, and then to Steventon for a fortnight, and it seems likely that she and her Aunt Martha may travel into Berkshire together.

We shall not have a month of Martha after your return, and that month will be a very interrupted and broken one, but we shall enjoy ourselves the more when we *can* get a quiet half-hour together.

To set against your new novel, of which nobody ever heard before, and perhaps never may again, we have got *"Ida of Athens,"* by Miss Owenson, which must be very clever, because it was written, as the authoress says, in three months. We have only read the preface yet, but her *Irish Girl* does not make me expect much. If the warmth of her language could affect the body it might be worth reading in this weather.

Adieu! I must leave off to stir the fire and call on Miss Murden.

Evening. – I have done them both, the first very often. We found our friend as comfortable as she can ever allow herself to be in cold weather. There is a very neat parlour behind the shop for her to sit in, not very light indeed, being *à la* Southampton, the middle of three deep, but very lively from the frequent sound of the pestle and mortar.

We afterwards called on the Miss Williamses, who lodge at Durantoy's. Miss Mary only was at home, and she is in very indifferent health. Dr. Hackett came in while we were there, and said that he never remembered such a severe winter as this in Southampton before. It is bad, but we do not suffer as we did last year, because the wind has been more N.E. than N.W.

For a day or two last week my mother was very poorly with a return of *one* of her old complaints, but it did not last long, and seems to have left nothing bad behind it. She began to talk of a serious illness, her two last having been preceded by the same symptoms, but, thank heaven! she is now quite as well as one can expect her to be in weather which deprives her of exercise.

Miss M. conveys to us a third volume of sermons, from Hamstall, just published, and which we are to like better than the two others; they are professedly *practical,* and for the use of country congregations. I have just received some verses in an unknown hand, and am desired to forward them to my nephew Edward at Godmersham.

> Alas! poor Brag, thou boastful game!
> What now avails thine empty name?
> Where now thy more distinguished fame?
> My day is o'er, and thine the same,
> For thou, like me, art thrown aside
> At Godmersham, this Christmas tide;
> And now across the table wide
> Each game save brag or spec. is tried.
> Such is the mild ejaculation
> Of tender-hearted speculation.

Wednesday. – I expected to have a letter from somebody to-day, but I have not. Twice every day I think of a letter from Portsmouth.

Miss Murden has been sitting with us this morning. As yet she seems very well pleased with her situation. The worst part of her being in Southampton will be the necessity of one walking with her now and then, for she talks so loud that one is quite ashamed; but our dining hours are luckily very different, which we shall take all reasonable advantage of.

The Queen's birthday moves the Assembly to this night instead of last, and, as it is always fully attended, Martha and I expect an amusing show. We were in hopes of being independent of other companions by having the attendance of Mr. Austen and Captain Harwood; but, as they fail us, we are obliged to look out for other help, and have fixed on the Wallops as least likely to be troublesome. I have called on them this morning and found them very willing, and I am sorry that you must wait a whole week for the particulars of the evening. I propose being asked to dance by our acquaintance Mr. Smith, now *Captain Smith,* who has lately re-appeared in Southampton, but I shall decline it. He saw Charles last August.

What an alarming bride Mrs. . . . . must have been; such a parade is one of the most immodest pieces of modesty that one can imagine. To *attract* notice could have been her only wish. It augurs ill for her family; it announces not *great* sense, and therefore ensures boundless influence.

I hope Fanny's visit is now taking place. You have said scarcely anything of her lately, but I trust you are as good friends as ever.

Martha sends her love, and hopes to have the pleasure of seeing you when you return to Southampton. You are to understand this message as being merely for the sake of a message to oblige me.

Yours affectionately,

J. AUSTEN.

Henry never sent his love to me in your last, but I send him mine.

Letter LIII – 1809

Castle Square: Tuesday (January 24).

MY DEAR CASSANDRA,

I will give you the indulgence of a letter on Thursday this week, instead of Friday, but I do not require you to write again before Sunday, provided I may believe you and your finger going on quite well. Take care of your precious self; do not work too hard. Remember that Aunt Cassandras are quite as scarce as Miss Beverleys.[13]

I had the happiness yesterday of a letter from Charles, but I shall say as little about it as possible, because I know *that* excruciating Henry will have had a letter likewise, to make all my intelligence valueless. It was written at Bermuda on the 7th and 10th of December. All well, and Fanny still only in expectation of being otherwise. He had taken a small prize in his late cruise – a French schooner, laden with sugar; but bad weather parted them, and she had not yet been heard of. His cruise ended December 1st. My September letter was the latest he had received.

---

13 "Cecilia" Beverley, the heroine of Miss Burney's novel.

This day three weeks you are to be in London, and I wish you better weather; not but that you may have worse, for we have now nothing but ceaseless snow or rain and insufferable dirt to complain of; no tempestuous winds nor severity of cold. Since I wrote last we have had something of each, but it is not genteel to rip up old grievances.

You used me scandalously by not mentioning Edward Cooper's sermons. I tell you everything, and it is unknown the mysteries you conceal from me; and, to add to the rest, you persevere in giving a final e to invalid, thereby putting it out of one's power to suppose Mrs. E. Leigh, even for a moment, a veteran soldier. She, good woman, is, I hope, destined for some further placid enjoyment of her own excellence in this world, for her recovery advances exceedingly well.

I had this pleasant news in a letter from Bookham last Thursday, but, as the letter was from Mary instead of her mother, you will guess her account was not equally good from home. Mrs. Cooke had been confined to her bed some days by illness, but was then better, and Mary wrote in confidence of her continuing to mend. I have desired to hear again soon.

You rejoice me by what you say of Fanny. I hope she will not turn good-for-nothing this ever so long. We thought of and talked of her yesterday with sincere affection, and wished her a long enjoyment of all the happiness to which she seems born. While she gives happiness to those about her she is pretty sure of her own share.

I am gratified by her having pleasure in what I write, but I wish the knowledge of my being exposed to her discerning criticism may not hurt my style, by inducing too great a solicitude. I begin already to weigh my words and sentences more than I did, and am looking about for a sentiment, an illustration, or a metaphor in every corner of the room. Could my ideas flow as fast as the rain in the store-closet it would be charming.

We have been in two or three dreadful states within the last week, from the melting of the snow, &c., and the contest between us and the closet has now ended in our defeat. I have been obliged to move almost everything out of it, and leave it to splash itself as it likes.

You have by no means raised my curiosity after Caleb. My disinclination for it before was affected, but now it is real. I do not like the evangelicals. Of course I shall be delighted when I read it, like other people, but till I do I dislike it.

I am sorry my verses did not bring any return from Edward. I was in hopes they might, but I suppose he does not rate them high enough. It might be partiality, but they seemed to me purely classical – just like Homer and Virgil, Ovid and Propria que Maribus.

I had a nice brotherly letter from Frank the other day, which, after an interval of nearly three weeks, was very welcome. No orders were come on Friday, and none were come yesterday, or we should have heard to-day. I had supposed Miss C. would share her cousin's room here, but a message in this letter proves the contrary. I will make the garret as comfortable as I can, but the possibilities of that apartment are not great.

My mother has been talking to Eliza about our future home, and *she,* making no difficulty at all of the sweetheart, is perfectly disposed to continue with us, but till she has written home for *mother's* approbation cannot quite decide. *Mother* does not like to have her so far off. At Chawton she will be nine or ten miles nearer, which I hope will have its due influence.

As for Sally, she means to play John Binns with us, in her anxiety to belong to our household again. Hitherto she appears a very good servant.

You depend upon finding all your plants dead, I hope. They look very ill, I understand.

Your silence on the subject of our ball makes me suppose your curiosity too great for words. We were very well entertained, and could have stayed longer but for the arrival of my list shoes to convey me home, and I did not like to keep them waiting in the cold. The room was tolerably full, and the ball opened by Miss Glyn. The Miss Lances had partners, Captain D'auvergne's friend appeared in regimentals, Caroline Maitland had an officer to flirt with, and Mr. John Harrison was deputed by Captain Smith, being himself absent, to ask me to dance. Everything went well, you see, especially after we had tucked Mrs. Lance's neckerchief in behind and fastened it with a pin.

We had a very full and agreeable account of Mr. Hammond's ball from Anna last night; the same fluent pen has sent similar information, I know, into Kent. She seems to have been as happy as one could wish her, and the complacency of her mamma in doing the honours of the evening must have made her pleasure almost as great. The grandeur of the meeting was beyond my hopes. I should like to have seen Anna's looks and performance, but that sad cropped head must have injured the former.

Martha pleases herself with believing that if *I* had kept her counsel you would never have heard of Dr. M.'s late behaviour, as if the very slight manner in which I mentioned it could have been all on which you found your judgment. I do not endeavour to un- deceive her, because I wish her happy, at all events, and know how highly she prizes happiness of any kind. She is, moreover, so full of kindness for us both, and sends you in particular so many good wishes about your finger, that I am willing to overlook a ve- nial fault, and as Dr. M. is a clergyman, their attach- ment, however immoral, has a decorous air. Adieu, sweet You. This is grievous news from Spain. It is well that Dr. Moore was spared the knowledge of such a son's death.

Yours affectionately,

J. AUSTEN.

Anna's hand gets better and better; it begins to be too good for any consequence.

We send best love to dear little Lizzy and Marianne in particular.

The Portsmouth paper gave a melancholy history of a poor mad woman, escaped from confinement, who said her husband and daughter, of the name of Payne, lived at Ashford, in Kent. Do you own them?

Letter LIV – 1809

Castle Square: Monday (January 30).

MY DEAR CASSANDRA,

I was not much surprised yesterday by the agreeable surprise of your letter, and extremely glad to receive the assurance of your finger being well again.

Here is such a wet day as never was seen. I wish the poor little girls had better weather for their journey; they must amuse themselves with watching the rain-drops down the windows. Sackree, I suppose, feels quite broken-hearted. I cannot have done with the weather without observing how delightfully mild it is; I am sure Fanny must enjoy it with us. Yesterday was a very blowing day; we got to church, however, which we had not been able to do for two Sundays before.

I am not at all ashamed about the name of the novel, having been guilty of no insult towards your handwriting; the diphthong I always saw, but knowing how fond you were of adding a vowel wherever you could, I attributed it to that alone, and the knowledge of the truth does the book no service; the only merit it could have was in the name of Caleb, which has an honest, un-pretending sound, but in Coelebs there is pedantry and affectation. Is it written only to classical scholars?

I shall now try to say only what is necessary, I am weary of meandering; so expect a vast deal of small matter, concisely told, in the next two pages.

Mrs. Cooke has been very dangerously ill, but is now, I hope, safe. I had a letter last week from George, Mary being too busy to write, and at that time the disorder was called of the typhus kind, and their alarm considerable, but yester-day brought me a much better account from Mary, the origin of the complaint being now ascertained to be bilious, and the strong medicines requisite promising to be effectual. Mrs. E. L. is so much recovered as to get into the dressing-room every day.

A letter from Hamstall gives us the history of Sir. Tho. Williams's return. The Admiral, whoever he might be, took a fancy to the "Neptune," and having only a worn-out 74 to offer in lieu of it, Sir Tho. declined such a command, and is come home passenger. Lucky man! to have so fair an opportunity of escape. I hope his wife allows herself to be happy on the occasion, and does not give all her thoughts to being nervous.

A great event happens this week at Hamstall in young Edward's removal to school. He is going to Rugby, and is very happy in the idea of it; I wish his happiness may last, but it will be a great change to become a raw school-boy from being a pompous sermon-writer and a domineering brother. It will do him good, I dare say.

Caroline has had a great escape from being burnt to death lately. As her husband gives the account, we must believe it true. Miss Murden is gone – called away by the critical state of Mrs. Pottinger, who has had another severe stroke, and is without sense or speech. Miss Murden wishes to return to Southampton if circumstances suit, but it must be very doubtful.

We have been obliged to turn away Cholles, he grew so very drunken and negligent, and we have a man in his place called Thomas.

Martha desires me to communicate something con-cerning herself which she knows will give you pleasure, as affording her very particular satisfaction – it is, that she is to be in town this spring with Mrs. Dundas. I need not dilate on the subject. You under-stand enough of the whys and wherefores to enter into her feelings, and to be conscious that of all possible arrangements it is the one most acceptable to her. She goes to Barton on leaving us, and the family remove to town in April.

What you tell me of Miss Sharpe is quite new, and surprises me a little; I feel, however, as you do. She is born, poor thing! to struggle with evil, and her continuing with Miss B. is, I hope, a proof that

308

matters are not always so very bad between them as her letters sometimes represent.

Jenny's marriage I had heard of, and supposed you would do so too from Steventon, as I knew you were corresponding with Mary at the time. I hope she will not sully the respectable name she now bears.

Your plan for Miss Curling is uncommonly considerate and friendly, and such as she must surely jump at. Edward's going round by Steventon, as I understand he promises to do, can be no reasonable objection; Mrs. J. Austen's hospitality is just of the kind to enjoy such a visitor.

We were very glad to know Aunt Fanny was in the country when we read of the fire. Pray give my best compliments to the Mrs. Finches, if they are at Gm. I am sorry to find that Sir J. Moore has a mother living, but though a very heroic son he might not be a very necessary one to her happiness. Deacon Morrell may be more to Mrs. Morrell

I wish Sir John had united something of the Christian with the hero in his death. Thank heaven! we have had no one to care for particularly among the troops – no one, in fact, nearer to us than Sir John himself. Col. Maitland is safe and well; his mother and sisters were of course anxious about him, but there is no entering much into the solicitudes of that family.

My mother is well, and gets out when she can with the same enjoyment, and apparently the same strength, as hitherto. She hopes you will not omit begging Mrs. Seward to get the garden cropped for us, supposing she leaves the house too early to make the garden any object to herself. We are very desirous of receiving *your* account of the house, for your observations will have a motive which can leave nothing to conjecture and suffer nothing from want of memory. For one's own dear self, one ascertains and remembers everything.

Lady Sondes is an impudent woman to come back into her old neighbourhood again; I suppose she pretends never to have married before, and wonders how her father and mother came to have her christened Lady Sondes.

The store closet, I hope, will never do so again, for much of the evil is proved to have proceeded from the gutter being choked up, and we have had it cleared. We had reason to rejoice in the child's absence at the time of the thaw, for the nursery was not habitable. We hear of similar disasters from almost everybody.

No news from Portsmouth. We are very patient. Mrs. Charles Fowle desires to be kindly remembered to you. She is warmly interested in my brother and his family.

Yours very affectionately,

J. AUSTEN.

Letter LV – 1811

Sloane St.: Thursday (April 18).

MY DEAR CASSANDRA,

I have so many little matters to tell you of, that I cannot wait any longer before I begin to put them down. I spent Tuesday in Bentinck Street. The Cookes called here and took me back, and it was quite a Cooke day, for the Miss Rolles paid a visit while I was there, and Sam Arnold dropped in to tea.

The badness of the weather disconcerted an excellent plan of mine – that of calling on Miss Beckford again; but from the middle of the day it rained incessantly. Mary and I, after disposing of her father and mother, went to the Liverpool Museum and the British Gallery, and I had some amusement at each, though my preference for men and women always inclines me to attend more to the company than the sight.

Mrs. Cooke regrets very much that she did not see you when you called; it was owing to a blunder among the servants, for she did not know of our visit till we were gone. She seems tolerably well, but the nervous part of her complaint, I fear, increases, and makes her more and more unwilling to part with Mary.

I have proposed to the latter that she should go to Chawton with me, on the supposition of my travelling the Guilford road, and *she,* I do believe, would be glad to do it, but perhaps it may be impossible; unless a brother can be at home at that time, it certainly must. George comes to them to-day.

I did not see Theo. till late on Tuesday; he was gone to Ilford, but he came back in time to show his usual nothing-meaning, harmless, heartless civility. Henry, who had been confined the whole day to the bank, took me in his way home, and, after putting life and wit into the party for a quarter of an hour, put himself and his sister into a hackney coach.

I bless my stars that I have done with Tuesday. But, alas! Wednesday was likewise a day of great doings, for Manon and I took our walk to Grafton House, and I have a good deal to say on that subject.

I am sorry to tell you that I am getting very extravagant, and spending all my money, and, what is worse for *you,* I have been spending yours too; for in a linendraper's shop to which I went for checked muslin, and for which I was obliged to give seven shillings a yard, I was tempted by a pretty-coloured muslin, and bought ten yards of it on the chance of your liking it; but, at the same time, if it should not suit you, you must not think yourself at all obliged to take it; it is only *3s. 6d.* per yard, and I should not in the least mind keeping the whole. In texture it is just what we prefer, but its resemblance to green crewels, I must own, is not great, for the pattern is a small red spot. And now I believe I have done all my commissions except Wedgwood.

I liked my walk very much; it was shorter than I had expected, and the weather was delightful. We set off immediately after breakfast, and must have reached Grafton House by half-past 11; but when we entered the shop the whole counter was thronged, and we waited *full* half an hour before we could be attended to. When we were served, however, I was very well satisfied with my purchases – my bugle trimming at *2s. 4d.* and three pair silk stockings for a little less than *12s.* a pair.

In my way back who should I meet but Mr. Moore, just come from Beckenham. I believe he would have passed me if I had not made him stop, but we were delighted to meet. I soon found, however, that he had nothing new to tell me, and then I let him go.

In my way back who should I meet but Mr. Moore, just come from Beckenham. I believe he would have passed me if I had not made him stop, but we were delighted to meet. I soon found, however, that he had nothing new to tell me, and then I let him go.

Miss Burton has made me a very pretty little bonnet, and now nothing can satisfy me but I must have a straw hat, of the riding-hat shape, like Mrs. Tilson's; and a young woman in this neighbourhood is actually making me one. I am really very shocking, but it will not be dear at a Guinea. Our pelisses are 17s. each; she charges only 8s. for the making, but the buttons seem expensive – I might have said, for the fact is plain enough.

We drank tea again yesterday with the Tilsons, and met the Smiths. I find all these little parties very pleasant. I like Mrs. S.; Miss Beaty is good-humour itself, and does not seem much besides. We spend to-morrow evening with them, and are to meet the Coln. and Mrs. *Cantelo* Smith you have been used to hear of, and, if she is in good humour, are likely to have excellent singing.

To-night I might have been at the play; Henry had kindly planned our going together to the Lyceum, but I have a cold which I should not like to make worse before Saturday, so I stay within all this day.

Eliza is walking out by herself. She has plenty of business on her hands just now, for the day of the party is settled, and drawing near. Above 80 people are invited for next Tuesday evening, and there is to be some very good music – five professionals, three of them glee singers, besides amateurs. Fanny will listen to this. One of the hirelings is a Capital on the harp, from which I expect great pleasure. The foundation of the party was a dinner to Henry Egerton and Henry Walter, but the latter leaves town the day before. I am sorry, as I wished *her* prejudice to be done away, but should have been more sorry if there had been no invitation.

I am a wretch, to be so occupied with all these things as to seem to have no thoughts to give to people and circumstances which really supply a far more lasting interest – the society in which you are; but I do think of you all, I assure you, and want to know all about everybody, and especially about your visit to the W. Friars; "mais le moyen" not to be occupied by one's own concerns?

Saturday. – Frank is superseded in the "Caledonia." Henry brought us this news yesterday from Mr. Daysh, and he heard at the same time that Charles may be in England in the course of a month. Sir Edward Pollen succeeds Lord Gambier in his command, and some captain of his succeeds Frank; and I believe the order is already gone out. Henry means to inquire farther to-day. He wrote to Mary on the occasion. This is something to think of. Henry is convinced that he will have the offer of something else, but does not think it will be at all incumbent on him to accept it; and then follows, what will he do? and where will he live?

I hope to hear from you to-day. How are you as to health, strength, looks, &c.? I had a very comfortable account from Chawton yesterday.

If the weather permits, Eliza and I walk into London this morning. She is in want of chimney lights for Tuesday, and I of an ounce of darning cotton. She has resolved not to venture to the play to-night. The D'Entraigues and Comte Julien cannot come to the party, which was at first a grief, but she has since supplied herself so well with performers that it is of no consequence; their not coming has produced our going to them to-morrow evening, which I like the idea of. It will be amusing to see the ways of a French circle.

I wrote to Mrs. Hill a few days ago, and have received a most kind and satisfactory answer. Any time the first week in May exactly suits her, and therefore I consider my going as tolerably fixed. I shall leave Sloane Street on the 1st or 2nd, and be ready for James on the 9th, and, if his plan alters, I can take care of myself. I have explained my views here, and everything is smooth and pleasant; and Eliza talks kindly of conveying me to Streatham.

We met the Tilsons yesterday evening, but the singing Smiths sent an excuse, which put our Mrs. Smith out of humour.

We are come back, after a good dose of walking and coaching, and I have the pleasure of your letter. I wish I had James's verses, but they were left at Chawton. When I return thither, if Mrs. K. will give me leave, I will send them to her.

Our first object to-day was Henrietta St., to consult with Henry in consequence of a very unlucky change of the play for this very night – "Hamlet" instead of "King John" – and we are to go on Monday to "Macbeth" instead; but it is a disappointment to us both.

Love to all.

Yours affectionately,

JANE.

Letter LVI – 1811

Sloane St.: Thursday (April 25).

MY DEAREST CASSANDRA,

I can return the compliment by thanking you for the unexpected pleasure of *your* letter yesterday, and as I like unexpected pleasure, it made me very happy; and, indeed, you need not apologise for your letter in any respect, for it is all very fine, but not *too* fine, I hope, to be written again, or something like it.

I think Edward will not suffer much longer from heat; by the look of things this morning I suspect the weather is rising into the balsamic north-east. It has been hot here, as you may suppose, since it was so hot with you, but I have not suffered from it at all, nor felt it in such a degree as to make me imagine it would be anything in the country. Everybody has talked of the heat, but I set it all down to London.

I give you joy of our new nephew, and hope if he ever comes to be hanged it will not be till we are too old to care about it. It is a great comfort to have it so safely and speedily over. The Miss Curlings must be hard worked in writing so many letters, but the novelty of it may recommend it to *them;* mine was from Miss Eliza, and she says that my brother may arrive to-day.

No, indeed, I am never too busy to think of *S. and S.* I can no more forget it than a mother can forget her sucking child; and I am much obliged to you for your inquiries. I have had two sheets to correct, but the last only brings us to Willoughby's first appearance. Mrs. K. regrets in the most flattering manner that she must wait *till* May, but I have scarcely a hope of its being out in June. Henry does not neglect it; he *has* hurried the printer, and says he will see him again to-day. It will not stand still during his absence, it will be sent to Eliza.

The *Incomes* remain as they were, but I will get them altered if I can. I am very much gratified by Mrs. K's interest in it; and whatever may be the event of it as to my credit with her, sincerely wish her curiosity could be satisfied sooner than is now probable. I think she will like my Elinor, but cannot build on anything else.

Our party went off extremely well. There were many solicitudes, alarms, and vexations, beforehand, of course, but at last everything was quite right. The rooms were dressed up with flowers, &c., and looked very pretty. A glass for the mantlepiece was lent by the man who is making their own. Mr. Egerton and

Mr. Walter came at half-past five, and the festivities began with a pair of very fine soals.

Yes, Mr. Walter – for he postponed his leaving London on purpose – which did not give much pleasure at the time, any more than the circumstance from which it rose – his calling on Sunday and being asked by Henry to take the family dinner on that day, which he did; but it is all smoothed over now, and she likes him very well.

At half-past seven arrived the musicians in two hackney coaches, and by eight the lordly company began to appear. Among the earliest were George and Mary Cooke, and I spent the greater part of the evening very pleasantly with them. The drawing-room being soon hotter than we liked, we placed ourselves in the connecting passage, which was comparatively cool, and gave us all the advantage of the music at a pleasant distance, as well as that of the first view of every new comer.

I was quite surrounded by acquaintances, especially gentlemen; and what with Mr. Hampson, Mr. Seymour, Mr. W. Knatchbull, Mr. Guillemarde, Mr. Cure, a Captain Simpson, brother to *the* Captain Simpson, besides Mr. Walter and Mr. Egerton, in addition to the Cookes, and Miss Beckford, and Miss Middleton, I had quite as much upon my hands as I could do.

Poor Miss B. has been suffering again from her old complaint, and looks thinner than ever. She certainly goes to Cheltenham the beginning of June. We were all delight and cordiality of course. Miss M. seems very happy, but has not beauty enough to figure in London.

Including everybody we were sixty-six – which was considerably more than Eliza had expected, and quite enough to fill the back drawing-room and leave a few to be scattered about in the other and in the passage.

The music was extremely good. It opened (tell Fanny) with "Poike de Parp pirs praise pof Prapela"; and of the other glees I remember, "In peace love tunes," "Rosabelle," "The Red Cross Knight," and "Poor In-sect." Between the songs were lessons on the harp, or harp and pianoforte together; and the harp-player was Wiepart, whose name seems famous, though new to me. There was one female singer, a short Miss Davis, all in blue, bringing up for the public line, whose voice was said to be very fine indeed; and all the performers gave great satisfaction by doing what they were paid for, and giving themselves no airs. No amateur could be persuaded to do anything.

The house was not clear till after twelve. If you wish to hear more of it, you must put your questions, but

I seem rather to have exhausted than spared the subject.

This said Captain Simpson told us, on the authority of some other Captain just arrived from Halifax, that Charles was bringing the "Cleopatra" home, and that she was probably by this time in the Channel; but, as Captain S. was certainly in liquor, we must not quite depend on it. It must give one a sort of expectation, however, and will prevent my writing to him any more. I would rather he should not reach England till I am at home, and the Steventon party gone.

My mother and Martha both write with great satisfaction of Anna's behaviour. She is quite an Anna with variations, but she cannot have reached her last, for that is always the most flourishing and showy; she is at about her third or fourth, which are generally simple and pretty.

Your lilacs are in leaf, *ours* are in bloom. The horse-chestnuts are quite out, and the elms almost. I had a pleasant walk in Kensington Gardens on Sunday with Henry, Mr. Smith, and Mr. Tilson; everything was fresh and beautiful.

We *did* go to the play after all on Saturday. We went to the Lyceum, and saw the "Hypocrite," an old play taken from Molière's "Tartuffe," and were well entertained. Dowton and Mathews were the good actors; Mrs. Edwin was the heroine, and her performance is just what it used to be. I have no chance of seeing Mrs. Siddons; she *did* act on Monday, but, as Henry was told by the boxkeeper that he did not think she would, the plans, and all thought of it, were given up. I should particularly have liked seeing her in "Constance," and could swear at her with little effort for disappointing me.

Henry has been to the Water-Colour Exhibition, which opened on Monday, and is to meet us there again some morning. If Eliza cannot go (and she has a cold at present) Miss Beaty will be invited to be my companion. Henry leaves town on Sunday afternoon, but he means to write soon himself to Edward, and will tell his own plans.

The tea is this moment setting out.

Do not have your coloured muslin unless you really want it, because I am afraid I could not send it to the coach without giving trouble here.

Eliza caught her cold on Sunday in our way to the D'Entraigues. The horses actually gibbed on this side of Hyde Park Gate: a load of fresh gravel made it a formidable hill to them, and they refused the collar; I believe there was a sore shoulder to irritate. Eliza was frightened and we got out, and were detained in the evening air several minutes. The cold is in her chest, but she takes care of herself, and I hope it may not last long.

This engagement prevented Mr. Walter's staying late – he had his coffee and went away. Eliza enjoyed her evening very much, and means to cultivate the acquaintance; and I see nothing to dislike in them but their taking quantities of snuff. Monsieur, the old Count, is a very fine-looking man, with quiet manners, good enough for an Englishman, and, I believe, is a man of great information and taste. He has some fine paintings, which delighted Henry as much as the son's music gratified Eliza; and among them a miniature of Philip V. of Spain, Louis XIV.'s grandson, which exactly suited *my* capacity. Count Julien's performance is very wonderful.

We met only Mrs. Latouche and Miss East, and we are just now engaged to spend next Sunday evening at Mrs. L.'s, and to meet the D'Entraigues, but M. le Comte must do without Henry. If he would but speak English, *I* would take to him.

Have you ever mentioned the leaving off tea to Mrs. K.? Eliza has just spoken of it again. The benefit *she* has found from it in sleeping has been very great.

I shall write soon to Catherine to fix my day, which will be Thursday. We have no engagement but for

Sunday. Eliza's cold makes quiet advisable. Her party is mentioned in this morning's paper. I am sorry to hear of poor Fanny's state. From *that* quarter, I suppose, is to be the alloy of her happiness. I will have no more to say.

Yours affectionately,

J. A.

Give my love particularly to my goddaughter.

Letter LVII – 1811

Sloane St.: Tuesday.

MY DEAR CASSANDRA,

I had sent off my letter yesterday before yours came, which I was sorry for; but as Eliza has been so good as to get me a frank, your questions shall be answered without much further expense to you.

The best direction to Henry at Oxford will be *The Blue Boar, Cornmarket.*

I do *not* mean to provide another trimming for my pelisse, for I am determined to spend no more money; so I shall wear it as it is, longer than I ought, and then – I do not know.

My head-dress was a bugle-band like the border to my gown, and a flower of Mrs. Tilson's. I depended upon hearing something of the evening from Mr. W. K., and am very well satisfied with his notice of me – "A pleasing-looking young woman" – that must do; one cannot pretend to anything better now; thankful to have it continued a few years longer!

It gives me sincere pleasure to hear of Mrs. Knight's having had a tolerable night at last, but upon this occasion I wish she had another name, for the two *nights* jingle very much.

We have tried to get *"Self-control,"* but in vain. I *should* like to know what her estimate is, but am always half afraid of finding a clever novel *too clever,* and of finding my own story and my own people all forestalled.

Eliza has just received a few lines from Henry to assure her of the good conduct of his mare. He slept at Uxbridge on Sunday, and wrote from Wheatfield.

We were not claimed by Hans Place yesterday, but are to dine there to-day. Mr. Tilson called in the evening, but otherwise we were quite alone all day; and, after having been out a great deal, the change was very pleasant.

I like your opinion of Miss Atten much better than I expected, and have now hopes of her staying a whole twelvemonth. By this time I suppose she is hard at it, governing away. Poor creature! I pity her, though they *are* my nieces.

Oh! yes, I remember Miss Emma Plumbtree's *local* consequence perfectly.

I am in a dilemma, for want of an Emma,

Escaped from the lips of Henry Gipps.

But, really, I was never much more put to it than in continuing an answer to Fanny's former message. What is there to be said on the subject? Pery pell, or pare pey? or po; or at the most, Pi, pope, pey, pike, pit.

I congratulate Edward on the Weald of Kent Canal Bill being put off till another Session, as I have just had the pleasure of reading. There is always something to be hoped from delay.

> Between Session and Session
> The first Prepossession
> May rouse up the Nation,
> And the villainous Bill
> May be forced to lie still.
> Against wicked men's will

There is poetry for Edward and his daughter. I am afraid I shall not have any for you.

I forgot to tell you in my last that our cousin, Miss Payne, called in on Saturday, and was persuaded to stay dinner. She told us a great deal about her friend Lady Cath. Brecknell, who is most happily married, and Mr. Brecknell is very religious, and has got black whiskers.

I am glad to think that Edward has a tolerable day for his drive to Goodnestone, and *very* glad to hear of his kind promise of bringing you to town. I hope everything will arrange itself favourably. The 16th is now to be Mrs. Dundas's day.

I mean, if I can, to wait for your return before I have my new gown made up, from a notion of their making up to more advantage together; and, as I find the muslin is not so wide as it *used to be,* some contrivance may be necessary. I expect the skirt to require one-half breadth cut in gores, besides two whole breadths.

Eliza has not yet quite resolved on inviting Anna, but I think she will.

Yours very affectionately,

JANE.

Letter LVIII – 1811

Chawton: Wednesday (May 29).

It was a mistake of mine, my dear Cassandra, to talk of a tenth child at Hamstall. I had forgot there were but eight already.

Your inquiry after my uncle and aunt were most happily timed, for the very same post brought an account of them. They are again at Gloucester House enjoying fresh air, which they seem to have felt the want of in Bath, and are tolerably well, but not more than tolerable. My aunt does not enter into particulars, but she does not write in spirits, and we imagine that she has never entirely got the better of her disorder in the winter. Mrs. Walby takes her out airing in her barouche, which gives her a headache – a comfortable proof, I suppose, of the uselessness of the new carriage when they have got it.

You certainly must have heard before I can tell you that Col. Orde has married our cousin, Margt. Beckford, the Marchess. of Douglas's sister. The papers say that her father disinherits her, but I think too well of an Orde to suppose that she has not a handsome independence of her own.

The chicken are all alive and fit for the table, but we save them for something grand. Some of the flower seeds are coming up very well, but your mignonette makes a wretched appearance. Miss Benn has been equally unlucky as to hers. She has seed from four different people, and none of it comes up. Our young piony at the foot of the fir-tree has just blown and looks very handsome, and the whole of the shrubbery border will soon be very gay with pinks and sweet-williams, in addition to the columbines already in bloom.

The syringas, too, are coming out. We are likely to have a great crop of Orleans plumbs, but not many greengages – on the standard scarcely any, three or four dozen, perhaps, against the wall. I believe I told you differently when I first came home, but I can now judge better than I could then.

I have had a medley and satisfactory letter this morning from the husband and wife at Cowes; and, in consequence of what is related of their plans, we have been talking over the possibility of inviting them here in their way from Steventon, which is what one should wish to do, and is, I daresay, what they expect; but, supposing Martha to be at home, it does not seem a very easy thing to accommodate so large a party. My mother offers to give up her room to Frank and Mary, but there will then be only the best for two maids and three children.

They go to Steventon about the 22nd, and I guess – for it is quite a guess – will stay there from a fortnight to three weeks.

I must not venture to press Miss Sharpe's coming at present; we may hardly be at liberty before August.

Poor John Bridges! we are very sorry for his situation and for the distress of the family. Lady B. is in *one way* severely tried. And our own dear brother suffers a great deal, I dare say, on the occasion.

I have not much to say of ourselves. Anna is nursing a cold caught in the arbour at Faringdon, that she may be able to keep her engagement to Maria M. this evening, when I suppose she will make it worse. She did not return from Faringdon till Sunday, when H. B. walked home with her, and drank tea here. She was with the Prowtings almost all Monday. She went to learn to make feather trimmings of Miss Anna, and they kept her to dinner, which was rather lucky, as we were called upon to meet Mrs. and Miss Terry the same evening at the Digweeds; and, though Anna was of course invited too, I think it always safest to keep her away from the family lest she should be doing too little or too much.

Mrs. Terry, Mary, and Robert, with my aunt Harding and her daughter, came from Dummer for a day and a night – all very agreeable and very much delighted with the new house and with Chawton in general.

We sat upstairs and had thunder and lightning as usual. I never knew such a spring for thunderstorms as it has been. Thank God! we have had no bad ones here. I thought myself in luck to have my uncomfortable feelings shared by the mistress of the house, as that procured blinds and candles. It had been excessively hot the whole day. Mrs. Harding is a good-looking woman, but not much like Mrs. Toke, inasmuch as she is very brown and has scarcely any teeth; she seems to have some of Mrs. Toke's civility. Miss H. is an elegant, pleasing, pretty-looking girl, about nineteen, I suppose, or nineteen and a half, or nineteen and a quarter, with flowers in her head and music at her finger ends. She plays very well indeed. I have seldom heard anybody with more pleasure. They were at Godington four or five years ago. My cousin, Flora Long, was there last year.

My name is Diana. How does Fanny like it? What a change in the weather! We have a fire again now.

Harriet Benn sleeps at the Great House to-night and spends to-morrow with us; and the plan is that we should all walk with her to drink tea at Faringdon, for her mother is now recovered, but the state of the weather is not very promising at present.

Miss Benn has been returned to her cottage since the beginning of last week, and has now just got another girl; she comes from Alton. For many days Miss B. had nobody with her but her niece Elizabeth, who was delighted to be her visitor and her maid. They both dined here on Saturday while Anna was at Faringdon; and last night an accidental meeting and a sudden impulse produced Miss Benn and Maria Middleton at our tea-table.

If you have not heard it is very fit you should, that Mr. Harrison has had the living of Fareham given him by the Bishop, and is going to reside there; and now it is said that Mr. Peach (beautiful wiseacre) wants to have the curacy of Overton, and, if he *does* leave Wootton, James Digweed wishes to go there. Fare you well,

Yours affectionately,

JANE AUSTEN.

The chimneys at the Great House are done. Mr. Prowting has opened a gravel pit, very conveniently for my mother, just at the mouth of the approach to his house; but it looks a little as if he meant to catch all his company. Tolerable gravel.

Letter LIX – 1811

Chawton: Friday (May 31).

MY DEAR CASSANDRA,

I have a magnificent project. The Cookes have put off their visit to us; they are not well enough to leave home at present, and we have no chance of seeing them till I do not know when – probably never, in this house.

This circumstances has made me think the present time would be favourable for Miss Sharpe's coming to us; it seems a more disengaged period with us than we are likely to have later in the summer. If Frank and Mary do come, it can hardly be before the middle of July, which will be allowing a reasonable length of visit for Miss Sharpe, supposing she begins it when you return; and if you and Martha do not dislike the plan, and she can avail herself of it, the opportunity of her being conveyed hither will be excellent.

I shall write to Martha by this post, and if neither you nor she make any objection to my proposal, I shall make the invitation directly, and as there is no time to lose, you must write by return of post if you have any reason for not wishing it done. It was her intention, I believe, to go first to Mrs. Lloyd, but such a means of getting here may influence her otherwise.

We have had a thunder-storm again this morning. Your letter came to comfort me for it.

I have taken your hint, slight as it was, and have written to Mrs. Knight, and most sincerely do I hope it will not be in vain. I cannot endure the idea of her giving away her own wheel, and have told her no more than the truth, in saying that I could never use it with comfort. I had a great mind to add that, if she persisted in giving it, I would spin nothing with it but a rope to hang myself, but I was afraid of making it appear less serious matter of feeling than it really is.

I am glad you are so well yourself, and wish everybody else were equally so. I will not say that your mulberry-trees are dead, but I am afraid they are not alive. We shall have pease soon. I mean to have them with a couple of ducks from Wood Barn, and Maria Middleton, towards the end of next week.

From Monday to Wednesday Anna is to be engaged at Faringdon, in order that she may come in for the gaieties of Tuesday (the 4th), on Selbourne Common, where there are to be volunteers and felicities of all kinds. Harriet B. is invited to spend the day with the John Whites, and her father and mother have very kindly undertaken to get Anna invited also.

Harriot and Eliza dined here yesterday, and we walked back with them to tea. Not my mother – she has a cold which affects her in the usual way, and was not equal to the walk. She is better this morning, and I hope will soon physick away the worst part of it. It has not confined her; she has got out every day that the weather has allowed her.

Poor Anna is also suffering from *her* cold, which is worse to-day, but as she has no sore throat I hope it may spend itself by Tuesday. She had a delightful evening with the Miss Middletons – syllabub, tea, coffee, singing, dancing, a hot supper, eleven o'clock, everything that can be imagined agreeable. She desires her best love to Fanny, and will answer her letter before she leaves Chawton, and engages to send her a particular account of the Selbourne day.

We cannot agree as to which is the eldest of the two Miss Plumbtrees; send us word. Have you remembered to collect pieces for the patchwork? We are now at a stand-still. I got up here to look for the old map, and can now tell you that it shall be sent to-morrow; it was among the great parcel in the dining-room. As to my debt of *3s. 6d.* to Edward, I must trouble you to pay it when you settle with him for your boots.

We began our China tea three days ago, and *I* find it very good. My companions know nothing of the matter. As to Fanny and her twelve pounds in a twelvemonth, she may talk till she is as black in the face as her own tea, but I cannot believe her – more likely twelve pounds to a quarter.

I have a message to you from Mrs. Cooke. The substance of it is that she hopes you will take Bookham in your way home and stay there as long as you can, and that when you must leave them they will convey you to Guildford. You may be sure that it is very kindly worded, and that there is no want of attendant compliments to my brother and his family.

I am very sorry for Mary, but I have some comfort in there being two curates now lodging in Bookham, besides their own Mr. Waineford from Dorking, so that I think she must fall in love with one or the other.

How horrible it is to have so many people killed! And what a blessing that one cares for none of them!

I return to my letter-writing from calling on Miss Harriot Webb, who is short and not quite straight, and cannot pronounce an R any better than her sisters; but she has dark hair, a complexion to suit, and, I think, has the pleasantest countenance and manner of the three – the most natural. She appears very well pleased with her new home, and they are all reading with delight Mrs. H. More's recent publication.

You cannot imagine – it is not in human nature to imagine – what a nice walk we have round the orchard. The row of beech look very well indeed, and so does the young quickset hedge in the garden. I hear to-day that an apricot has been detected on one of the trees. My mother is perfectly convinced *now* that she shall not be overpowered by her cleftwood, and I believe would rather have more than less.

Strange to tell, Mr. Prowting was *not* at Miss Lee's wedding, but his daughters had some cake, and Anna had her share of it.

I continue to like our old cook quite as well as ever, and, but that I am afraid to write in her praise, I could say that she seems just the servant for us. Her cookery is at least tolerable; her pastry is the only deficiency.

God bless you, and I hope June will find you well, and bring us together.

Yours ever,

JANE.

I hope you understand that I do not expect you to write on Sunday if you like my plan. I shall consider silence as consent.

Letter LXI – 1813

Chawton: Thursday (June 6).

By this time, my dearest Cassandra, you know Martha's plans. I was rather disappointed, I confess, to find that she could not leave town till after ye 24th, as I had hoped to see you here the week before. The delay, however, is not great, and everything seems generally arranging itself for your return very comfortably.

I found Henry perfectly pre-disposed to bring you to London if agreeable to yourself; he has not fixed his day for *going* into Kent, but he must be back again before ye 20th. You may, therefore, think with something like certainty of the close of your Godmersham visit, and will have, I suppose, about a week for Sloane Street. He travels in his gig, and should the weather be tolerable I think you must have a delightful journey.

I have given up all idea of Miss Sharpe's travelling with you and Martha, for though you are both all compliance with my scheme, yet as *you* knock off a week from the end of her visit, *Martha* rather more from the beginning, the thing is out of the question.

I have written to her to say that after the middle of July we shall be happy to receive her, and I have added a welcome if she could make her way hither *directly,* but I do not expect that she will. I have also sent our invitation to Cowes.

We are very sorry for the disappointment you have all had in Lady B.'s illness; but a division of the proposed party is with you by this time, and I hope may have brought you a better account of the rest.

Give my love and thanks to Harriot, who has written me charming things of your looks, and diverted me very much by poor Mrs. C. Milles's continued perplexity.

I had a few lines from Henry on Tuesday to prepare us for himself and his friend, and by the time that I had made the sumptuous provision of a neck of mutton on the occasion, they drove into the court; but lest you should not immediately recollect in how many hours a neck of mutton may be certainly procured, I add that they came a little after twelve, both tall and well, and in their different degrees agreeable.

It was a visit of only twenty-four hours, but very pleasant while it lasted. Mr. Tilson took a sketch of the Great House before dinner, and after dinner we all three walked to Chawton Park,[14] meaning to go into it, but it was too dirty, and we were obliged to keep on the outside. Mr. Tilson admired the trees very much, but grieved that they should not be turned into money.

My mother's cold is better, and I believe she only wants dry weather to be very well. It was a great distress to her that Anna should be absent during her uncle's visit, a distress which I could not share. She does not return from Faringdon till this evening, and I doubt not has had plenty of the miscellaneous, unsettled sort of happiness which seems to suit her best. We hear from Miss Benn, who was on the Common with the Prowtings, that she was very much admired by the gentlemen in general.

I like your new bonnets exceedingly; yours is a shape which always looks well, and I think Fanny's particularly becoming to her.

On Monday I had the pleasure of receiving, unpacking, and approving our Wedgwood ware. It all came very safely, and upon the whole is a good match, though I think they might have allowed us rather larger leaves, especially in such a year of fine foliage as this.

---

14 A large beech wood extending for a long distance upon a hill about a mile from Chawton: the trees are magnificent.

One is apt to suppose that the woods about Birmingham must be blighted. There was no bill with the goods, but that shall not screen them from being paid. I mean to ask Martha to settle the account. It will be quite in her way, for she is just now sending my mother a breakfast set from the same place.

I hope it will come by the waggon to-morrow; it is certainly what we want, and I long to know what it is like, and as I am sure Martha has great pleasure in making the present, I will not have any regret. We have considerable dealings with the waggons at present: a hamper of port and brandy from Southampton is now in the kitchen.

Your answer about the Miss Plumbtrees proves you as fine a Daniel as ever Portia was; for I maintained Emma to be the eldest.

We began pease on Sunday, but our gatherings are very small, not at all like the gathering in the "Lady of the Lake." Yesterday I had the agreeable surprise of finding several scarlet strawberries quite ripe; had *you* been at home, this would have been a pleasure lost. There are more gooseberries and fewer currants than I thought at first. We must buy currants for our wine.

The Digweeds are gone down to see the Stephen Terrys at Southampton, and catch the King's birthday at Portsmouth. Miss Papillon called on us yesterday, looking handsomer than ever. Maria Middleton and Miss Benn dine here to-morrow.

We are not to enclose any more letters to Abingdon Street, as perhaps Martha has told you,

I had just left off writing and put on my things for walking to Alton, when Anna and her friend Harriot called in their way thither, so we went together. Their business was to provide mourning against the King's death, and my mother has had a bombasin bought for her. I am not sorry to be back again, for the young ladies had a great deal to do, and without much method in doing it.

Anna does not come home till to-morrow morning. She has written I find to Fanny, but there does not seem to be a great deal to relate of Tuesday. I had hoped there might be dancing.

Mrs. Budd died on Sunday evening. I saw her two days before her death, and thought it must happen soon. She suffered much from weakness and restlessness almost to the last. Poor little Harriot seems truly grieved. You have never mentioned Harry; how is he?

With love to you all,

Yours affectionately,

J. A.

Letter LXI – 1813

Sloane St.: Monday (May 24)

MY DEAREST CASSANDRA,

I am very much obliged to you for writing to me. You must have hated it after a worrying morning. Your letter came just in time to save my going to Remnant's, and fit me for Christian's, where I bought Fanny's dimity.

I went the day before (Friday) to Layton's, as I proposed, and got my mother's gown – seven yards at 6*s*. 6*d*. I then walked into No. 10, which is all dirt and confusion, but in a very promising way, and after being present at the opening of a new account, to my great amusement, Henry and I went to the exhibition in Spring Gardens. It is not thought a good collection, but I was very well pleased, particularly (pray tell Fanny) with a small portrait of Mrs. Bingley, excessively like her.

I went in hopes of seeing one of her sister, but there was no Mrs. Darcy. Perhaps, however, I may find her in the great exhibition, which we shall go to if we have time. I have no chance of her in the collection of Sir Joshua Reynolds's paintings, which is now showing in Pall Mall, and which we are also to visit.

Mrs. Bingley's is exactly herself – size, shaped face, features, and sweetness; there never was a greater likeness. She is dressed in a white gown, with green ornaments, which convinces me of what I had always supposed, that green was a favourite colour with her. I dare say Mrs. D. will be in yellow.

Friday was our worst day as to weather. We were out in a very long and very heavy storm of hail, and there had been others before, but I heard no thunder. Saturday was a good deal better; dry and cold.

I gave 2s. 6d. for the dimity. I do not boast of any bargains, but think both the sarsenet and dimity good of their sort.

I have bought your locket, but was obliged to give 18s. for it, which must be rather more than you intended. It is neat and plain, set in gold.

We were to have gone to the Somerset House Exhibition on Saturday, but when I reached Henrietta Street Mr. Hampson was wanted there, and Mr. Tilson and I were obliged to drive about town after him, and by the time we had done it was too late for anything but home. We never found him after all.

I have been interrupted by Mrs. Tilson. Poor woman! She is in danger of not being able to attend Lady Drummond Smith's party to night. Miss Burdett was to have taken her, and now Miss Burdett has a cough and will not go. My cousin *Caroline* is her sole dependence.

The events of yesterday were, our going to Belgrave Chapel in the morning, our being prevented by the rain from going to evening service at St. James, Mr. Hampson's calling, Messrs. Barlow and Phillips dining here, and Mr. and Mrs. Tilson's coming in the evening *à l'ordinaire. She* drank tea with us both Thursday and Saturday; *he* dined out each day, and on Friday we were with them, and they wish us to go to them to-morrow evening, to meet Miss Burdett, but I do not know how it will end. Henry talks of a drive to Hampstead, which may interfere with it.

I should like to see Miss Burdett very well, but that I am rather frightened by hearing that she wishes to be introduced to *me.* If I *am* a wild beast I cannot help it. It is not my own fault.

There is no change in our plan of leaving London, but we shall not be with you before Tuesday. Henry thinks Monday would appear too early a day. There is no danger of our being induced to stay longer.

I have not quite determined how I shall manage about my clothes; perhaps there may be only my trunk to send by the coach, or there may be a band-box with it. I have taken your gentle hint, and written to Mrs. Hill.

The Hoblyns want us to dine with them, but we have refused. When Henry returns he will be dining out a great deal, I dare say; as he will then be alone, it will be more desirable; he will be more welcome at every table, and every invitation more welcome to him. He will not want either of us again till he is settled in Henrietta Street. This is my present persuasion. And he will not be settled there really settled – till late in the autumn; "he will not be come to bide" till after September.

There is a gentleman in treaty for this house. Gentleman himself is in the country, but gentleman's friend came to see it the other day, and seemed pleased on the whole. Gentleman would rather prefer an increased rent to parting with five hundred guineas at once, and if that is the only difficulty it will not be minded. Henry is indifferent as to the which.

Get us the best weather you can for Wednesday, Thursday, and Friday. We are to go to Windsor in our way to Henley, which will be a great delight. We shall be leaving Sloane Street about 12, two or three hours after Charles's party have begun their journey. You will miss them, but the comfort of getting back into your own room will be great. And then the tea and sugar!

I fear Miss Clewes is not better, or you would have mentioned it. I shall not write again unless I have any unexpected communication or opportunity to tempt me. I enclose Mr. Herington's bill and receipt.

I am very much obliged to Fanny for her letter; it made me laugh heartily, but I cannot pretend to answer it. Even had I more time, I should not feel at all sure of the sort of letter that Miss D.[15] would write. I hope Miss Benn is got well again, and will have a comfortable dinner with you to-day.

Monday Evening. – We have been both to the exhibition and Sir J. Reynolds's, and I am disappointed, for there was nothing like Mrs. D. at either. I can only imagine that Mr. D. prizes any picture of her too much to like it should be exposed to the public eye. I can imagine he would have that sort of feeling – that mixture of love, pride, and delicacy.

Setting aside this disappointment, I had great amusement among the pictures; and the driving about, the carriage being open, was very pleasant. I liked my solitary elegance very much, and was ready to laugh all the time at my being where I was. I could

---

15 Miss Darcy.

not but feel that I had naturally small right to be parading about London in a barouche.

Henry desires Edward may know that he has just bought three dozen of claret for him (cheap), and ordered it to be sent down to Chawton.

I should not wonder if we got no farther than Reading on Thursday evening, and so reach Steventon only to a reasonable dinner hour the next day; but whatever I may write or you may imagine we know it will be something different. I shall be quiet to-morrow morning; all my business is done, and I shall only call again upon Mrs. Hoblyn, &c.

Love to your much . . . party.

Yours affectionately,

J. AUSTEN.

Letter LXII – 1813

Henrietta St.: Wednesday (Sept. 15, 1/2 past 8).

Here I am, my dearest Cassandra, seated in the breakfast, dining, sitting-room, beginning with all my might. Fanny will join me as soon as she is dressed and begin her letter.

We had a very good journey, weather and roads excellent; the three first stages for 1*s*. 6*d.*, and our only misadventure the being delayed about a quarter of an hour at Kingston for horses, and being obliged to put up with a pair belonging to a hackney coach and their coachman, which left no room on the barouche box for Lizzy, who was to have gone her last stage there as she did the first; consequently we were all four within, which was a little crowded.

We arrived at a quarter-past four, and were kindly welcomed by the coachman, and then by his master, and then by William, and then by Mrs. Pengird, who all met us before we reached the foot of the stairs. Mde. Bigion was below dressing us a most comfortable dinner of soup, fish, bouillée, partridges, and an apple tart, which we sat down to soon after five, after cleaning and dressing ourselves and feeling that we were most commodiously disposed of. The little adjoining dressing-room to our apartment makes Fanny and myself very well off indeed, and as we have poor Eliza's[16] bed our space is ample every way.

Sace arrived safely about half-past six. At seven we set off in a coach for the Lyceum; were at home again in about four hours and a half; had soup and wine and water, and then went to our holes.

Edward finds his quarters very snug and quiet. I must get a softer pen. This is harder. I am in agonies. I have not yet seen Mr. Crabbe. Martha's letter is gone to the post.

I am going to write nothing but short sentences. There shall be two full stops in every line. Layton and Shear's *is* Bedford House. We mean to get there before breakfast if it's possible; for we feel more and more how much we have to do and how little time. This house looks very nice. It seems like Sloane Street moved here. I believe Henry is just rid of Sloane Street. Fanny does not come, but I have Edward seated by me beginning a letter, which looks natural.

Henry has been suffering from the pain in the face which he has been subject to before. He caught cold at Matlock, and since his return has been paying a little for past pleasure. It is nearly removed now, but

---

16 Eliza, Henry Austen's first wife, who had died in the earlier part of this year.

he looks thin in the face, either from the pain or the fatigues of his tour, which must have been great.

Lady Robert is delighted with P. and P.,[17] and really was so, as I understand, before she knew who wrote it, for, of course, she knows now. He told her with as much satisfaction as if it were my wish. He did not tell me this, but he told Fanny. And Mr. Hastings! I am quite delighted with what such a man writes about it. Henry sent him the books after his return from Daylesford, but you will hear the letter too.

Let me be rational, and return to my two full stops.

I talked to Henry at the play last night. We were in a private box – Mr. Spencer's – which made it much more pleasant. The box is directly on the stage. One is infinitely less fatigued than in the common way. But Henry's plans are not what one could wish. He does not mean to be at Chawton till the 29th. He must be in town again by Oct. 5. His plan is to get a couple of days of pheasant shooting and then return directly. His wish was to bring you back with him. I have told him your scruples. He wishes you to suit yourself as to time, and if you cannot come till later, will send for you at any time as far as Bagshot. He presumed you would not find difficulty in getting so far. I could not say you would. He proposed your

---

17 "Pride and Prejudice."

going with him into Oxfordshire. It was his own thought at first. I could not but catch at it for you.

We have talked of it again this morning (for now we have breakfasted), and I am convinced that if you can make it suit in other respects you need not scruple on his account. If you cannot come back with him on the 3rd or 4th, therefore, I do hope you will contrive to go to Adlestrop. By not beginning your absence till about the middle of this month I think you may manage it very well. But you will think all this over. One could wish he had intended to come to you earlier, but it cannot be helped.

I said nothing to him of Mrs. H. and Miss B., that he might not suppose difficulties. Shall not you put *them* into our own room? This seems to me the best plan, and the maid will be most conveniently near.

Oh, dear me! when I shall ever have done. We *did* go to Layton and Shear's before breakfast. Very pretty English poplins at 4*s.* 3*d.*; Irish, ditto at 6*s.*; *more* pretty, certainly – beautiful.

Fanny and the two little girls are gone to take places for to-night at Covent Garden; "Clandestine Marriage" and "Midas." The latter will be a fine show for L. and M.[18] They revelled last night in "Don Juan," whom we

---

18 Lizzie and Marianne.

left in hell at half-past eleven. We had scaramouch and a ghost, and were delighted. I speak of *them; my* delight was very tranquil, and the rest of us were sober-minded. "Don Juan" was the last of three musical things. "Five hours at Brighton," in three acts – of which one was over before we arrived, none the worse – and the "Beehive," rather less flat and trumpery.

I have this moment received 5*l.* from kind, beautiful Edward. Fanny has a similar gift. I shall save what I can of it for your better leisure in this place. *My* letter was from Miss Sharpe – nothing particular. A letter from Fanny Cage this morning.

Four o'clock. – We are just come back from doing Mrs. Tickars, Miss Hare, and Mr. Spence. Mr. Hall is here, and, while Fanny is under his hands, I will try to write a little more.

Miss Hare had some pretty caps, and is to make me one like one of them, only white satin instead of blue. It will be *white* satin and lace, and a little white flower perking out of the left ear, like Harriot Byron's feather. I have allowed her to go as far as 1*l.* 16*s.* My gown is to be trimmed everywhere with white ribbon plaited on somehow or other. She says it will look well. I am not sanguine. They trim with white very much.

I learnt from Mrs. Tickars's young lady, to my high amusement, that the stays now are not made to force the bosom up at all; *that* was a very unbecoming, unnatural fashion. I was really glad to hear that they are not to be so much off the shoulders as they were.

Going to Mr. Spence's was a sad business and cost us many tears; unluckily we were obliged to go a second time before he could do more than just look. We went first at half-past twelve and afterwards at three; papa with us each time; and, alas! we are to go again to-morrow. Lizzy is not finished yet. There have been no teeth taken out, however, nor will be, I believe, but he finds *hers* in a very bad state, and seems to think particularly ill of their durableness. They have been all cleaned, *hers* filed, and are to be filed again. There is a very sad hole between two of her front teeth.

Thursday Morning, Half-past Seven. – Up and dressed and downstairs in order to finish my letter in time for the parcel. At eight I have an appointment with Madame B., who wants to show me something downstairs. At nine we are to set off for Grafton House, and get that over before breakfast. Edward is so kind as to walk there with us. We are to be at Mr. Spence's again at 11:05; from that time shall be driving about I suppose till four o'clock at least. We are, if possible, to call on Mrs. Tilson.

Mr. Hall was very punctual yesterday, and curled me out at a great rate. I thought it looked hideous, and longed for a snug cap instead, but my companions silenced me by their admiration. I had only a bit of velvet round my head. I did not catch cold, however. The weather is all in my favour. I have had no pain in my face since I left you.

We had very good places in the box next the stage-box, front and second row; the three old ones behind of course. I was particularly disappointed at seeing nothing of Mr. Crabbe. I felt sure of him when I saw that the boxes were fitted up with crimson velvet. The new Mr. Terry was Lord Ogleby, and Henry thinks he may do; but there was no acting more than moderate, and I was as much amused by the remembrances connected with "Midas" as with any part of it. The girls were very much delighted, but still prefer "Don Juan"; and I must say that I have seen nobody on the stage who has been a more interesting character than that compound of cruelty and lust.

It was not possible for me to get the worsteds yesterday. I heard Edward last night pressing Henry to come to you, and I think Henry engaged to go there after his November collection. Nothing has been done as to *S. and S.*[19]

---

[19] "Sense and Sensibility."

The books came to hand too late for him to have time for it before he went. Mr. Hastings never *hinted* at Eliza in the smallest degree. Henry knew nothing of Mr. Trimmer's death. I tell you these things that you may not have to ask them over again.

There is a new clerk sent down to Alton, a Mr. Edmund Williams, a young man whom Henry thinks most highly of, and he turns out to be a son of the luckless Williamses of Grosvenor Place.

I long to have you hear Mr. H.'s opinion of *P. and P.* His admiring my Elizabeth so much is particularly welcome to me.

Instead of saving my superfluous wealth for you to spend, I am going to treat myself with spending it myself. I hope, at least, that I shall find some poplin at Layton and Shear's that will tempt me to buy it. If I do, it shall be sent to Chawton, as half will be for you; for I depend upon your being so kind as to accept it, being the main point. It will be a great pleasure to me. Don't say a word. I only wish you could choose too. I shall send twenty yards.

Now for Bath. Poor F. Cage has suffered a good deal from her accident. The noise of the White Hart was terrible to her. They will keep her quiet, I dare say. *She* is not so much delighted with the place as the rest of the party; probably, as she says herself, from having been less well, but she thinks she should like it better in the season. The streets are very empty now, and the shops not so gay as she expected. They are at No. 1 Henrietta Street, the corner of Laura Place, and have no acquaintance at present but the Bramstons.

Lady Bridges drinks at the Cross Bath, her son at the Hot, and Louisa is going to bathe. Dr. Parry seems to be half starving Mr. Bridges, for he is restricted to much such a diet as James's bread, water and meat, and is never to eat so much of that as he wishes, and he is to walk a great deal – walk till he drops, I believe gout or no gout. It really is to that purpose. I have not exaggerated.

Charming weather for you and us, and the travellers, and everybody. You will take your walk this afternoon, and...

Letter LXIII – 1813

Henrietta St.: Thursday (Sept. 16, after dinner).

Thank you, my dearest Cassandra, for the nice long letter I sent off this morning. I hope you have had it by this time, and that it has found you all well, and my mother no more in need of leeches. Whether this will be delivered to you by Henry on Saturday evening, or by the postman on Sunday morning, I know not, as he has lately recollected something of an engagement for Saturday, which perhaps may delay his visit. He seems determined to come to you soon however.

I hope you will receive the gown to-morrow, and may be able with tolerable honesty to say that you like the colour. It was bought at Grafton House, where, by going very early, we got immediate attendance and went on very comfortably. I only forgot the one particular thing which I had always resolved to buy there – a white silk handkerchief – and was therefore obliged to give six shillings for one at Crook and Besford's; which reminds me to say that the worsteds ought also to be at Chawton to-morrow, and that I shall be very happy to hear they are approved. I had not much time for deliberation.

We are now all four of us young ladies sitting round the circular table in the inner room writing our letters, while the two brothers are having a comfortable cose in the room adjoining. It is to be a quiet evening, much to the satisfaction of four of the six. My eyes are quite tired of dust and lamps.

The letter you forwarded from Edward, junr., has been duly received. He has been shooting most prosperously at home, and dining at Chilham Castle and with Mr. Scudamore.

My cap is come home, and I like it very much. Fanny has one also; hers is white sarsenet and lace, of a different shape from mine, more fit for morning carriage wear, which is what it is intended for, and is in shape exceedingly like our own satin and lace of last winter; shaped round the face exactly like it, with pipes and more fulness, and a round crown inserted behind. *My* cap has a peak in front. Large full bows of very narrow ribbon (old twopenny) are the thing. One over the right temple, perhaps, and another at the left ear.

Henry is not quite well. His stomach is rather deranged. You must keep him in rhubarb, and give him plenty of port and water. He caught his cold farther back than I told you; before he got to Matlock, somewhere in his journey from the North, but the ill effects of *that* I hope are nearly gone.

We returned from Grafton House only just in time for breakfast, and had scarcely finished breakfast when the carriage came to the door. From 11 to half-past 3 we were hard at it; we *did* contrive to get to Hans Place for ten minutes. Mrs. T. was as affectionate and pleasing as ever.

After our return Mr. Tilson walked up from the Compting House and called upon us, and these have been all our visitings.

I have rejoiced more than once that I bought my writing-paper in the country; we have not had a quarter of an hour to spare.

I enclose the eighteen-pence due to my mother. The rose colour was 6*s.* and the other 4*s.* per yard. There was but two yards and a quarter of the dark slate in the shop, but the man promised to match it and send it off correctly.

Fanny bought her Irish at Newton's in Leicester Square, and I took the opportunity of thinking about your Irish, and seeing one piece of the yard wide at 4*s.,* and it seemed to me very good, good enough for your purpose. It might at least be worth your while to go there, if you have no other engagements. Fanny is very much pleased with the stockings she has bought of Remmington, silk at 12*s.,* cotton at 4*s. 3d.* She thinks them great bargains, but I have not seen them yet, as my hair was dressing when the man and the stockings came.

The poor girls and their teeth! I have not mentioned them yet, but we were a whole hour at Spence's, and Lizzy's were filed and lamented over again, and poor Marianne had two taken out after all, the two just beyond the eye teeth, to make room for those in front. When her doom was fixed, Fanny, Lizzy, and I walked into the next room, where we heard each of the two sharp and hasty screams.

The little girls' teeth I can suppose in a critical state, but I think he must be a lover of teeth and money and mischief, to parade about Fanny's. I would not have had him look at mine for a shilling a tooth and double it. It was a disagreeable hour.

We then went to Wedgwood's, where my brother and Fanny chose a dinner set. I believe the pattern is a small lozenge in purple, between lines of narrow gold, and it is to have the crest.

We must have been three-quarters of an hour at Grafton House, Edward sitting by all the time with wonderful patience. There Fanny bought the net for Anna's gown, and a beautiful square veil for herself. The edging there is very cheap. I was tempted by some, and I bought some very nice plaiting lace at 3s. 4d.

Fanny desires me to tell Martha, with her kind love, that Birchall assured her that there was no second set of Hook's Lessons for Beginners, and that, by my advice, she has therefore chosen her a set by another composer. I thought she would rather have something than not. It costs six shillings.

With love to you all, including Triggs, I remain

Yours very affectionately,

J. AUSTEN.

Letter LXIV – 1813

Godmersham Park: Thursday (Sept 23).

MY DEAREST CASSANDRA,

Thank you five hundred and forty times for the exquisite piece of workmanship which was brought into the room this morning, while we were at break-fast, with some very inferior works of art in the same way, and which I read with high glee, much delighted with everything it told, whether good or bad. It is so rich in striking intelligence that I hardly know what to reply to first. I believe finery must have it.

I am extremely glad that you like the poplin. I thought it would have my mother's approbation, but was not so confident of yours. Remember that it is a present. Do not refuse me. I am very rich.

Mrs. Clement is very welcome to her little boy, and to my congratulations into the bargain, if ever you think of giving them. I hope she will do well. Her sister in Lucina, Mrs. H. Gipps, does too well, we think. Mary P. wrote on Sunday that she had been three days on the sofa. Sackree does not approve it.

Well, there is some comfort in the Mrs. Hulbart's not coming to you, and I am happy to hear of the honey. I was thinking of it the other day. Let me know when you begin the new tea, and the new white wine. My present elegancies have not yet made me indifferent to such matters. I am still a cat if I see a mouse.

I am glad you like our caps, but Fanny is out of conceit with hers already; she finds that she has been buying a new cap without having a new pattern, which is true enough. She is rather out of luck to like neither her gown nor her cap, but I do not much mind it, because besides that I like them both myself, I consider it as a thing of course at her time of life – one of the sweet taxes of youth to choose in a hurry and make bad bargains.

I wrote to Charles yesterday, and Fanny has had a letter from him to-day, principally to make inquiries about the time of their visit here, to which mine was an answer beforehand; so he will probably write again soon to fix his week. I am best pleased that Cassy does not go to you.

Now, what have we been doing since I wrote last? The Mr. K.'s[20] came a little before dinner on Monday, and Edward went to the church with the two seniors, but there is no inscription yet drawn up. They are

20 Knatchbulls.

very good-natured you know, and civil, and all that, but are not particularly superfine; however, they ate their dinner and drank their tea, and went away, leaving their lovely Wadham in our arms, and I wish you had seen Fanny and me running backwards and forwards with his breeches from the little chintz to the white room before we went to bed, in the greatest of frights lest he should come upon us before we had done it all. There had been a mistake in the house-maids' preparation, and *they* were gone to bed.

He seems a very harmless sort of young man, nothing to like or dislike in him – goes out shooting or hunting with the two others all the morning, and plays at whist and makes queer faces in the evening.

On Tuesday the carriage was taken to the painter's; at one time Fanny and I were to have gone in it, chiefly to call on Mrs. C. – Milles and *Moy*[21] – but we found that they were going for a few days to Sandling, and would not be at home; therefore my brother and Fanny went to Eastwell in the chair instead. While

---

21 Mrs. C. Milles was the mother of Mr. R. Milles of Nackington and Elmham, Norfolk. "Moy" means "Molly" Milles – probably an imitation of her mother's way of pronouncing her name. She was sister to Mr. R. Milles, and "the Nackington Milles'" refers to his widow who lived there after his death

they were gone the Nackington Milles's called and left their cards. Nobody at home at Eastwell.

We hear a great deal of Geo. H.'s wretchedness. I suppose he has quick feelings, but I dare say they will not kill him. He is so much out of spirits, however, that his friend John Plumptre is gone over to comfort him, at Mr. Hatton's desire. He called here this morning in his way. A handsome young man certainly, with quiet, gentlemanlike manners. I set him down as sensible rather than brilliant. There is nobody brilliant nowadays. He talks of staying a week at Eastwell, and then comes to Chilham Castle for a day or two, and my brother invited him to come here afterwards, which he seemed very agreeable to.

"'Tis night, and the landscape is lovely no more," but to make amends for that, our visit to the Tylden's is over. My brother, Fanny, Edwd., and I went; Geo. stayed at home with W. K. There was nothing entertaining, or out of the common way. We met only Tyldens and double Tyldens. A whist-table for the gentlemen, a grown-up musical young lady to play backgammon with Fanny, and engravings of the Colleges at Cambridge for me. In the morning we returned Mrs. Sherer's visit. I like *Mr.* S. very much.

Well, I have not half done yet, I am not come up with myself. My brother drove Fanny to Nackington and Canty. yesterday, and while they were gone the Faggs paid their duty. Mary Oxenden is staying at Canty. with the Blairs, and Fanny's object was to see her.

The Deedes want us to come to Sandling for a few days, or at least a day and night. At present Edwd. does not seem well affected – he would rather not be asked to go anywhere – but I rather expect he will be persuaded to go for the one day and night.

I read him the chief of your letter; he was interested and pleased, as he ought, and will be happy to hear from you himself. Your finding so much comfort from his cows gave him evident pleasure. I wonder Henry did not go down on Saturday; he does not in general fall *within* a doubtful intention.

My face is very much as it was before I came away; for the first two or three days it was rather worse. I caught a small cold in my way down, and had some pain every evening, not to last long, but rather severer than it had been lately. This has worn off, however, and I have scarcely felt anything for the last two days.

Sackree is pretty well again, only weak. Much obliged to you for your message, &c.; it was very true that she blessed herself the whole time that the pain was not in her stomach. I read all the scraps I could of your letter to her. She seemed to like it, and says she shall always like to hear anything of Chawton now, and I am to make you Miss Clewes's assurance to the same effect, with thanks and best respects, &c.

The girls are much disturbed at Mary Stacey's not admitting Dame L. Miss C. and I are sorry, but not angry; we acknowledge Mary Stacey's right, and can suppose her to have reason.

Oh! the church must have looked very forlorn. We all thought of the empty pew. How Bentigh is grown! and the Canty. Hill Plantation! And the improvements *within* are very great. I admire the chintz room very much. We live in the library except at meals, and have a fire every evening. The weather is set about changing; we shall have a settled wet season soon. I must go to bed.

Friday. – I am sorry to find that one of the nightcaps here belongs to you – sorry, because it must be in constant wear.

Great doings again to-day. Fanny, Lizzy, and Marnne. are going to Goodnestone for the fair, which is to-morrow, and stay till Monday, and the gentlemen are all to dine at Evington. Edwd. has been repenting ever since he promised to go, and was hoping last night for a wet day, but the morning is fair. I shall dine with Miss Clewes, and I dare say find her very agreeable. The invitation to the fair was general.

Edwd. positively declined his share of that, and I was very glad to do the same. It is likely to be a baddish fair – not much upon the stall, and neither Mary O.[22] nor Mary P.[23]

It is hoped that the portfolio may be in Canty. this morning. Sackree's sister found it at Croydon and took it to town with her, but unluckily did not send it down till she had directions. Fanny C.'s screens can be done nothing with, but there are parts of workbags in the parcel, very important in their way. Three of the Deedes girls are to be at Goodnestone.

We shall not be much settled till this visit is over, settled as to employment I mean. Fanny and I are to go on with Modern Europe together, but hitherto have advanced only twenty-five pages. Something or other has always happened to delay or curtail the reading hour.

I ought to have told you before of a purchase of Edward's in town; he desired you might hear of it – a *thing* for measuring timber with, so that you need not have the trouble of finding him in tapes any longer. He treated himself with this seven-shilling

---

22 Mary Oxenden.

23 Mary Plumptre.

purchase, and bought a new watch and new gun for George. The new gun shoots very well.

Apples are scarce in this country – 1*l*. 5*s.* a sack. Miss Hinton should take Hannah Knight. Mrs. Driver has not yet appeared. J. Littleworth and the grey pony reached Bath safely.

A letter from Mrs. Cooke: they have been at Brighton a fortnight; stay at least another, and Mary is already much better.

Poor Dr. Isham is obliged to admire P. and P.,[24] and to send me word that he is sure he shall not like Madame D'Arblay's new novel half so well. Mrs. C. invented it all, of course. He desires his compliments to you and my mother.

Of the Adlestrop living business, Mrs. C. says: "It can be now no secret, as the papers for the necessary dispensations are going up to the Archbishop's Secretary. However, be it known that we all wish to have it understood that George takes this trust *entirely* to oblige Mr. Leigh, and never will be a shilling benefited by it. Had my consent been necessary, believe me, I should have withheld it, for I do think it on the part of the patron a very shabby piece of business. All these and other *Scrapings* from dear

24 "Pride and Prejudice."

Mrs. E. L. are to accumulate no doubt to help Mr. Twisleton to a secure admission again into England." I would wish you, therefore, to make it known to my mother as if *this* were the first time of Mrs. Cooke's mentioning it to me.

I told Mrs. C. of my mother's late oppressions in *her head.* She says on that subject: "Dear Mrs. Austen's is, I believe, an attack frequent at her age and mine. Last year I had for some time the sensation of a peck loaf resting on my head, and they talked of cupping me, but I came off with a dose or two of calomel, and have never heard of it since."

The three Miss Knights and Mrs. Sayce are just off; the weather has got worse since the early morning, and whether Mrs. Clewes and I are to be *tête-à-tête,* or to have four gentlemen to admire us, is uncertain.

I am now alone in the library, mistress of all I survey; at least I may say so, and repeat the whole poem if I like it, without offence to anybody.

Martha will have wet races and catch a bad cold; in other respects I hope she will have much pleasure at them, and that she is free from ear-ache now. I am glad she likes my cap so well. I assure you my old one looked so smart yesterday that I was asked two or three times before I set off whether it was not my new one.

I have *this* moment seen Mrs. Driver driven up to the kitchen door. I cannot close with a grander circumstance of greater wit.

Yours affectionately,

J. A.

I am going to write to Steventon, so you need not send any news of me there.

Louisa's best love and a hundred thousand million kisses.

Letter LXV – 1813

Godmersham Park: Monday (Oct 11).

[MY DEAREST AUNT CASS.,

I have just asked Aunt Jane to let me write a little in her letter, but she does not like it, so I won't. Good-bye!]

You will have Edward's letter to-morrow. He tells me that he did not send you any news to interfere with mine, but I do not think there is much for anybody to send at present.

We had our dinner party on Wednesday, with the addition of Mrs. and Miss Milles, who were under a promise of dining here in their return from Eastwell, whenever they paid their visit of duty there, and it happened to be paid on that day. Both mother and daughter are much as I have always found them. I like the mother – first, because she reminds me of Mrs. Birch; and, secondly, because she is cheerful and grateful for what she is at the age of ninety and upwards. The day was pleasant enough. I sat by Mr. Chisholme, and we talked away at a great rate about nothing worth hearing.

It was a mistake as to the day of the Sherers going being fixed; *they* are ready, but are waiting for Mr. Paget's answer.

I inquired of Mrs. Milles after Jemima Brydges, and was quite grieved to hear that she was obliged to leave Canterbury some months ago on account of her debts, and is nobody knows where. What an unprosperous family!

On Saturday, soon after breakfast, Mr. J. P. left us for Norton Court. I like him very much. He gives me the idea of a very amiable young man, only too diffident to be so agreeable as he might be. He was out the chief of each morning with the other two, shooting and getting wet through. To-morrow we are to know whether he and a hundred young ladies will come here for the ball. I do not much expect any.

The Deedes cannot meet us; they have engagements at home. I will finish the Deedes by saying that they are not likely to come here till quite late in my stay – the very last week perhaps; and I do not expect to see the Moores at all. They are not solicited till after Edward's return from Hampshire.

Monday, November 15, is the day now fixed for our setting out.

Poor Basingstoke races! There seem to have been two particularly wretched days on purpose for them; and Weyhill week does not begin much happier.

We were quite surprised by a letter from Anna at Tollard Royal, last Saturday; but perfectly approve her going, and only regret they should all go so far to stay so few days.

We had thunder and lightning here on Thursday morning, between five and seven; no very bad thunder, but a great deal of lightning. It has given the commencement of a season of wind and rain, and perhaps for the next six weeks we shall not have two dry days together.

Lizzy is very much obliged to you for your letter and will answer it soon, but has so many things to do that it may be four or five days before she can. This is quite her own message, spoken in rather a desponding tone. Your letter gave pleasure to all of us; we had all the reading of it of course, I *three times,* as I undertook, to the great relief of Lizzy, to read it to Sackree, and afterwards to Louisa.

Sackree does not at all approve of Mary Doe and her nuts – on the score of propriety rather than health. She saw some signs of going after her in George and Henry, and thinks if you could give the girl a check, by rather reproving her for taking anything seriously about nuts which they said to her, it might be of use. This, of course, is between our three discreet selves, a scene of triennial bliss.

Mrs. Breton called here on Saturday. I never saw her before. She is a large, ungenteel woman, with self-satisfied and would-be elegant manners.

We are certain of some visitors to-morrow. Edward Bridges comes for two nights in his way from Lenham to Ramsgate, and brings a friend – name unknown – but supposed to be a Mr. Harpur, a neighbouring clergyman; and Mr. R. Mascall is to shoot with the young men, which it is to be supposed will end in his staying dinner.

On Thursday, Mr. Lushington, M.P. for Canterbury, and manager of the Lodge Hounds, dines here, and stays the night. He is chiefly young Edward's acquaintance. If I can I will get a frank from him, and write to you all the sooner. I suppose the Ashford ball will furnish something.

As I wrote of my nephews with a little bitterness in my last, I think it particularly incumbent on me to do them justice now, and I have great pleasure in saying that they were both at the Sacrament yesterday. After having much praised or much blamed anybody, one is generally sensible of something just the reverse soon afterwards. Now these two boys who are out with the foxhounds will come home and disgust me again by some habit of luxury or some proof of sporting mania, unless I keep it off by this prediction. They amuse themselves very comfortably in the evening by netting; they are each about a rabbit net, and sit as deedily to it, side by side, as any two Uncle Franks could do.

I am looking over "Self Control" again, and my opinion is confirmed of its being an excellently-meant, elegantly-written work, without anything of nature or probability in it. I declare I do not know whether Laura's passage down the American river is not the most natural, possible, everyday thing she ever does.

Tuesday. – Dear me! what is to become of me? Such a long letter! Two-and-forty lines in the second page. Like Harriot Byron, I ask, what am I to do with my gratitude? I can do nothing but thank you and go on. A few of your inquiries, I think, are replied to *en avance.*

The name of F. Cage's drawing-master is O'Neil. We are exceedingly amused with your Shalden news, and your self-reproach on the subject of Mrs. Stockwell made me laugh heartily. I rather wondered that Johncock,[25] the only person in the room, could

---

25   The butler at Godmersham.

help laughing too. I had not heard before of her having the measles. Mrs. H. and Alethea's staying till Friday was quite new to me; a good plan however. I could not have settled it better myself, and am glad they found so much in the house to approve, and I hope they will ask Martha to visit them. I admire the sagacity and taste of Charlotte Williams. Those large dark eyes always judge well. I will compliment her by naming a heroine after her.

Edward has had all the particulars of the building, &c., read to him twice over, and seems very well satisfied. A narrow door to the pantry is the only subject of solicitude; it is certainly just the door which should not be narrow, on account of the trays; but, if a case of necessity, it must be borne.

I *knew* there was sugar in the tin, but had no idea of there being enough to last through your company. All the better. You ought not to think this new loaf better than the other, because *that* was the first of five which all came together. Something of fancy, perhaps, and something of Imagination.

Dear Mrs. Digweed! I cannot bear that she should not be foolishly happy after a ball. I hope Miss Yates and her companions were all well the day after their arrival. I am thoroughly rejoiced that Miss Benn has placed herself in lodgings, though I hope they may not be long necessary.

No letter from Charles yet.

Southey's "Life of Nelson": I am tired of "Lives of Nelson," being that I never read any. I will read this, however, if Frank is mentioned in it.

Here am I in Kent, with one brother in the same county and another brother's wife, and see nothing of them, which seems unnatural. It will not last so forever, I trust. I should like to have Mrs. F. A. and her children here for a week, but not a syllable of that nature is ever breathed. I wish her last visit had not been so long a one.

I wonder whether Mrs. Tilson has ever lain-in. Mention it if it ever comes to your knowledge, and we shall hear of it by the same post from Henry.

Mr. Rob. Mascall breakfasted here; he eats a great deal of butter. I dined upon goose yesterday, which, I hope, will secure a good sale of my second edition. Have you any tomatas? Fanny and I regale on them every day.

Disastrous letters from the Plumptres and Oxendens. Refusals everywhere – a blank *partout* – and it is not quite certain whether we go or not; something may depend upon the disposition of Uncle Edward when he comes, and upon what we hear at Chilham Castle this morning, for we are going to pay visits. We are going to each house at Chilham and to Mystole. I shall like seeing the Faggs. I shall like it all, except that we are to set out so early that I have not time to write as I would wish.

Edwd. Bridges's friend is a Mr. Hawker, I find, not Harpur. I would not have you sleep in such an error for the world.

My brother desires his best love and thanks for all your information. He hopes the roots of the old beech have been dug away enough to allow a proper covering of mould and turf. He is sorry for the necessity of building the new coin, but hopes they will contrive that the doorway should be of the usual width – if it must be contracted on one side, by widening it on the other. The appearance need not signify. And he desires me to say that your being at Chawton when he is will be quite necessary. You cannot think it more indispensable than he does. He is very much obliged to you for your attention to everything. Have you any idea of returning with him to Henrietta Street and finishing your visit then? Tell me your sweet little innocent ideas.

Everything of love and kindness, proper and improper, must now suffice.

Yours very affectionately,

J. AUSTEN.

Letter LXVI – 1813

Godmersham Park: Thursday (Oct. 14).

MY DEAREST CASSANDRA,

Now I will prepare for Mr. Lushington, and as it will be wisest also to prepare for his not coming, or my not getting a frank, I shall write very close from the first, and even leave room for the seal in the proper place. When I have followed up my last with this I shall feel somewhat less unworthy of you than the state of our correspondence now requires.

I left off in a great hurry to prepare for our morning visits. Of course was ready a good deal the first, and need not have hurried so much. Fanny wore her new gown and cap. I was surprised to find Mystole so pretty.

The ladies were at home. I was in luck, and saw Lady Fagg and all her five daughters, with an old Mrs. Hamilton, from Canterbury, and Mrs. and Miss Chapman, from Margate, into the bargain. I never saw so plain a family – five sisters so very plain! They are as plain as the Foresters, or the Franfraddops, or the Seagraves, or the Rivers, excluding Sophy. Miss Sally Fagg has a pretty figure, and that comprises all the good looks of the family.

It was stupidish; Fanny did her part very well, but there was a lack of talk altogether, and the three friends in the house only sat by and looked at us. However, Miss Chapman's name is Laura, and she had a double flounce to her gown. You really must get some flounces. Are not some of your large stock of white morning gowns just in a happy state for a flounce – too short? Nobody at home at either house in Chilham.

Edward Bridges and his friend did not forget to arrive. The friend is a Mr. Wigram, one of the three-and-twenty children of a great rich mercantile, Sir Robert Wigram, an old acquaintance of the Footes, but very recently known to Edward B. The history of his coming here is, that, intending to go from Ramsgate to Brighton, Edw. B. persuaded him to take Lenham on his way, which gave him the convenience of Mr. W.'s gig, and the comfort of not being alone there; but, probably thinking a few days of Gm. would be the cheapest and pleasantest way of entertaining his friend and himself, offered a visit here, and here they stay till to-morrow.

Mr. W. is about five or six-and-twenty, not ill-looking, and not agreeable. He is certainly no addition. A sort of cool, gentlemanlike manner, but very silent. They say his name is Henry, a proof how unequally the gifts of fortune are bestowed. I have seen many a John and Thomas much more agreeable.

We have got rid of Mr. R. Mascall, however. I did not like *him* either. He talks too much, and is conceited, besides having a vulgarly shaped mouth. He slept here on Tuesday, so that yesterday Fanny and I sat down to breakfast with six gentlemen to admire us.

We did not go to the ball. It was left to her to decide, and at last she determined against it. She knew that it would be a sacrifice on the part of her father and brothers if they went, and I hope it will prove that *she* has not sacrificed much. It is not likely that there should have been anybody there whom she would care for. *I* was very glad to be spared the trouble of dressing and going, and being weary before it was half over, so my gown and my cap are still unworn. It will appear at last, perhaps, that I might have done without either. I produced my brown bombazine yesterday, and it was very much admired indeed, and I like it better than ever.

You have given many particulars of the state of Chawton House, but still we want more. Edward wants to be expressly told that all the round tower, &c., is entirely down, and the door from the best room stopped up; he does not know enough of the appearance of things in that quarter.

He heard from Bath yesterday. Lady B. continues very well, and Dr. Parry's opinion is, that while the water agrees with her she ought to remain there, which throws their coming away at a greater uncertainty than we had supposed. It will end, perhaps, in a fit of the gout, which may prevent her coming away. Louisa thinks her mother's being so well may be quite as much owing to her being so much out of doors as to the water. Lady B. is going to try the hot pump, the Cross bath being about to be painted. Louisa is particularly well herself, and thinks the water has been of use to her. She mentioned our inquiries, &c., to Mr. and Mrs. Alex. Evelyn, and had their best compliments and thanks to give in return. Dr. Parry does not expect Mr. E. to last much longer.

Only think of Mrs. Holder's being dead! Poor woman, she has done the only thing in the world she could possibly do to make one cease to abuse her. Now, if you please, Hooper must have it in his power to do more by his uncle. Lucky for the little girl. An Anne Ekins can hardly be so unfit for the care of a child as a Mrs. Holder.

A letter from Wrotham yesterday offering an early visit here, and Mr. and Mrs. Moore and one child are to come on Monday for ten days. I hope Charles and Fanny may not fix the same time, but if they come at all in October they *must.* What is the use of hoping? The two parties of children is the chief evil.

To be sure, here we are; the very thing has happened, or rather worse – a letter from Charles this very morning, which gives us reason to suppose they may come here to-day. It depends upon the weather, and the weather now is very fine. No difficulties are made, however, and, indeed, there will be no want of room; but I wish there were no Wigrams and Lushingtons in the way to fill up the table and make us such a motley set. I cannot spare Mr. Lushington either, because of his frank, but Mr. Wigram does no good to anybody. I cannot imagine how a man can have the impudence to come into a family party for three days, where he is quite a stranger, unless he knows himself to be agreeable on undoubted authority. He and Edw. B. are going to ride to Eastwell, and as the boys are hunting, and my brother is gone to Canty., Fanny and I have a quiet morning before us.

Edward has driven off poor Mrs. Salkeld. It was thought a good opportunity of doing something towards clearing the house. By her own desire Mrs. Fanny[26] is to be put in the room next the nursery, her baby in a little bed by her; and as Cassy is to have the closet within, and Betsey William's little hole, they will be all very snug together. I shall be most happy to see dear Charles, and he will be as happy as he can with a cross child, or some such care, pressing on him at the time. I should be very happy in the idea of seeing little Cassy again, too, did not I fear

---

[26] Mrs. Charles Austen, née Fanny Palmer

she would disappoint me by some immediate disagreeableness.

We had the good old original Brett and Toke calling here yesterday, separately. Mr. Toke I am always very fond of. He inquired after you and my mother, which adds esteem to passion. The Charles Cages are staying at Godington. I knew they must be staying somewhere soon. Ed. Hussey is warned out of Pett, and talks of fixing at Ramsgate. Bad taste! He is very fond of the sea, however. Some taste in that, and some judgment, too, in fixing on Ramsgate, as being by the sea.

The comfort of the billiard-table here is very great; it draws all the gentlemen to it whenever they are within, especially after dinner, so that my brother, Fanny, and I have the library to ourselves in delightful quiet. There is no truth in the report of G. Hatton being to marry Miss Wemyss. He desires it may be contradicted.

Have you done anything about our present to Miss Benn? I suppose she must have a bed at my mother's whenever she dines there. How will they manage as to inviting her when you are gone? and if they invite, how will they continue to entertain her?

Let me know as many of your parting arrangements as you can, as to wine, &c. I wonder whether the ink-bottle has been filled. Does butcher's meat keep up at the same price, and is not bread lower than 2*s.* 6*d.?* Mary's blue gown! My mother must be in agonies. I have a great mind to have *my* blue gown dyed some time or other. I proposed it once to you, and you made some objection, I forget what. It is the fashion of flounces that gives it particular expediency.

Mrs. and Miss Wildman have just been here. Miss is very plain. I wish Lady B. may be returned before we leave Gm., that Fanny may spend the time of her father's absence at Goodnestone, which is what she would prefer.

Friday. – They came last night at about seven. We had given them up, but I *still* expected them to come. Dessert was nearly over; a better time for arriving than an hour and a-half earlier. They were late because they did not set out earlier, and did not allow time enough. Charles did not *aim* at more than reaching Sittingbourne by three, which could not have brought them here by dinner time. They had a very rough passage; he would not have ventured if he had known how bad it would be.

However, here they are, safe and well, just like their own nice selves, Fanny looking as neat and white this morning as possible, and dear Charles all affectionate, placid, quiet, cheerful, good humour. They are both looking very well, but poor little Cassy is grown extremely thin, and looks poorly. I hope a week's country air and exercise may do her good. I am sorry to say it can be but a week. The baby does not appear so large in proportion as she was, nor quite so pretty, but I have seen very little of her. Cassy was too tired and bewildered just at first to seem to know anybody. We met them in the hall – the women and girl part of us – but before we reached the library she kissed me very affectionately, and has since seemed to recollect me in the same way.

It was quite an evening of confusion, as you may suppose. At first we were all walking about from one part of the house to the other; then came a fresh dinner in the breakfast-room for Charles and his wife, which Fanny and I attended; then we moved into the library, were joined by the dining-room people, were introduced, and so forth; and then we had tea and coffee, which was not over till past 10. Billiards again drew all the odd ones away, and Edward, Charles, the two Fannies, and I sat snugly talking. I shall be glad to have our numbers a little reduced, and by the time you receive this we shall be only a family, though a large family, party. Mr. Lushington goes to-morrow.

Now I must speak of *him,* and I like him very much. I am sure he is clever, and a man of taste. He got a volume of Milton last night, and spoke of it with warmth. He is quite an M.P., very smiling, with an exceeding good address and readiness of language. I am rather in love with him. I dare say he is ambitious and insincere. He puts me in mind of Mr. Dundas. He has a wide smiling mouth, and very good teeth, and something the same complexion and nose. He is a much shorter man, with Martha's leave. Does Martha never hear from Mrs. Craven? Is Mrs. Craven never at home?

We breakfasted in the dining-room to-day, and are now all pretty well dispersed and quiet. Charles and George are gone out shooting together, to Winni-gates and Seaton Wood. I asked on purpose to tell Henry. Mr. Lushington and Edwd. are gone some other way. I wish Charles may kill something, but this high wind is against their sport.

Lady Williams is living at the Rose at Sittingbourne; they called upon her yesterday; she cannot live at Sheerness, and as soon as she gets to Sittingbourne is quite well. In return for all your matches, I announce that her brother William is going to marry a Miss Austen, of a Wiltshire family, who say they are related to us.

I talk to Cassy about Chawton; she remembers much, but does not volunteer on the subject. Poor little love! I wish she were not so very Palmery, but it seems stronger than ever. I never knew a wife's family features have such undue influence.

Papa and mamma have not yet made up their mind as to parting with her or not; the chief, indeed the only, difficulty with mamma is a very reasonable one, the child's being very unwilling to leave them. When it was mentioned to her she did not like the idea of it at all. At the same time, she has been suffering so much lately from sea-sickness that her mamma cannot bear to have her much on board this winter. Charles is less inclined to part with her. I do not know how it will end, or what is to determine it. He desires his best love to you, and has not written because he has not been able to decide. They are both very sensible of your kindness on the occasion.

I have made Charles furnish me with something to say about young Kendall. He is going on very well. When he first joined the "Namur" my brother did not find him forward enough to be what they call put in the office, and therefore placed him under the schoolmaster, but he is very much improved, and goes into the office now every afternoon, still attending school in the morning.

This cold weather comes very fortunately for Edward's nerves, with such a house full; it suits him exactly; he is all alive and cheerful. Poor James, on the contrary, must be running his toes into the fire. I find that Mary Jane Fowle was very near returning with her brother and paying them a visit on board. I forget exactly what hindered her; I believe the Cheltenham scheme. I am glad something did. They are to go to Cheltenham on Monday se'nnight. I don't vouch for their going, you know; it only comes from one of the family.

Now I think I have written you a good-sized letter, and may deserve whatever I can get in reply. Infinities of love. I must distinguish that of Fanny, senior, who particularly desires to be remembered to you all.

Yours very affectionately,

J. AUSTEN.

Letter LXVII – 1813

Godmersham Park (Oct. 18).

MY DEAR AUNT CASSANDRA,

I am very much obliged to you for your long letter and for the nice account of Chawton. We are all very glad to hear that the Adams are gone and hope Dame Libscombe will be more happy now with her deaffy child, as she calls it, but I am afraid there is not much chance of her remaining long sole mistress of her house.

I am sorry you had not any better news to send us of our hare, poor little thing! I thought it would not live long in that *Pondy House;* I don't wonder that Mary Doe is very sorry it is dead, because we promised her that if it was alive when we came back to Chawton, we would reward her for her trouble.

Papa is much obliged to you for ordering the scrubby firs to be cut down; I think he was rather frightened at first about the great oak. Fanny quite believed it, for she exclaimed: "Dear me, what a pity, how could they be so stupid!" I hope by this time they have put up some hurdles for the sheep, or turned out the cart-horses from the lawn.

Pray tell grandmamma that we have begun getting seeds for her; I hope we shall be able to get her a nice collection, but I am afraid this wet weather is very much against them. How glad I am to hear she has had such good success with her chickens, but I wish there had been more bantams amongst them. I am very sorry to hear of poor Lizzie's fate.

I must now tell you something about our poor people. I believe you know old Mary Croucher, she gets *maderer* and *maderer* every day. Aunt Jane has been to see her, but it was on one of her rational days. Poor Will Amos hopes your skewers are doing well; he has left his house in the poor Row, and lives in a barn at Builting. We asked him why he went away, and he said the fleas were so starved when he came back from Chawton that they all flew upon him and *eenermost* eat him up.

How unlucky it is that the weather is so wet! Poor uncle Charles has come home half drowned every day.

I don't think little Fanny is quite so pretty as she was; one reason is because she wears short petticoats, I believe. I hope Cook is better; she was very unwell the day we went away. Papa has given me half-a-dozen new pencils, which are very good ones indeed; I draw every other day. I hope you go and whip Lucy Chalcraft every night.

Miss Clewes begs me to give her very best respects to you; she is very much obliged to you for your kind inquiries after her. Pray give my duty to grandmamma and love to Miss Floyd. I remain, my dear Aunt Cassandra,

Your very affectionate niece,

ELIZTH. KNIGHT.

Thursday. – I think Lizzy's letter will entertain you. Thank you for yours just received. To-morrow shall be fine if possible. You will be at Guildford before our party set off. They only go to Key Street, as Mr. Street the Purser lives there, and they have promised to dine and sleep with him.

Cassy's looks are much mended. She agrees pretty well with her cousins, but is not quite happy among them; they are too many and too boisterous for her. I have given her your message, but she said nothing, and did not look as if the idea of going to Chawton again was a pleasant one. They have Edward's carriage to Ospringe.

I think I have just done a good deed – extracted Charles from his wife and children upstairs, and made him get ready to go out shooting, and not keep Mr. Moore waiting any longer.

Mr. and Mrs. Sherer and Joseph dined here yesterday very prettily. Edw. and Geo. were absent – gone for a night to Eastling. The two Fannies went to Canty. in the morning, and took Lou. and Cass. to try on new stays. Harriot and I had a comfortable walk together. She desires her best love to you and kind remembrance to Henry. Fanny's best love also. I fancy there is to be another party to Canty. to-morrow – Mr. and Mrs. Moore and me.

Edward thanks Henry for his letter. We are most happy to hear he is so much better. I depend upon you for letting me know what he wishes as to my staying with him or not; you will be able to find out, I dare say. I had intended to beg you would bring one of my nightcaps with you, in case of my staying, but forgot it when I wrote on Tuesday. Edward is much concerned about his pond: he cannot now doubt the fact of its running out, which he was resolved to do as long as possible.

I suppose my mother will like to have me write to her. I shall try at least.

No; I have never seen the death of Mrs. Crabbe. I have only just been making out from one of his prefaces that he probably was married. It is almost ridiculous. Poor woman! I will comfort *him* as well as I can, but I do not undertake to be good to her children. She had better not leave any.

Edw. and Geo. set off this day week for Oxford. Our party will then be very small, as the Moores will be going about the same time. To enliven us, Fanny proposes spending a few days soon afterwards at Fredville. It will really be a good opportunity, as her father will have a companion. We shall all three go to Wrotham, but Edwd. and I stay only a night perhaps. Love to Mr. Tilson.

Yours very affectionately,

J. A.

Letter LXVIII – 1813

Godmersham Park: Tuesday (Oct. 26).

MY DEAREST CASSANDRA,

You will have had such late accounts from this place as (I hope) to prevent your expecting a letter from me immediately, as I really do not think I have wherewithal to fabricate one to-day. I suspect this will be brought to you by our nephews; tell me if it is. It is a great pleasure to me to think of you with Henry. I am sure your time must pass most comfortably, and I trust you are seeing improvement in him every day. I shall be most happy to hear from you again. Your Saturday's letter, however, was quite as long and as particular as I could expect. I am not at all in a humour for writing; I must write on till I am.

I congratulate Mr. Tilson, and hope everything is going on well. Fanny and I depend upon knowing what the child's name is to be; as soon as you can tell us. I guess Caroline.

Our gentlemen are all gone to their Sittingbourne meeting, East and West Kent, in one barouche together – rather, West Kent driving East Kent. I believe that is not the usual way of the county. We breakfasted before nine, and do not dine till half-past six on the occasion, so I hope we three shall have a long morning enough.

Mr. Deedes and Sir Brook – I do not care for Sir Brook's being a baronet; I will put Mr. Deedes first because I like him a great deal the best. They arrived together yesterday, for the Bridges' are staying at Sandling, just before dinner; both gentlemen much as they used to be, only growing a little older. They leave us to-morrow.

You were clear of Guildford by half-an-hour, and were winding along the pleasant road to Ripley when the Charleses set off on Friday. I hope we shall have a visit from them at Chawton in the spring or early part of the summer. They seem well inclined. Cassy had recovered her looks almost entirely, and I find they do not consider the "Namur" as disagreeing with her in general, only when the weather is so rough as to make her sick.

Our Canterbury scheme took place as proposed, and very pleasant it was – Harriot and I and little George within, my brother on the box with the master coachman. I was most happy to find my brother included in the party. It was a great improvement, and he and Harriot and I walked about together very happily, while Mr. Moore took his little boy with him to tailor's and hair-cutter's.

Our chief business was to call on Mrs. Milles, and we had, indeed, so little else to do that we were obliged to saunter about anywhere and go backwards and forwards as much as possible to make out the time and keep ourselves from having two hours to sit with the good lady – a most extraordinary circumstance in a Canterbury morning.

Old Toke came in while we were paying our visit. I thought of Louisa. Miss Milles was queer as usual, and provided us with plenty to laugh at. She undertook in *three words* to give us the history of Mrs. Scudamore's reconciliation, and then talked on about it for half-an-hour, using such odd expressions, and so foolishly minute, that I could hardly keep my countenance. The death of Wyndham Knatchbull's son will rather supersede the Scudamores. I told her that he was to be buried at Hatch. She had heard, with military honours, at Portsmouth. We may guess how that point will be discussed evening after evening.

Owing to a difference of clocks the coachman did not bring the carriage so soon as he ought by half-an-hour; anything like a breach of punctuality was a great offence, and Mr. Moore was very angry, which I was rather glad of. I wanted to see him angry; and, though he spoke to his servant in a very loud voice and with a good deal of heat, I was happy to perceive that he did not scold

Harriot at all. Indeed, there is nothing to object to in his manners to her, and I do believe that he makes her – or she makes herself – very happy. They do not spoil their boy.

It seems now quite settled that we go to Wrotham on Saturday, the 13th, spend Sunday there, and proceed to London on Monday, as before intended. I like the plan. I shall be glad to see Wrotham. Harriot is quite as pleasant as ever. We are very comfortable together, and talk over our nephews and nieces occasionally, as may be supposed, and with much unanimity; and I really like Mr. M. better than I expected – see less in him to dislike.

I begin to perceive that you will have this letter to-morrow. It is throwing a letter away to send it by a visitor; there is never convenient time for reading it, and visitor can tell most things as well. I *had* thought with delight of saving you the postage, but money is dirt. If *you* do not regret the loss of Oxfordshire and Gloucestershire *I* will not, though I certainly had wished for your going very much. "Whatever is, is best." There has been one infallible Pope in the world.

George Hatton called yesterday, and I saw him, saw him for ten minutes; sat in the same room with him, heard him talk, saw him bow, and was not in raptures. I discerned nothing extraordinary. I should speak of him as a gentlemanlike young man – *eh! bien tout est dit.* We are expecting the ladies of the family this morning.

How do you like your flounce? We have seen only *plain* flounces. I hope you have not cut off the train of your bombazin. I cannot reconcile myself to giving them up as morning gowns; they are so very sweet by candlelight. I would rather sacrifice my blue one for that purpose; in short, I do not know and I do not care.

Thursday or Friday is now mentioned from Bath as the day of setting off. The Oxford scheme is given up. They will go directly to Harefield. Fanny does not go to Fredville, not yet at least.

She has had a letter of excuse from Mary Plumptre to-day. The death of Mr. Ripley, their uncle by marriage, and Mr. P.'s very old friend, prevents their receiving her. Poor blind Mrs. Ripley must be felt for, if there is any feeling to be had for love or money.

We have had another of Edward Bridges' Sunday visits. I think the pleasantest part of his married life must be the dinners, and breakfasts, and luncheons, and billiards that he gets in this way at Gm. Poor wretch! he is quite the dregs of the family as to luck.

I long to know whether you are buying stockings or what you are doing. Remember me most kindly to Mde. B. and Mrs. Perigord. You will get acquainted with my friend, Mr. Philips, and hear him talk from books, and be sure to have something odd happen to you, see somebody that you do not expect, meet with some surprise or other, find some old friend sitting with Henry when you come into the room. Do something clever in that way. Edward and I settled that you went to St. Paul's, Covent Garden, on Sunday. Mrs. Hill will come and see you, or else she won't come and see you and will write instead.

I have had a late account from Steventon, and a baddish one, as far as Ben is concerned. He has declined a curacy (apparently highly eligible), which he might have secured against his taking orders; and, upon its being made rather a serious question, says he has not made up his mind as to taking orders so early, and that, if her father makes a point of it, he must give Anna up rather than do what he does not approve. They are going on again at present as before, but it cannot last. Mary says that Anna is very unwilling to go to Chawton and will get home again as soon as she can.

Good-bye. Accept this indifferent letter and think it long and good. Miss Clewes is better for some prescription of Mr. Scudamore's, and, indeed, seems tolerably stout now. I find time in the midst of port and

Madeira to think of the fourteen bottles of mead very often.

Yours very affectionately,

J. A.

Lady Elizabeth, her second daughter, and the two Mrs. Finches have just left us; the two latter friendly, and talking, and pleasant as usual.

Harriot and Fanny's best love.

Letter LXIX – 1813

Godmersham Park: Wednesday (Nov. 3).

MY DEAREST CASSANDRA,

I will keep this celebrated birthday by writing to you, and as my pen seems inclined to write large, I will put my lines very close together. I had but just time to enjoy your letter yesterday before Edward and I set off in the chair for Canty., and I allowed him to hear the chief of it as we went along.

We rejoice sincerely in Henry's gaining ground as he does, and hope there will be weather for him to get out every day this week, as the likeliest way of making him equal to what he plans for the next. If he is tolerably well, the going into Oxford-shire will make him better, by making him happier.

Can it be, that I have not given you the minutiæ of Edward's plans? See, here they are: To go to Wrotham on Saturday the 13th, spend Sunday there, and be in town on Monday to dinner, and, if agreeable to Henry, spend one whole day with him, which day is likely to be Tuesday, and so go down to Chawton on Wednesday.

But now I cannot be quite easy without staying a little while with Henry, unless he wishes it otherwise; his illness and the dull time of year together make me feel that it would be horrible of me not to offer to remain with him, and therefore unless you know of any objection, I wish you would tell him with my best love that I shall be most happy to spend ten days or a fortnight in Henrietta St., if he will accept me. I do not offer more than a fortnight, because I shall then have been some time from home; but it will be a great pleasure to be with him, as it always is. I have the less regret and scruple on your account, because I shall see you for a day and a-half, and because you will have Edward for at least a week. My scheme is to take Bookham in my way home for a few days, and my hope that Henry will be so good as to send me some part of the way thither. I have a most kind repetition of Mrs. Cooke's two or three dozen invitations, with the offer of meeting me anywhere in one of her airings.

Fanny's cold is much better. By dosing and keeping her room on Sunday, she got rid of the worst of it, but I am rather afraid of what this day may do for her; she is gone to Canty. with Miss Clewes, Liz., and Marnne., and it is but roughish weather for any one in a tender state. Miss Clewes has been going to Canty. ever since her return, and it is now just accomplishing.

Edward and I had a delightful morning for our drive *there,* I enjoyed it thoroughly; but the day turned off before we were ready, and we came home in some rain and the apprehension of a great deal. It has not done us any harm, however. He went to inspect the gaol, as a visiting magistrate, and took me with him. I was gratified, and went through all the feelings which people must go through, I think, in visiting such a building. We paid no other visits, only walked about snugly together and shopped. I bought a concert ticket and a sprig of flowers for my old age.

To vary the subject from gay to grave with inimitable address, I shall now tell you something of the Bath party – and still a Bath party they are, for a fit of the gout came on last week. The accounts of Lady B. are as good as can be under such a circumstance; Dr. P. says it appears a good sort of gout, and her spirits are better than usual, but as to her coming away, it is of course all uncertainty. I have very little doubt of Edward's going down to Bath, if they have not left it when he is in Hampshire; if he does, he will go on from Steventon, and then return direct to London, without coming back to Chawton. This detention does not suit his feelings. It may be rather a good thing, however, that Dr. P. should see Lady B. with the gout on her. Harriot was quite wishing for it.

The day seems to improve. I wish my pen would, too.

Sweet Mr. Ogle. I dare say he sees all the panoramas for nothing, has free admittance everywhere; he is so delightful! Now, you need not see anybody else.

I am glad to hear of our being likely to have a peep at Charles and Fanny at Christmas, but do not force poor Cass. to stay if she hates it. You have done very right as to Mrs. F. A. Your tidings of *S. and S.* give me pleasure. I have never seen it advertised.

Harriot, in a letter to Fanny to-day, inquires whether they sell cloths for pelisses at Bedford House, and, if they do, will be very much obliged to you to desire them to send her down patterns, with the width and prices; they may go from Charing Cross almost any day in the week, but if it is a *ready money* house it will not do, for the *bru* of *feu*[27] the Archbishop says she cannot pay

---

[27] It is clearly written "Bru of feu" or "face," and may have been some joke in connection with the fact that "Harriot" was the daughter-in-law of Archbishop Moore, but, if so, the joke is lost. In French bru is "daughter in law", while one of the many meanings of feu is "deceased".

for it immediately. Fanny and I suspect they do not deal in the article.

The Sherers, I believe, are now really going to go; Joseph has had a bed here the two last nights, and I do not know whether this is not the day of moving. Mrs. Sherer called yesterday to take leave. The weather looks worse again.

We dine at Chilham Castle to-morrow, and I expect to find some amusement, but more from the concert the next day, as I am sure of seeing several that I want to see. We are to meet a party from Goodnestone, Lady B., Miss Hawley, and Lucy Foote, and I am to meet Mrs. Harrison, and we are to talk about Ben and Anna. "My dear Mrs. Harrison," I shall say, "I am afraid the young man has some of your family madness, and though there often appears to be something of madness in Anna too, I think she inherits more of it from her mother's family than from ours." That is what I shall say, and I think she will find it difficult to answer me.

I took up your letter again to refresh me, being somewhat tired and was struck with the prettiness of the hand: it is really a very pretty hand now and – so small and so neat! I wish I could get as much into a sheet of paper. Another time I will take two days to make a letter in: it is fatiguing to write a whole long one at once. I hope to hear from you again on

Sunday and again on Friday, the day before we move. On Monday, I suppose, you will be going to Streatham, to see quiet Mr. Hill and eat very bad baker's bread.

A fall in bread by-the-bye. I hope my mother's bill next week will show it. I have had a very comfortable letter from her, one of her foolscap sheets quite full of little home news. Anna was there the first of the two days. An Anna sent away and an Anna fetched are different things. This will be an excellent time for Ben to pay his visit, now that we, the formidables, are absent.

I did not mean to eat, but Mr. Johncock has brought in the tray, so I must. I am all alone. Edward is gone into his woods. At this present time I have five tables, eight-and-twenty chairs, and two fires all to myself.

Miss Clewes is to be invited to go to the concert with us; there will be my brother's place and ticket for her, as he cannot go. He and the other connections of the Cages are to meet at Milgate that very day, to consult about a proposed alteration of the Maidstone road, in which the Cages are very much interested. Sir Brook comes here in the morning, and they are to be joined by Mr. Deedes at Ashford. The loss of the concert will be no great evil to the Squire. We shall be a party of three ladies therefore, and to meet three ladies.

What a convenient carriage Henry's is, to his friends in general! Who has it next? I am glad William's going is voluntary, and on no worse grounds. An inclination for the country is a venial fault. He has more of Cowper than of Johnson in him – fonder of tame hares and blank verse than of the full tide of human existence at Charing Cross.

Oh! I have more of such sweet flattery from Miss Sharp. She is an excellent kind friend. I am read and admired in Ireland, too. There is a Mrs. Fletcher, the wife of a judge, an old lady, and very good and very clever, who is all curiosity to know about me – what I am like, and so forth. I am not known to her by *name,* however. This comes through Mrs. Carrick, not through Mrs. Gore. You are quite out there.

I do not despair of having my picture in the Exhibition at last – all white and red, with my head on one side; or perhaps I may marry young Mr. D'Arblay. I suppose in the meantime I shall owe dear Henry a great deal of money for printing, &c.

I hope Mrs. Fletcher will indulge herself with *S. and S.* If I *am* to stay stay in H. S., and if you should be writing home soon, I wish you would be so good as to give a hint of it, for I am not likely to write there again these ten days, having written yesterday.

Fanny has set her heart upon its being a Mr. Brett who is going to marry a Miss Dora Best, of this country. I dare say Henry has no objection. Pray, where did the boys sleep?

The Deedes come here on Monday to stay till Friday, so that we shall end with a flourish the last canto. They bring Isabella and one of the grown-ups, and will come in for a Canty. ball on Thursday. I shall be glad to see them. Mrs. Deedes and I must talk rationally together, I suppose.

Edward does not write to Henry, because of my writing so often. God bless you. I shall be so glad to see you again, and I wish you many happy returns of this day. Poor Lord Howard! How he does cry about it!

Yours very truly,

J. A.

Letter LXX – 1813

Godmersham Park: Saturday (Nov. 6).

MY DEAR CASSANDRA,

Having half-an-hour before breakfast (very, snug, in my own room, lovely morning, excellent fire – fancy me!) I will give you some account of the last two days. And yet, what is there to be told? I shall get foolishly minute unless I cut the matter short.

We met only the Bretons at Chilham Castle, besides a Mr. and Mrs. Osborne and a Miss Lee staying in the house, and were only fourteen altogether. My brother and Fanny thought it the pleasantest party they had ever known there, and I was very well entertained by bits and scraps. I had long wanted to see Dr. Breton, and his wife amuses me very much with her affected refinement and elegance. Miss Dee I found very conversable; she admires Crabbe as she ought. She is at an age of reason, ten years older than myself at least. She was at the famous ball at Chilham Castle, so of course you remember her.

By-the-bye, as I must leave off being young, I find many *douceurs* in being a sort of *chaperon,* for I am put on the sofa near the fire, and can drink as much wine as I like. We had music in the evening: Fanny and Miss Wildman played, and Mr. James Wildman sat close by and listened, or pretended to listen.

Yesterday was a day of dissipation all through: first came Sir Brook to dissipate us before breakfast; then there was a call from Mr. Sherer, then a regular morning visit from Lady Honeywood in her way home from Eastwell; then Sir Brook and Edward set off; then we dined (five in number) at half-past four; then we had coffee; and at six Miss Clewes, Fanny, and I drove away. We had a beautiful night for our frisks. We were earlier than we need have been, but after a time Lady B. and her two companions appeared – we had kept places for them; and there we sat, all six in a row, under a side wall, I between Lucy Foote and Miss Clewes.

Lady B. was much what I expected; I could not determine whether she was rather handsome or very plain. I liked her for being in a hurry to have the concert over and get away, and for getting away at last with a great deal of decision and promptness, not waiting to compliment and dawdle and fuss about seeing *dear Fanny,* who was half the evening in another part of the room with her friends the Plumptres. I am growing too minute, so I will go to breakfast.

When the concert was over, Mrs. Harrison and I found each other out, and had a very comfortable little complimentary friendly chat. She is a sweet woman

– still quite a sweet woman in herself, and so like her sister! I could almost have thought I was speaking to Mrs. Lefroy. She introduced me to her daughter, whom I think pretty, but most dutifully inferior to *la Mère Beauté.* The Faggs and the Hammonds were there – Wm. Hammond the only young man of renown. *Miss* looked very handsome but I prefer her little smiling flirting sister Julia.

I was just introduced at last to Mary Plumptre, but should hardly know her again. She was delighted with *me,* however, good enthusiastic soul! And Lady B. found me handsomer than she expected, so you see I am not so very bad as you might think for.

It was 12 before we reached home. We were all dog-tired, but pretty well to-day: Miss Clewes says she has not caught cold, and Fanny's does not seem worse. I was so tired that I began to wonder how I should get through the ball next Thursday, but there will be so much more variety then in walking about, and probably so much less heat, that perhaps I may not feel it more. My China crape is still kept for the ball. Enough of the concert.

I had a letter from Mary yesterday. They travelled down to Cheltenham last Monday very safely, and are certainly to be there a month. Bath is still Bath. The H. Bridges' must quit them early next week, and Louisa seems not quite to despair of their all moving together, but to those who see at a distance there appears no chance of it. Dr. Parry does not want to keep Lady B. at Bath when she can once move. That is lucky. You will see poor Mr. Evelyn's death.

Since I wrote last, my 2nd edit. has stared me in the face. Mary tells me that Eliza means to buy it. I wish she may. It can hardly depend upon any more Fyfield Estates. I cannot help hoping that *many* will feel themselves obliged to buy it. I shall not mind imagining it a disagreeable duty to them, so as they do it. Mary heard before she left home that it was very much admired at Cheltenham, and that it was given to Miss Hamilton. It is pleasant to have such a respectable writer named. I cannot tire *you,* I am sure, on this subject, or I would apologise.

What weather, and what news! We have enough to do to admire them both. I hope you derive your full share of enjoyment from each.

I have extended my lights and increased my acquaintance a good deal within these two days. Lady Honeywood you know; I did not sit near enough to be a perfect judge, but I thought her extremely pretty, and her manners have all the recommendations of ease and good humour and unaffectedness; and, going about with four horses and nicely dressed herself, she is altogether a perfect sort of woman.

Oh, and I saw Mr. Gipps last night – the useful Mr. Gipps, whose attentions came in as acceptably to us in handing us to the carriage, for want of a better man, as they did to Emma Plumptre. I thought him rather a good-looking little man.

I long for your letter to-morrow, particularly that I may know my fate as to London. My first wish is that Henry should really choose what he likes best; I shall certainly not be sorry if he does not want me. Morning church tomorrow; I shall come back with impatient feelings.

The Sherers are gone, but the Pagets are not come; we shall therefore have Mr. S. again. Mr. Paget acts like an unsteady man. Dr. Mant, however, gives him a very good character; what is wrong is to be imputed to the lady. I dare say the house likes female government.

I have a nice long black and red letter from Charles, but not communicating much that I did not know.

There is some chance of a good ball next week, as far as females go. Lady Bridges may perhaps be there with some Knatchbulls. Mrs. Harrison, perhaps, with Miss Oxenden and the Miss Papillons; and if Mrs. Harrison, then Lady Fagg will come.

The shades of evening are descending, and I resume my interesting narrative. Sir Brook and my brother came back about four, and Sir Brook almost immediately set forward again to Goodnestone. We are to have Edwd. B. tomorrow, to pay us another Sunday's visit – the last, for more reasons than one; they all come home on the same day that we go. The Deedes do not come till Tuesday; Sophia is to be the comer. She is a disputable beauty that I want much to see. Lady Eliz. Hatton and Annamaria called here this morning. Yes, they called; but I do not think I can say anything more about them. They came, and they sat, and they went.

Sunday. – Dearest Henry! What a turn he has for being ill, and what a thing bile is! This attack has probably been brought on in part by his previous confinement and anxiety; but, however it came, I hope it is going fast, and that you will be able to send a very good account of him on Tuesday. As I hear on Wednesday, of course I shall not expect to hear again on Friday. Perhaps a letter to Wrotham would not have an ill effect.

We are to be off on Saturday before the post comes in, as Edward takes his own horses all the way. He talks of 9 o'clock. We shall bait at Lenham.

Excellent sweetness of you to send me such a nice long letter; it made its appearance, with one from my mother, soon after I and my impatient feelings walked in. How glad I am that I did what I did! I was only afraid that you might think the offer superfluous, but you have set my heart at ease. Tell Henry that I *will* stay with him, let it be ever so disagreeable to him.

Oh, dear me! I have not time on paper for half that I want to say. There have been two letters from Oxford – one from George yesterday. They got there very safely – Edwd. two hours behind the coach, having lost his way in leaving London. George writes cheerfully and quietly; hopes to have Utterson's rooms soon; went to lecture on Wednesday, states some of his expenses, and concludes with saying, "I am afraid I shall be poor." I am glad he thinks about it so soon. I believe there is no private tutor yet chosen, but my brother is to hear from Edwd. on the subject shortly.

You, and Mrs. H., and Catherine, and Alethea going about together in Henry's carriage seeing sights – I am not used to the idea of it yet. All that you are to see of Streatham, seen already! Your Streatham and my Bookham may go hang. The prospect of being taken down to Chawton by Henry perfects the plan to me. I was in hopes of your seeing some illuminations, and you have seen them. "I thought you would come, and you did come." I am sorry he is not to come from the Baltic sooner. Poor Mary!

My brother has a letter from Louisa to-day of an unwelcome nature; they are to spend the winter at Bath. It was just decided on. Dr. Parry wished it, not from thinking the water necessary to Lady B., but so that he might be better able to judge how far his treatment of her, which is totally different from anything she had been used to, is right; and I suppose he will not mind having a few more of her Ladyship's guineas. His system is a lowering one. He took twelve ounces of blood from her when the gout appeared, and forbids wine, &c. Hitherto, the plan agrees with her. *She* is very well satisfied to stay, but it is a sore disappointment to Louisa and Fanny.

The H. Bridges leave them on Tuesday, and they mean to move into a smaller house; you may guess how Edward feels. There can be no doubt of his going to Bath now; I should not wonder if he brought Fanny Cage back with him.

You shall hear from me once more, some day or other.

Yours very affectionately,

J. A.

We do not like Mr. Hampson's scheme.

Letter LXXI – 1814

Henrietta Street: Saturday (March 5).

MY DEAR CASSANDRA,

Do not be angry with me for beginning another letter to you. I have read the *"Corsair,"* mended my petticoat, and have nothing else to do. Getting out is impossible. It is a nasty day for everybody. Edward's spirits will be wanting sunshine, and here is nothing but thickness and sleet; and though these two rooms are delightfully warm, I fancy it is very cold abroad.

Young Wyndham accepts the invitation. He is such a nice, gentlemanlike, unaffected sort of young man, that I think he may do for Fanny; has a sensible, quiet look, which one likes. Our fate with Mrs. L. and Miss E. is fixed for this day se'nnight. A civil note is come from Miss H. Moore, to apologise for not returning my visit to-day, and ask us to join a small party this evening. Thank ye, but we shall be better engaged.

I was speaking to Mde. B. this morning about a boiled loaf, when it appeared that her master has no raspberry jam; *she* has some, which of course she is determined he shall have; but cannot you bring a pot when you come?

Sunday. – I find a little time before breakfast for writing. It was considerably past four when they arrived yesterday, the roads were so very bad! As it was, they had four horses from Cranford Bridge. Fanny was miserably cold at first, but they both seem well.

No possibility of Edwd.'s writing. His opinion, however, inclines *against* a second prosecution; he thinks it would be a vindictive measure. He might think differently, perhaps, on the spot. But things must take their chance.

We were quite satisfied with Kean. I cannot imagine better acting, but the part was too short; and, excepting him and Miss Smith, and *she* did not quite answer my expectation, the parts were ill filled and the play heavy. We were too much tired to stay for the whole of "Illusion" ("Nour-jahad"), which has three acts; there is a great deal of finery and dancing in it, but I think little merit. Elliston was "Nour-jahad," but it is a solemn sort of part, not at all calculated for his powers. There was nothing of the *best* Elliston about him. I might not have known him but for his voice.

A grand thought has struck me as to our gowns. This six weeks' mourning makes so great a difference that I shall not go to Miss Hare till you can come and help choose yourself, unless you particularly wish the contrary. It may be hardly worth while perhaps to have the gowns so expensively made up. We may buy a cap or a *veil* instead; but we can talk more of this together.

Henry is just come down; he seems well, his cold does not increase. I expected to have found Edward seated at a table writing to Louisa, but I was first. Fanny I left fast asleep. She was doing about last night when *I* went to sleep, a little after one. I am most happy to find there were but *five* shirts. She thanks you for your note, and reproaches herself for not having written to you, but I assure her there was no occasion.

The accounts are not capital of Lady B. Upon the whole, I believe, Fanny liked Bath very well. They were only out three evenings, to one play and each of the rooms. Walked about a good deal, and saw a good deal of the Harrisons and Wildmans. All the Bridges are likely to come away together, and Louisa will probably turn off at Dartford to go to Harriot. Edward is quite–[28]

Now we are come from church, and all going to write. Almost everybody was in mourning last night, but my brown gown did very well. Genl. Chowne was introduced to me; he has not much remains of Frederick. This young Wyndham does not come after all; a very

---

[28] MS. torn

long and very civil note of excuse is arrived. It makes one moralise upon the ups and downs of this life.

I have determined to trim my lilac sarsenet with black satin ribbon just as my China crape is, 6*d.* width at the bottom, 3*d.* or 4*d.,* at top. Ribbon trimmings are all the fashion at Bath, and I dare say the fashions of the two places are alike enough in that point to content *me.* With this addition it will be a very useful gown, happy to go anywhere.

Henry has this moment said that he likes my M. P.[29] better and better; he is in the third volume. I believe now he has changed his mind as to foreseeing the end; he said yesterday, at least, that he defied anybody to say whether H. C.[30] would be reformed, or would forget Fanny in a fortnight.

I shall like to see Kean again excessively, and to see him with you too. It appeared to me as if there were no fault in him anywhere; and in his scene with "Tubal" there was exquisite acting.

Edward has had a correspondence with Mr. Wickham on the Baigent business, and has been showing me some letters enclosed by Mr. W. from a friend of his,

---

29   "Mansfield Park."

30   Henry Crawford.

a lawyer, whom he had consulted about it, and whose opinion is *for* the prosecution for assault, supposing the boy is acquitted on the first, which he rather expects. Excellent letters; and I am sure he must be an excellent man. They are such thinking, clear, considerate letters as Frank might have written. I long to know who he is, but the name is always torn off. He was consulted only as a friend. When Edwd. gave me *his* opinions against the second prosecution he had not read this letter, which was waiting for him here. Mr. W. is to be on the grand jury. This business must hasten an intimacy between his family and my brothers.

Fanny cannot answer your question about button-holes till she gets home.

I have never told you, but soon after Henry and I began our journey he said, talking of yours, that he should desire you to come post at his expense, and added something of the carriage meeting you at Kingston. He has said nothing about it since.

Now I have just read Mr. Wickham's letter, by which it appears that the letters of his friend were sent to my brother quite confidentially, therefore don't tell. By his expression, this friend must be one of the judges.

A cold day, but bright and clear. I am afraid your planting can hardly have begun. I am sorry to hear that there has been a rise in tea. I do not mean to pay Twining till later in the day, when we may order a fresh supply. I long to know something of the mead, and how you are off for a cook.

Monday. – Here's a day! The ground covered with snow! What is to become of us? We were to have walked out early to near shops, and had the carriage for the more distant. Mr. Richard Snow is dreadfully fond of us. I dare say he has stretched himself out at Chawton too.

Fanny and I went into the park yesterday and drove about, and were very much entertained; and our dinner and evening went off very well. Messrs. J. Plumptre and J. Wildman called while we were out, and we had a glimpse of them both, and of G. Hatton too, in the park. *I* could not produce a single acquaintance.

By a little convenient listening, I now know that Henry wishes to go to Gm. for a few days before Easter, and has indeed promised to do it. This being the case, there can be no time for your remaining in London after your return from Adlestrop. You must not put off your coming therefore; and it occurs to me that, instead of my coming here again from Streatham, it will be better for you to join me there. It is a great comfort to have got at the truth. Henry finds he cannot set off for Oxfordshire before the Wednesday, which will be the 23rd; but we shall not have too many days together here previously. I shall write to Catherine very soon.

Well, we have been out as far as Coventry St.; Edwd. escorted us there and back to Newton's, where he left us, and I brought Fanny safe home. It was snowing the whole time. We have given up all idea of the carriage. Edward and Fanny stay another day, and both seem very well pleased to do so. Our visit to the Spencers is, of course, put off.

Edwd. heard from Louisa this morning. Her mother does not get better, and Dr. Parry talks of her beginning the waters again; this will be keeping them longer in Bath, and of course is not palatable.

You cannot think how much my ermine tippet is admired both by father and daughter. It was a noble gift.

Perhaps you have not heard that Edward has a good chance of escaping his lawsuit. His opponent "knocks under." The terms of agreement are not quite settled.

We are to see "The Devil to Pay" to-night. I expect to be very much amused. Excepting Miss Stephens, I daresay "Artaxerxes" will be very tiresome.

A great many pretty caps in the windows of Cranbourn Alley. I hope when you come we shall both be tempted. I have been ruining myself in black satin ribbon with a proper pearl edge, and now I am trying to draw it up into kind of roses instead of putting it in plain double plaits.

Tuesday. – My dearest Cassandra, – In ever so many hurries I acknowledge the receipt of your letter last night, just before we set off for Covent Garden. I have no mourning come, but it does not signify. This very moment has Richd. put it on the table. I have torn it open and read your note. Thank you, thank you, thank you.

Edwd. is amazed at the sixty-four trees. He desires his love, and gives you notice of the arrival of a study table for himself. It ought to be at Chawton this week. He begs you to be so good as to have it inquired for and fetched by the cart, but wishes it not to be unpacked till he is on the spot himself. It may be put in the hall.

Well, Mr. Hampson dined here, and all that. I was very tired of "Artaxerxes," highly amused with the farce, and, in an inferior way, with the pantomime that followed. Mr. J. Plumptre joined in the latter part of the evening, walked home with us, ate some soup, and is very earnest for our going to Covent Garden again to-night to see Miss Stephens in the "Farmer's Wife." He is to try for a box. I do not particularly wish him to succeed. I have had enough for the present. Henry dines to-day with Mr. Spencer.

Yours very affectionately,

J. AUSTEN.

Letter LXXII – 1814

Henrietta St.: Wednesday (March 9).

Well, we went to the play again last night, and as we were out a great part of the morning too, shopping, and seeing the Indian jugglers, I am very glad to be quiet now till dressing time. We are to dine at the Tilsons', and to-morrow at Mr. Spencer's.

We had not done breakfast yesterday when Mr. J. Plumptre appeared to say that he had secured a box. Henry asked him to dine here, which I fancy he was very happy to do, and so at five o'clock we four sat down to table together while the master of the house was preparing for going out himself. The "Farmer's Wife" is a musical thing in three acts, and, as Edward was steady in not staying for anything more, we were at home before ten.

Fanny and Mr. J. P. are delighted with Miss S., and her merit in singing is, I dare say, very great; that she gave *me* no pleasure is no reflection upon her, nor, I hope, upon myself, being what Nature made me on that article. All that I am sensible of in Miss S. is a pleasing person and no skill in acting. We had Mathews, Liston, and Emery; of course, some amusement.

Our friends were off before half-past eight this morning, and had the prospect of a heavy cold journey before them. I think they both liked their visit very much. I am sure Fanny did. Henry sees decided attachment between her and his new acquaintance.

I have a cold, too, as well as my mother and Martha. Let it be a generous emulation between us which can get rid of it first.

I wear my gauze gown to-day, long sleeves and all. I shall see how they succeed, but as yet I have no reason to suppose long sleeves are allowable. I have lowered the bosom, especially at the corners, and plaited black satin ribbon round the top. Such will be my costume of vine-leaves and paste.

Prepare for a play the very first evening, I rather think Covent Garden, to see Young in "Richard." I have answered for your little companion's being conveyed to Keppel St. immediately. I have never yet been able to get there myself, but hope I shall soon.

What cruel weather this is! and here is Lord Portsmouth married, too, to Miss Hanson.[31]

---

[31] His second wife. He died in 1853, and was succeeded by his brother, the father of the present earl.

Henry has finished *"Mansfield Park,"* and his approbation has not lessened. He found the last half of the last volume *extremely interesting.*

I suppose my mother recollects that she gave me no money for paying Brecknell and Twining, and *my* funds will not supply enough.

We are home in such good time that I can finish my letter to-night, which will be better than getting up to do it to-morrow, especially as, on account of my cold, which has been very heavy in my head this evening, I rather think of lying in bed later than usual. I would not but be well enough to go to Hertford St. on any account.

We met only Genl. Chowne to-day, who has not much to say for himself. I was ready to laugh at the remembrance of Frederick, and such a different Frederick as we chose to fancy him to the real Christopher!

Mrs. Tilson had long sleeves, too, and she assured me that they are worn in the evening by many. I was glad to hear this. She dines here, I believe, next Tuesday.

On Friday we are to be snug with only Mr. Barlowe and an evening of business. I am so pleased that the mead is brewed. Love to all. I have written to Mrs. Hill, and care for nobody.

Yours affectionately,

J. AUSTEN.

Letter LXXIII – 1814

Chawton: Tuesday (June 13).

MY DEAREST CASSANDRA,

Fanny takes my mother to Alton this morning, which gives me an opportunity of sending you a few lines without any other trouble than that of writing them.

This is a delightful day in the country, and I hope not much too hot for town. Well, you had a good journey, I trust, and all that, and not rain enough to spoil your bonnet. It appeared so likely to be a wet evening that I went up to the Gt. House between three and four, and dawdled away an hour very comfortably, though Edwd. was not very brisk. The air was clearer in the evening and he was better. We all five walked together into the kitchen garden and along the Gosport road, and they drank tea with us.

You will be glad to hear that G. Turner has another *situation,* something in the cow line, near Rumsey, and he wishes to move immediately, which is not likely to be inconvenient to anybody.

The new nurseryman at Alton comes this morning to value the crops in the garden.

The only letter to-day is from Mrs. Cooke to me. They do not leave home till July, and want me to come to them, according to my promise. And, after considering everything, I have resolved on going. My companions promote it. I will not go, however, till after Edward is gone, that he may feel he has a somebody to give memorandums to, to the last. I must give up all help from his carriage, of course. And, at any rate, it must be such an excess of expense that I have quite made up my mind to it and do not mean to care.

I have been thinking of Triggs and the chair, you may be sure, but I know it will end in posting. They will meet me at Guildford.

In addition to their standing claims on me they admire *"Mansfield Park"* exceedingly. Mr. Cooke says "it is the most sensible novel he ever read," and the manner in which I treat the clergy delights them very much. Altogether, I must go, and I want you to join me there when your visit in Henrietta St. is over. Put this into your capacious head.

Take care of yourself, and do not be trampled to death in running after the Emperor. The report in Alton yesterday was that they would certainly travel this road either to or from Portsmouth. I long to know what this bow of the Prince's will produce.

I saw Mrs. Andrews yesterday. Mrs. Browning had seen her before. She is very glad to send an Elizabeth.

Miss Benn continues the same. Mr. Curtis, however, saw her yesterday and said her hand was going on as well as possible. Accept our best love.

Yours very affectionately,

J. AUSTEN.

Letter LXXIV – 1814

Thursday (June 23).

DEAREST CASSANDRA,

I received your pretty letter while the children were drinking tea with us, as Mr. Louch was so obliging as to walk over with it. Your good account of everybody made us very happy.

I heard yesterday from Frank. When he began his letter he hoped to be here on Monday, but before it was ended he had been told that the naval review would not take place till Friday, which would probably occasion him some delay, as he cannot get some necessary business of his own attended to while Portsmouth is in such a bustle. I hope Fanny has seen the Emperor, and then I may fairly wish them all away. I go to-morrow, and hope for some delays and adventures.

My mother's wood is brought in, but, by some mistake, no Bavins. She must therefore buy some.

Henry at White's! Oh, what a Henry! I do not know what to wish as to Miss B., so I will hold my tongue and my wishes.

Sackree and the children set off yesterday, and have not been returned back upon us. They were all very well the evening before. We had handsome presents from the Gt. House yesterday – a ham and the four leeches. Sackree has left some shirts of her master's at the school, which, finished or unfinished, she begs to have sent by Henry and Wm. Mr. Hinton is expected home soon, which is a good thing for the shirts.

We have called upon Miss Dusantoy and Miss Papillon, and been very pretty. Miss D. has a great idea of being Fanny Price – she and her youngest sister together, who is named Fanny.

Miss Benn has drank tea with the Prowtings, and, I believe, comes to us this evening. She has still a swelling about the fore-finger and a little discharge, and does not seem to be on the point of a perfect cure, but her spirits are good, and she will be most happy, I believe, to accept any invitation. The Clements are gone to Petersfield to look.

Only think of the Marquis of Granby being dead. I hope, if it please Heaven there should be another son, they will have better sponsors and less parade.

I certainly do not *wish* that Henry should think again of getting me to town. I would rather return straight from Bookham; but, if he really does propose it, I cannot say No to what will be so kindly intended. It could be but for a few days, however, as my mother would be quite disappointed by my exceeding the fortnight which I now talk of as the outside – at least, we could not both remain longer away comfortably.

The middle of July is Martha's time, as far as she has any time. She has left it to Mrs. Craven to fix the day. I wish she could get her money paid, for I fear her going at all depends upon that.

Instead of Bath the Deans Dundases have taken a house at Clifton – Richmond Terrace – and she is as glad of the change as even you and I should be, or almost. She will now be able to go on from Berks and visit them without any fears from heat.

This post has brought me a letter from Miss Sharpe. Poor thing! she has been suffering indeed, but is now in a comparative state of comfort. She is at Sir W. P.'s, in Yorkshire, with the children, and there is no appearance of her quitting them. Of course we lose the pleasure of seeing her here. She writes highly of Sir Wm. I do so want him to marry her. There is a Dow. Lady P. presiding there to make it all right. The *Man* is the same; but she does not mention what he is by profession or trade. She does not think Lady P. was privy to his scheme on her, but, on being in his power, yielded. Oh, Sir Wm.! Sir Wm.! how I will love you if you will love Miss Sharp!

Mrs. Driver, &c., are off by Collier, but so near being too late that she had not time to call and leave the keys herself. I have them, however. I suppose one is the key of the linen-press, but I do not know what to guess the other.

The coach was stopped at the blacksmith's, and they came running down with Triggs and Browning, and trunks, and birdcages. Quite amusing.

My mother desires her love, and hopes to hear from you.

Yours very affectionately,

J. AUSTEN.

Frank and Mary are to have Mary Goodchild to help as *Under* till they can get a cook. *She* is delighted to go.

Best love at Streatham.

Letter LXXV – 1814

23 Hans Place: Tuesday morning (August).

MY DEAR CASSANDRA,

I had a very good journey, not crowded, two of the three taken up at Bentley being children, the others of a reasonable size; and they were all very quiet and civil. We were late in London, from being a great load, and from changing coaches at Farnham; it was nearly four, I believe, when we reached Sloane Street. Henry himself met me, and as soon as my trunk and basket could be routed out from all the other trunks and baskets in the world, we were on our way to Hans Place in the luxury of a nice, large, cool, dirty hackney coach.

There were four in the kitchen part of Yalden, and I was told fifteen at top, among them Percy Benn. We met in the same room at Egham, but poor Percy was not in his usual spirits. He would be more chatty, I dare say, in his way *from* Woolwich. We took up a young Gibson at Holybourn, and, in short, everybody either *did* come up by Yalden yesterday, or wanted to come up. It put me in mind of my own coach between Edinburgh and Stirling.

Henry is very well, and has given me an account of the Canterbury races, which seem to have been as pleasant as one could wish. Everything went well. Fanny had good partners, Mr. – was her second on Thursday, but he did not dance with her any more.

This will content you for the present. I must just add, however, that there were no Lady Charlottes, they were gone off to Kirby, and that Mary Oxenden, instead of dying, is going to marry Wm. Hammond.

No James and Edward yet. Our evening yesterday was perfectly quiet; we only talked a little to Mr. Tilson across the intermediate gardens; *she* was gone out airing with Miss Burdett. It is a delightful place – more than answers my expectation. Having got rid of my unreasonable ideas, I find more space and comfort in the rooms than I had supposed, and the garden is quite a love. I am in the front attic, which is the bedchamber to be preferred.

Henry wants you to see it all, and asked whether you would return with him from Hampshire; I encouraged him to think you would. He breakfasts here early, and then rides to Henrietta St. If it continues fine John is to drive me there by-and-bye, and we shall take an airing together; and I do not mean to take any other exercise, for I feel a little tired after my long jumble. I live in his room downstairs; it is particularly pleasant from opening upon the garden. I go and refresh myself every now and then, and then come back to solitary coolness. There is *one* maidservant only, a very creditable, clean-looking young woman. Richard remains for the present.

Wednesday morning. – My brother and Edwd. arrived last night. They could not get places the day before. Their business is about teeth and wigs, and they are going to breakfast to Scarman's and Tavistock St., and they are to return to go with me afterwards in the barouche. I hope to do some of my errands to-day.

I got the willow yesterday, as Henry was not quite ready when I reached Hena. St. I saw Mr. Hampson there for a moment. He dines here to-morrow and proposed bringing his son; so I must submit to seeing George Hampson, though I had hoped to go through life without it. It was one of my vanities, like your not reading *"Patronage."*

After leaving H. St. we drove to Mrs. Latouche's; *they* are always at home, and they are to dine here on Friday. We could do no more, as it began to rain.

We dine at half-past four to-day, that our visitors may go to the play, and Henry and I are to spend the evening with the Tilsons, to meet Miss Burdett, who leaves town to-morrow. Mrs. T. called on me yesterday.

Is not this all that can have happened or been arranged? Not quite. Henry wants me to see more of his Hanwell favourite, and has written to invite her to spend a day or two here with me. His scheme is to fetch her on Saturday. I am more and more convinced that he will marry again soon, and like the idea of *her* better than of anybody else at hand.

Now, I have breakfasted and have the room to myself again. It is likely to be a fine day. How do you all do?

Henry talks of being at Chawton *about* the 1st of Sept. He has once mentioned a scheme, which I should rather like – calling on the Birches and the Crutchleys in our way. It may never come to anything, but I must provide for the possibility by troubling you to send up my silk pelisse by Collier on Saturday. I feel it would be necessary on such an occasion; and be so good as to put up a clean dressing-gown which will come from the wash on Friday. You need not direct it to be left anywhere. It may take its chance.

We are to call for Henry between three and four, and I must finish this and carry it with me, as he is not always there in the morning before the parcel is made up. And, before I set off, I must return Mrs. Tilson's visit. I hear nothing of the Hoblyns, and abstain from all inquiry.

I hope Mary Jane and Frank's gardens go on well. Give my love to them all – Nunna Hat's love to George. A great many people wanted to run up in the Poach as well as me. The wheat looked very well all the way, and James says the same of *his* road.

The same good account of Mrs. C.'s health continues, and her circumstances mend. She gets farther and farther from poverty. What a comfort! Good-bye to you.

Yours very truly and affectionately,

JANE.

All well at Steventon. I hear nothing particular of Ben, except that Edward is to get him some pencils.

Letter LXXVI – 1815

Hans Place: Friday (Nov 24).

MY DEAREST CASSANDRA,

I have the pleasure of sending you a much better account of *my affairs,* which I know will be a great delight to you.

I wrote to Mr. Murray yesterday myself, and Henry wrote at the same time to Roworth. Before the notes were out of the house, I received three sheets and an apology from R. We sent the notes, however, and I had a most civil one in reply from Mr. M. He is so very polite, indeed, that it is quite overcoming. The printers have been waiting for paper – the blame is thrown upon the stationer; but he gives his word that I shall have no farther cause for dissatisfaction. He has lent us *Miss Williams* and *Scott,* and says that any book of his will always be at *my* service. In short, I am soothed and complimented into tolerable comfort.

We had a visit yesterday from Edwd. Knight, and Mr. Mascall joined him here; and this morning has brought Mr. Mascall's compliments and two pheasants. We have some hope of Edward's coming to dinner to-day; he will, if he can, I believe. He is looking extremely well.

To-morrow Mr. Haden is to dine with us. There is happiness! We really grow so fond of Mr. Haden that I do not know what to expect. He, and Mr. Tilson, and Mr. Philips made up our circle of wits last night; Fanny played, and he sat and listened and suggested improvements, till Richard came in to tell him that "the doctor was waiting for him at Captn. Blake's"; and then he was off with a speed that you can imagine. He never does appear in the least above his profession, or out of humour with it, or I should think poor Captn. Blake, whoever he is, in a very bad way.

I must have misunderstood Henry when I told you that *you* were to hear from him to-day. He read me what he wrote to Edward: part of it must have amused him, I am sure – one part, alas! cannot be very amusing to anybody. I wonder that with such business to worry him he can be getting better, but he certainly does gain strength, and if you and Edwd. were to see him now I feel sure that you would think him improved since Monday.

He was out yesterday; it was a fine sunshiny day *here* (in the country perhaps you might have clouds and fogs. Dare I say so? I shall not deceive *you,* if I do, as to my estimation of the climate of London), and he ventured first on the balcony and then as far as the greenhouse. He caught no cold, and therefore has done more to-day, with great delight and self-persuasion of improvement.

He has been to see Mrs. Tilson and the Malings. By-the-bye, you may talk to Mr. T. of his wife's being better; I saw her yesterday, and was sensible of her having gained ground in the last two days.

Evening. – We have had no Edward. Our circle is formed – only Mr. Tilson and Mr. Haden. We are not so happy as we were. A message came this afternoon from Mrs. Latouche and Miss East, offering themselves to drink tea with us to-morrow, and, as it was accepted, here is an end of our extreme felicity in our dinner guest. I am heartily sorry they are coming; it will be an evening spoilt to Fanny and me.

Another little disappointment: Mr. H. advises Henry's *not* venturing with us in the carriage to-morrow; if it were spring, he says, it would be a different thing. One would rather this had not been. He seems to think his going out today rather imprudent, though acknowledging at the same time that he is better than he was in the morning.

Fanny has had a letter full of commissions from Goodnestone; we shall be busy about them and her own matters, I dare say, from 12 to 4. Nothing I trust will keep us from Keppel Street.

This day has brought a most friendly letter from Mr. Fowle, with a brace of pheasants. I did not know before that Henry had written to him a few days ago to ask for them. We shall live upon pheasants – no bad life!

I send you five one-pound notes, for fear you should be distressed for little money. Lizzy's work is charmingly done; shall you put it to your chintz? A *sheet* came in this moment; 1st and 3rd vols. are now at 144; 2nd at 48. I am sure you will like particulars. We are not to have the trouble of returning the sheets to Mr. Murray's any longer, the printer's boys bring and carry.

I hope Mary continues to get well fast, and I send my love to little Herbert. You will tell me more of Martha's plans, of course, when you write again. Remember me most kindly to everybody, and Miss Benn besides.

Yours very affectionately,

J. AUSTEN.

Letter LXXVII – 1815

Hans Place: Sunday (Nov. 26).

MY DEAREST,

The parcel arrived safely, and I am much obliged to you for your trouble. It cost 2*s.* 10*d.,* but, as there is a certain saving of 2*s.* 4 1/2*d.* on the other side, I am sure it is well worth doing. I send four pair of silk stockings, but I do not want them washed at present. In the three neck-handkerchiefs I include the one sent down before. These things, perhaps, Edwd. may be able to bring, but even if he is not, I am extremely pleased with his returning to you from Steventon. It is much better; far preferable.

I *did* mention the P. R. in my note to Mr. Murray; it brought me a fine compliment in return. Whether it has done any good I do not know, but Henry thought it worth trying.

The printers continue to supply me very well. I am advanced in Vol. III. to my *arra*-root, upon which peculiar style of spelling there is a modest query in the margin. I will not forget Anna's arrowroot. I hope you have told Martha of my first resolution of letting nobody know that I *might* dedicate, &c., for fear of being obliged to do it, and that she is thoroughly convinced of my being influenced now by nothing but the most mercenary motives. I have paid nine shillings on her account to Miss Palmer; there was no more owing.

Well, we were very busy all yesterday; from half-past 11 till 4 in the streets, working almost entirely for other people, driving from place to place after a parcel for Sandling, which we could never find, and encountering the miseries of Grafton House to get a purple frock for Eleanor Bridges. We got to Keppel St., however, which was all I cared for, and though we could stay only a quarter-of-an-hour, Fanny's calling gave great pleasure, and her sensibility still greater, for she was very much affected at the sight of the children. Poor little F. looked heavy. We saw the whole party.

Aunt Harriet hopes Cassy will not forget to make a pincushion for Mrs. Kelly, as *she* has spoken of its being promised her several times. I hope we shall see Aunt H. and the dear little girls here on Thursday.

So much for the morning. Then came the dinner and Mr. Haden, who brought good manners and clever conversation. From 7 to 8 the harp; at 8 Mrs. L. and Miss E. arrived, and for the rest of the evening the drawing-room was thus arranged: on the sofa side the two ladies, Henry, and myself, making the best of it; on the opposite side Fanny and Mr. Haden, in two chairs (I *believe,* at least, they had *two* chairs), talking together uninterruptedly. Fancy the scene! And what is to be fancied next? Why, that Mr. H. dines here again to-morrow. Today we are to have Mr. Barlow. Mr. H. is reading *"Mansfield Park"* for the first time, and prefers it to *P. and P.*

A hare and four rabbits from Gm. yesterday, so that we are stocked for nearly a week. Poor Farmer Andrews! I am very sorry for him, and sincerely wish his recovery.

A better account of the sugar than I could have expected. I should like to help you break some more. I am glad you cannot wake early; I am sure you must have been under great arrears of rest.

Fanny and I have been to B. Chapel, and walked back with Maria Cuthbert. We have been very little plagued with visitors this last week. I remember only Miss Herries, the aunt, but I am in terror for to-day, a fine bright Sunday; plenty of mortar, and nothing to do.

Henry gets out in his garden every day, but at present his inclination for doing more seems over, nor has he now any plan for leaving London before Dec. 18, when he thinks of going to Oxford for a few days; to-day, indeed, his feelings are for continuing where he is through the next two months.

456

One knows the uncertainty of all this, but, should it be so, we must think the best, and hope the best, and do the best; and my idea in that case is, that when *he* goes to Oxford *I* should go home, and have nearly a week of *you* before you take my place. This is only a silent project, you know, to be gladly given up if better things occur. Henry calls himself stronger every day, and Mr. H. keeps on approving his pulse, which seems generally better than ever, but still they will not let him be well. Perhaps when Fanny is gone he will be allowed to recover faster.

I am not disappointed: I never thought the little girl at Wyards very pretty, but she will have a fine complexion and curly hair, and pass for a beauty. We are glad the mamma's cold has not been worse, and send her our love and good wishes by every convenient opportunity. Sweet, amiable Frank! why does he have a cold too? Like Captain Mirvan to Mr. Duval,[32] "I wish it well over with him."

Fanny has heard all that I have said to you about herself and Mr. H. Thank you very much for the sight of dearest Charles's letter to yourself. How pleasantly and how naturally he writes! and how perfect a picture of his disposition and feelings his style conveys! Poor dear fellow! Not a present! I have a great mind to send him all the twelve copies which were to have

---

32 Characters in Miss Burney's "Evelina."

been dispersed among my near connections, beginning with the P. R. and ending with Countess Morley. Adieu.

Yours affectionately,

J. AUSTEN.

Give my love to Cassy and Mary Jane. Caroline will be gone when this reaches you.

Letter LXXVIIII – 1815

Hans Place: Saturday (Dec. 2).

MY DEAR CASSANDRA,

Henry came back yesterday, and might have returned the day before if he had known as much in time. I had the pleasure of hearing from Mr. T. on Wednesday night that Mr. Seymour thought there was not the least occasion for his absenting himself any longer.

I had also the comfort of a few lines on Wednesday morning from Henry himself, just after your letter was gone, giving so good an account of his feelings as made me perfectly easy. He met with the utmost care and attention at Hanwell, spent his two days there very quietly and pleasantly, and, being certainly in no respect the worse for going, we may believe that he must be better, as he is quite sure of being himself. To make his return a complete gala Mr. Haden was secured for dinner. I need not say that our evening was agreeable.

But you seem to be under a mistake as to Mr. H. You call him an apothecary. He is no apothecary; he has never been an apothecary; there is not an apothecary in this neighbourhood – the only inconvenience of the situation perhaps – but so it is; we have not a medical man within reach. He is a Haden, nothing but a Haden, a sort of wonderful nondescript creature on two legs, something between a man and an angel, but without the least spice of an apothecary. He is, perhaps, the only person *not* an apothecary here-abouts. He has never sung to us. He will not sing without a pianoforte accompaniment.

Mr. Meyers gives his three lessons a week, altering his days and his hours, however, just as he chooses, never very punctual, and never giving good measure. I have not Fanny's fondness for masters, and Mr. Meyers does not give me any longing after them. The truth is, I think, that they are all, at least music-masters, made of too much consequence and allowed to take too many liberties with their scholars' time.

We shall be delighted to see Edward on Monday, only sorry that you must be losing him. A turkey will be equally welcome with himself. He must prepare for his own proper bedchamber here, as Henry moved down to the one below last week; he found the other cold.

I am sorry my mother has been suffering, and am afraid this exquisite weather is too good to agree with her. *I* enjoy it all over me, from top to toe, from right to left, longitudinally, perpendicularly, diagonally; and I cannot but selfishly hope we are to have it last till

Christmas – nice, unwholesome, unseasonable, relaxing, close, muggy weather.

Oh, thank you very much for your long letter; it did me a great deal of good. Henry accepts your offer of making his nine gallon of mead thankfully. The mistake of the dogs rather vexed him for a moment, but he has not thought of it since. To-day he makes a third attempt at his strengthening plaister, and, as I am sure he will now be getting out a great deal, it is to be wished that he may be able to keep it on. He sets off this morning by the Chelsea coach to sign bonds and visit Henrietta St., and I have no doubt will be going every day to Henrietta St.

Fanny and I were very snug by ourselves as soon as we were satisfied about our invalid's being safe at Hanwell. By manoeuvring and good luck we foiled all the Malings' attempts upon us. Happily I caught a little cold on Wednesday, the morning we were in town, which we made very useful, and we saw nobody but our precious[33] and Mr. Tilson.

This evening the Malings are allowed to drink tea with us. We are in hopes – that is, we *wish* – Miss Palmer and the little girls may come this morning. You know, of course, that she could *not* come on Thursday, and she will not attempt to *name* any other day.

---

33 Probably a playful allusion to Mr. Haden.

God bless you. Excuse the shortness of this, but I must finish it now that I may save you *2d.* Best love.

Yours affectionately,

J. A.

It strikes me that I have no business to give the P. R. a binding, but we will take counsel upon the question.

I am glad you have put the flounce on your chintz; I am sure it must look particularly well, and it is what I had thought of.

Letter LXXIX – 1816

Chawton: Sunday (Sept 8).

MY DEAREST CASSANDRA,

I have borne the arrival of your letter to-day extremely well; anybody might have thought it was giving me pleasure. I am very glad you find so much to be satisfied with at Cheltenham. While the waters agree, everything else is trifling.

A letter arrived for you from Charles last Thursday. They are all safe and pretty well in Keppel St., the children decidedly better for Broadstairs; and he writes principally to ask when it will be convenient to us to receive Miss P., the little girls, and himself. They would be ready to set off in ten days from the time of his writing, to pay their visits in Hampshire and Berkshire, and he would prefer coming to Chawton *first.*

I have answered him, and said that we hoped it might suit them to wait till the last week in *Septr.,* as we could not ask them sooner, either on your account or the want of room. I mentioned the 23rd as the probable day of your return. When you have once left Cheltenham I shall grudge every half-day wasted on the road. If there were but a coach from Hungerford to Chawton! I have desired him to let me hear again soon.

He does not include a maid in the list to be accommodated, but if they bring one, as I suppose they will, we shall have no bed in the house even then for Charles himself – let alone Henry. But what can we do?

We shall have the Gt. House quite at our command; it is to be cleared of the Papillons' servants in a day or two. They themselves have been hurried off into Essex to take possession – not of a large estate left them by an uncle – but to scrape together all they can, I suppose, of the effects of a Mrs. Rawstorn, a rich old friend and cousin, suddenly deceased, to whom they are joint executors. So there is a happy end of the Kentish Papillons coming here.

No morning service to-day, wherefore I am writing between twelve and one o'clock. Mr. Benn in the afternoon, and likewise more rain again, by the look and the sound of things. You left us in doubt of Mrs. Benn's situation, but she has bespoke her nurse. Mrs. F. A. seldom either looks or appears quite well. Little Embryo is troublesome, I suppose. They dined with us yesterday, and had fine weather both for coming and going home, which has hardly ever happened to them before. She is still unprovided with a housemaid.

Our day at Alton was very pleasant, venison quite right, children well-behaved, and Mr. and Mrs. Digweed taking kindly to our charades and other games. I must also observe, for his mother's satisfaction, that Edward at my suggestion devoted himself very properly to the entertainment of Miss S. Gibson. Nothing was wanting except Mr. Sweeney, but he, alas! had been ordered away to London the day before. We had a beautiful walk home by moonlight.

Thank you, my back has given me scarcely any pain for many days. I have an idea that agitation does it as much harm as fatigue, and that I was ill at the time of your going from the very circumstance of your going. I am nursing myself up now into as beautiful a state as I can, because I hear that Dr. White means to call on me before he leaves the country.

Evening. – Frank and Mary and the children visited us this morning. Mr. and Mrs. Gibson are to come on the 23rd, and there is too much reason to fear they will stay above a week. Little George could tell me where you were gone to, as well as what you were to bring him, when I asked him the other day.

Sir Tho. Miller is dead. I treat you with a dead baronet in almost every letter.

So you have C. Craven among you, as well as the Duke of Orleans and Mr. Pocock. But it mortifies me that *you* have not added one to the stock of common acquaintance. Do pray meet with somebody belonging to yourself. I am quite weary of your knowing nobody.

Mrs. Digweed parts with both Hannah and old cook; the former will not give up her lover, who is a man of bad character; the latter is guilty only of being unequal to anything.

Miss Terry was to have spent this week with her sister, but as usual it is put off. My amiable friend knows the value of her company. I have not seen Anna since the day you left us; her father and brother visited her most days. Edward and Ben called here on Thursday. Edward was in his way to Selborne. We found him very agreeable. He is come back from France, thinking of the French as one could wish – disappointed in everything. He did not go beyond Paris.

I have a letter from Mrs. Perigord; she and her mother are in London again. She speaks of France as a scene of general poverty and misery: no money, no trade, nothing to be got but by the innkeepers, and as to her own present prospects she is not much less melancholy than before.

I have also a letter from Miss Sharp, quite one of her letters; she has been again obliged to exert herself more than ever, in a more distressing, more harassed state, and has met with another excellent old physician and his wife, with every virtue under heaven, who takes to her and cures her from pure love and benevolence. Dr. and Mrs. Storer are *their* Mrs. and Miss Palmer – for they are at Bridlington. I am happy to say, however, that the sum of the account is better than usual. Sir William is returned; from Bridlington they go to Chevet, and she *is* to have a young governess under her.

I enjoyed Edward's company very much, as I said before, and yet I was not sorry when Friday came. It had been a busy week, and I wanted a few days quiet and exemption from the thought and contrivancy which any sort of company gives. I often wonder how *you* can find time for what you do, in addition to the care of the house; and how good Mrs. West could have written such books and collected so many hard works, with all her family cares, is still more a matter of astonishment. Composition seems to me impossible with a head full of joints of mutton and doses of rhubarb.

Monday. – Here is a sad morning. I fear you may not have been able to get to the Pump. The two last days were very pleasant. I enjoyed them the more for your sake. But to-day it is really bad enough to make you all cross. I hope Mary will change her lodgings at the fortnight's end; I am sure, if you looked about well, you would find others in some odd corner to suit you better. Mrs. Potter charges for the *name* of the High St.

Success to the pianoforte! I trust it will drive you away. We hear now that there is to be *no honey* this year. Bad news for us. We must husband our present stock of mead, and I am sorry to perceive that our twenty gallons is very nearly out. I cannot comprehend how the fourteen gallons could last so long.

We do not much like Mr. Cooper's new sermons. They are fuller of regeneration and conversion than ever, with the addition of his zeal in the cause of the Bible Society.

Martha's love to Mary and Caroline, and she is extremely glad to find they like the pelisse. The Debarys are indeed odious! We are to see my brother to-morrow, but for only one night. I had no idea that he would care for the races *without* Edward. Remember me to all.

Yours very affectionately,

J. AUSTEN.

Letters to Her Niece Fanny Knight, 1814–1816.

Letter LXXX – 1814

Chawton: Friday (Nov. 18).

I feel quite as doubtful as you could be, my dearest Fanny, as to *when* my letter may be finished, for I can command very little quiet time at present; but yet I must begin, for I know you will be glad to hear as soon as possible, and I really am impatient myself to be writing something on so very interesting a subject, though I have no hope of writing anything to the purpose. I shall do very little more, I dare say, than say over again what you have said before.

was certainly a good deal surprised *at first,* as I had no suspicion of any change in your feelings, and I have no scruple in saying that you cannot be in love. My dear Fanny, I am ready to laugh at the idea, and yet it is no laughing matter to have had you so mistaken as to your own feelings. And with all my heart I wish I had cautioned you on that point when first you spoke to me; but, though I did not think you then so *much* in love, I did consider you as being attached in a degree quite sufficiently for happiness, as I had no doubt it would increase with opportunity, and from the time of our being in London together I thought you really very much in love. But you certainly are not at all – there is no concealing it.

What strange creatures we are! It seems as if your being secure of him had made you indifferent. There was a little disgust, I suspect, at the races, and I do not wonder at it. His expressions then would not do for one who had rather more acuteness, penetration, and taste, than love, which was your case. And yet, after all, I *am* surprised that the change in your feelings should be so great. He is just what he ever was, only more evidently and uniformly devoted to *you.* This is all the difference. How shall we account for it?

My dearest Fanny, I am writing what will not be of the smallest use to you. I am feeling differently every moment, and shall not be able to suggest a single thing that can assist your mind. I could lament in one sentence and laugh in the next, but as to opinion or counsel I am sure that none will be extracted worth having from this letter.

I read yours through the very evening I received it, getting away by myself. I could not bear to leave off when I had once begun. I was full of curiosity and concern. Luckily your At. C. dined at the other house; therefore I had not to manoeuvre away from *her,* and as to anybody else, I do not care.

Poor dear Mr. A.! Oh, dear Fanny! your mistake has been one that thousands of women fall into. He was the *first* young man who attached himself to you. That was the charm, and most powerful it is. Among the multitudes, however, that make the same mistake with yourself, there can be few indeed who have so little reason to regret it; *his* character and *his* attachment leave you nothing to be ashamed of.

Upon the whole, what is to be done? You have no inclination for any other person. His situation in life, family, friends, and, above all, his character, his uncommonly amiable mind, strict principles, just notions, good habits, *all* that *you* know so well how to value, *all* that is really of the first importance, everything of this nature pleads his cause most strongly. You have no doubt of his having superior abilities, he has proved it at the University; he is, I dare say, such a scholar as your agreeable, idle brothers would ill bear a comparison with.

Oh, my dear Fanny! the more I write about him, the warmer my feelings become – the more strongly I feel the sterling worth of such a young man and the desirableness of your growing in love with him again. I recommend this most thoroughly.

There *are* such beings in the world, perhaps one in a thousand, as the creature you and I should think perfection, where grace and spirit are united to worth, where the manners are equal to the heart and understanding, but such a person may not come in your way, or, if he does, he may not be the eldest son of a man of fortune, the near relation of your particular friend and belonging to your own county.

Think of all this, Fanny. Mr. A. has advantages which do not often meet in one person. His only fault, indeed, seems modesty. If he were less modest he would be more agreeable, speak louder, and look impudenter; and is not it a fine character of which modesty is the only defect? I have no doubt he will get more lively and more like yourselves as he is more with you; he will catch your ways if he belongs to you. And, as to there being any objection from his *goodness,* from the danger of his becoming even evangelical, I cannot admit *that.* I am by no means convinced that we ought not all to be evangelicals, and am at least persuaded that they who are so from reason and feeling must be happiest and safest. Do not be frightened from the connection by your brothers having most wit – wisdom is better than wit, and in the long run will certainly have the laugh on her side; and don't be frightened by the idea of his acting more strictly up to the precepts of the New Testament than others.

And now, my dear Fanny, having written so much on one side of the question, I shall turn round and entreat you not to commit yourself farther, and not to think of accepting him unless you really do like him. Anything is to be preferred or endured rather than marrying without affection; and if his deficiencies of manner, &c. &c., strike you more than all his good qualities, if you continue to think strongly of them, give him up at once. Things are now in such a state that you must resolve upon one or the other – either to allow him to go on as he has done, or whenever you are together behave with a coldness which may convince him that he has been deceiving himself. I have no doubt of his suffering a good deal for a time – a great deal when he feels that he must give you up; but it is no creed of mine, as you must be well aware, that such sort of disappointments kill anybody.

Your sending the music was an admirable device, it made everything easy, and I do not know how I could have accounted for the parcel otherwise; for though your dear papa most conscientiously hunted about till he found me alone in the dining-parlour, your Aunt C. had seen that he *had* a parcel to deliver. As it was, however, I do not think anything was suspected.

We have heard nothing fresh from Anna. I trust she is very comfortable in her new home. Her letters have been very sensible and satisfactory, with no *parade* of happiness, which I liked them the better for. I have often known young married women write in a way I did not like in that respect.

You will be glad to hear that the first edition of *M. P.*[34] is all sold. Your uncle Henry is rather wanting me to come to town to settle about a second edition, but as I could not very conveniently leave home now, I have written him my will and pleasure, and, unless he still urges it, shall not go. I am very greedy and want to make the most of it, but as you are much above caring about money I shall not plague you with any particulars. The pleasures of vanity are more within your comprehension, and you will enter into mine at receiving the *praise* which every now and then comes to me through some channel or other.

Saturday. – Mr. Palmer spent yesterday with us, and is gone off with Cassy this morning. We have been expecting Miss Lloyd the last two days, and feel sure of her to-day. Mr. Knight and Mr. Edwd. Knight are to dine with us, and on Monday they are to dine with us again, accompanied by their respectable host and hostess.

Sunday. – Your papa had given me messages to you, but they are unnecessary, as he writes by this post to Aunt Louisa. We had a pleasant party yesterday, at least we found it so. It is delightful to see him so

---

34 Mansfield Park.

cheerful and confident. Aunt Cass. and I dine at the Great House today. We shall be a snug half-dozen. Miss Lloyd came, as we expected, yesterday, and desires her love. She is very happy to hear of your learning the harp. I do not mean to send you what I owe Miss Hare, because I think you would rather not be paid beforehand.

Yours very affectionately,

JANE AUSTEN.

Letter LXXXI – 1814

23 Hans Place: Wednesday (Nov. 30).

I am very much obliged to you, my dear Fanny, for your letter, and I hope you will write again soon, that I may know you to be all safe and happy at home.

Our visit to Hendon will interest you, I am sure, but I need not enter into the particulars of it, as your papa will be able to answer *almost* every question. I certainly *could* describe her bedroom, and her drawers, and her closet, better than he can, but I do not feel that I can stop to do it. I was rather sorry to hear that she *is* to have an instrument; it seems throwing money away. They will wish the twenty-four guineas in the shape of sheets and towels six months hence; and as to her playing, it never can be anything.

Her purple pelisse rather surprised me. I thought we had known all paraphernalia of that sort. I do not mean to blame her; it looked very well, and I dare say she wanted it. I suspect nothing worse than its being got in secret, and not owned to anybody. I received a very kind note from her yesterday, to ask me to come again and stay a night with them. I cannot do it, but I was pleased to find that she had the *power* of doing so right a thing. My going was to give them *both* pleasure very properly.

I just saw Mr. Hayter at the play, and think his face would please me on acquaintance. I was sorry he did not dine here. It seemed rather odd to me to be in the theatre with nobody to *watch* for. I was quite composed myself, at leisure for all the agitation Isabella could raise.

Now, my dearest Fanny, I will begin a subject which comes in very naturally. You frighten me out of my wits by your reference. Your affection gives me the highest pleasure, but indeed you must not let anything depend on my opinion; your own feelings, and none but your own, should determine such an important point. So far, however, as answering your question, I have no scruple. I am perfectly convinced that your present feelings, supposing you were to marry *now,* would be sufficient for his happiness; but when I think how very, very far it is from a *"now,"* and take everything that *may be* into consideration, I dare not say, "Determine to accept him;" the risk is too great for *you,* unless your own sentiments prompt it.

You will think me perverse perhaps; in my last letter I was urging everything in his favour, and now I am inclining the other way, but I cannot help it; I am at present more impressed with the possible evil that may arise to *you* from engaging yourself to him – in word or mind – than with anything else. When I consider how few young men you have yet seen much of; how capable you are (yes, I do still think you *very* capable) of being really in love; and how full of temptation the next six or seven years of your life will probably be (it is the very period of life for the *strongest* attachments to be formed), – I cannot wish you, with your present very cool feelings, to devote yourself in honour to him. It is very true that you never may attach another man his equal altogether; but if that other man has the power of attaching you *more,* he will be in your eyes the most perfect.

I shall be glad if you *can* revive past feelings, and from your unbiassed self resolve to go on as you have done, but this I do not expect; and without it I cannot wish you to be fettered. I should not be afraid of your *marrying* him; with all his worth you would soon love him enough for the happiness of both; but I should dread the continuance of this sort of tacit engagement, with such an uncertainty as there is of *when* it may be completed. Years may pass before he is independent; you like him well enough to marry, but not well enough to wait; the unpleasantness of appearing fickle is certainly great; but if you think you want punishment for past illusions, there it is, and nothing can be compared to the misery of being bound *without* love – bound to one, and preferring another; *that* is a punishment which you do *not* deserve.

I know you did not meet, or rather will not meet, to-day, as he called here yesterday; and I am glad of it. It does not seem very likely, at least, that he should be in time for a dinner visit sixty miles off. We did not see him, only found his card when we came home at four. Your Uncle H. merely observed that he was a day *after "the fair."* He asked your brother on Monday (when Mr. Hayter was talked of) why he did not invite *him* too; saying, "I know he is in town, for I met him the other day in Bond St." Edward answered that he did not know where he was to be found. "Don't you know his chambers?" "No."

I shall be most glad to hear from you again, my dearest Fanny, but it must not be later than Saturday, as we shall be off Monday long before the letters are delivered; and write *something* that may do to be read or told. I am to take the Miss Moores back on Saturday, and when I return I shall hope to find your pleasant little flowing scrawl on the table. It will be a relief to me after playing at ma'ams, for though I like Miss H. M. as much as one can at my time of life after a day's acquaintance, it is uphill work to be talking to those whom one knows so little.

Only *one* comes back with me to-morrow, probably Miss Eliza, and I rather dread it. We shall not have two ideas in common. She is young, pretty, chattering, and thinking chiefly, I presume, of dress, company, and admiration. Mr. Sanford is to join us at dinner, which will be a comfort, and in the evening, while your uncle and Miss Eliza play chess, he shall tell me comical things and I will laugh at them, which will be a pleasure to both.

I called in Keppel Street and saw them all, including dear Uncle Charles, who is to come and dine with us quietly to-day. Little Harriot sat in my lap, and seemed as gentle and affectionate as ever, and as pretty, except not being quite well. Fanny is a fine stout girl, talking incessantly, with an interesting degree of lisp and indistinctness, and very likely may be the handsomest in time. That puss Cassy did not show more pleasure in seeing me than her sisters, but I expected no better. She does not shine in the tender feelings. She will never be a Miss O'Neil, more in the Mrs. Siddons line.

Thank you, but it is not settled yet whether I *do* hazard a second edition. We are to see Egerton to-day, when it will probably be determined. People are more ready to borrow and praise than to buy, which I cannot wonder at; but though I like praise as well as anybody, I like what Edward calls *"Pewter,"* too. I hope he continues careful of his eyes and finds the good effect of it. I cannot suppose we differ in our ideas of the Christian religion. You have given an excellent description of it. We only affix a different meaning to the word *evangelical.*

Yours most affectionately,

J. AUSTEN.

Letter LXXXII – 1816*

[* This letter and the two following are actually from 1817.]

Chawton: (Feb. 20).

MY DEAREST FANNY,

You are inimitable, irresistible. You are the delight of my life. Such letters, such entertaining letters, as you have lately sent! such a description of your queer little heart! such a lovely display of what imagination does. You are worth your weight in gold, or even in the new silver coinage. I cannot express to you what I have felt in reading your history of yourself – how full of pity and concern, and admiration and amusement, I have been! You are the paragon of all that is silly and sensible, commonplace and eccentric, sad and lively, provoking and interesting. Who can keep pace with the fluctuations of your fancy, the capprizios of your taste, the contradictions of your feelings? You are so odd, and all the time so perfectly natural! – so peculiar in yourself, and yet so like everybody else!

It is very, very gratifying to me to know you so intimately. You can hardly think what a pleasure it is to me to have such thorough pictures of your heart. Oh, what a loss it will be when you are married! You are too agreeable in your single state – too agreeable as a niece. I shall hate you when your delicious play of mind is all settled down in conjugal and maternal affections.

Mr. B– frightens me. He will have you. I see you at the altar. I have *some* faith in Mrs. C. Cage's observation, and still more in Lizzy's; and, besides, I know it *must* be so. He must be wishing to attach you. It would be too stupid and too shameful in him to be otherwise; and all the family are seeking your acquaintance.

Do not imagine that I have any real objection; I have rather taken a fancy to him than not, and I like the house for you. I only do not like you should marry anybody. And yet I do wish you to marry very much, because I know you will never be happy till you are; but the loss of a Fanny Knight will be never made up to me. My "affec. niece F. C. B–" will be but a poor substitute. I do not like your being nervous, and so apt to cry – it is a sign you are not quite well; but I hope Mr. Scud – as you always write his name (your Mr. Scuds amuse me very much) – will do you good.

What a comfort that Cassandra should be so recovered! It was more than we had expected. I can easily believe she was very patient and very good. I always loved Cassandra, for her fine dark eyes and sweet temper. I am almost entirely cured of my rheumatism

– just a little pain in my knee now and then, to make me remember what it was, and keep on flannel. Aunt Cassandra nursed me so beautifully.

I enjoy your visit to Goodnestone, it must be a great pleasure to you; you have not seen Fanny Cage in comfort so long. I hope she represents and remonstrates and reasons with you properly. Why should you be living in dread of his marrying somebody else? (Yet, how natural!) You did not choose to have him yourself, why not allow him to take comfort where he can? In your conscience you *know* that he could not bear a comparison with a more animated character. You cannot forget how you felt under the idea of its having been possible that he might have dined in Hans Place.

My dearest Fanny, I cannot bear you should be unhappy about him. Think of his principles; think of his father's objection, of want of money, &c. But I am doing no good; no, all that I urge against him will rather make you take his part more, sweet, perverse Fanny.

And now I will tell you that we like your Henry to the utmost, to the very top of the glass, quite brimful. He is a very pleasing young man. I do not see how he could be mended. He does really bid fair to be everything his father and sister could wish; and William I love very much indeed, and so we do all;

484

he is quite our own William. In short, we are very comfortable together; that is, we can answer for *ourselves.*

Mrs. Deedes is as welcome as May to all our benevolence to her son; we only lamented that we could not do more, and that the 50*l.* note we slipped into his hand at parting was necessarily the limit of our offering. Good Mrs. Deedes! Scandal and gossip; yes, I dare say you are well stocked, but I am very fond of Mrs. – for reasons good. Thank you for mentioning her praise of *"Emma,"* &c.

I have contributed the marking to Uncle H.'s shirts, and now they are a complete memorial of the tender regard of many.

Friday. – I had no idea when I began this yesterday of sending it before your brother went back, but I have written away my foolish thoughts at such a rate that I will not keep them many hours longer to stare me in the face.

Much obliged for the quadrilles, which I am grown to think pretty enough, though of course they are very inferior to the cotillions of my own day.

Ben and Anna walked here last Sunday to hear Uncle Henry, and she looked so pretty, it was quite a pleasure to see her, so young and so blooming, and so innocent, as if she had never had a wicked thought in her life, which yet one has some reason to suppose she must have had, if we believe the doctrine of original sin . I hope Lizzy will have her play very kindly arranged for her. Henry is generally thought very good-looking, but not so handsome as Edward. I think *I* prefer his face. Wm. is in excellent looks, has a fine appetite, and seems perfectly well. You will have a great break up at Godmersham in the spring. You *must* feel their all going. It is very right, however! Poor Miss C.! I shall pity her when she begins to understand herself.

Your objection to the quadrilles delighted me exceedingly. Pretty well, for a lady irrecoverably attached to *one* person! Sweet Fanny, believe no such thing of yourself, spread no such malicious slander upon your understanding, within the precincts of your imagination. Do not speak ill of your sense merely for the gratification of your fancy; yours is sense which deserves more honourable treatment. You are *not* in love with him; you never *have* been really in love with him.

Yours very affectionately,

J. AUSTEN.

Letter LXXXIII – 1816

Chawton: Thursday (March 13).

AS to making any adequate return for such a letter as yours, my dearest Fanny, it is absolutely impossible. If I were to labour at it all the rest of my life, and live to the age of Methuselah, I could never accomplish anything so long and so perfect; but I cannot let William go without a few lines of acknowledgment and reply.

I have pretty well done with Mr. –. By your description, he *cannot* be in love with you, however he may try at it; and I could not wish the match unless there were a great deal of love on his side. I do not know what to do about Jemima Branfill. What does her dancing away with so much spirit mean? That she does not care for *him,* or only wishes to *appear* not to care for him? Who can understand a young lady?

Poor Mrs. C. Milles, that she should die on the wrong day at last, after being about it so long! It was unlucky that the Goodnestone party could not meet you, and I hope her friendly, obliging, social spirit, which delighted in drawing people together, was not conscious of the division and disappointment she was occasioning. I am sorry and surprised that you speak of her as having little to leave, and must feel for Miss

Milles, though she is Molly, if a material loss of income is to attend her other loss. Single women have a dreadful propensity for being poor, which is one very strong argument in favour of matrimony, but I need not dwell on such arguments with *you,* pretty dear

To you I shall say, as I have often said before, Do not be in a hurry, the right man will come at last; you will in the course of the next two or three years meet with somebody more generally unexceptionable than anyone you have yet known, who will love you as warmly as possible, and who will so completely attach you that you will feel you never really loved before.

Do none of the A.'s ever come to balls now? You have never mentioned them as being at any. And what do you hear of the Gipps, or of Fanny and her husband?

Aunt Cassandra walked to Wyards yesterday with Mrs. Digweed. Anna has had a bad cold, and looks pale. She has just weaned Julia.

I have also heard lately from your Aunt Harriot, and cannot understand their plans in parting with Miss S., whom she seems very much to value now that Harriot and Eleanor are both of an age for a governess to be so useful to, especially as, when Caroline was sent to school some years, Miss *Bell* was still retained, though the others even then were nursery children. They have some good reason, I dare say, though I cannot penetrate it, and till I know what it is I shall invent a bad one, and amuse myself with accounting for the difference of measures by supposing Miss S. to be a superior sort of woman, who has never stooped to recommend herself to the master of the family by flattery, as Miss Bell did.

I *will* answer your kind questions more than you expect. "Miss Catherine" is put upon the shelf for the present, and I do not know that she will ever come out; but I have a something ready for publication, which may, perhaps, appear about a twelvemonth hence. It is short – about the length of "Catherine." This is for yourself alone. Neither Mr. Salusbury nor Mr. Wildman is to know of it.

I am got tolerably well again, quite equal to walking about and enjoying the air, and by sitting down and resting a good while between my walks, I get exercise enough. I have a scheme, however, for accomplishing more, as the weather grows spring-like. I mean to take to riding the donkey; it will be more independent and less troublesome than the use of the carriage, and I shall be able to go about with Aunt Cassandra in her walks to Alton and Wyards.

I hope you will think Wm. looking well; he was bilious the other day, and At. Cass. supplied him with a dose at his own request. I am sure *you* would have approved it. Wm. and I are the best of friends. I love him very much. Everything is so *natural* about him – his affections, his manners, and his drollery. He entertains and interests us extremely.

Mat. Hammond and A. M. Shaw are people whom I cannot care for, in themselves, but I enter into their situation, and am glad they are so happy. If I were the Duchess of Richmond, I should be very miserable about my son's choice.

Our fears increase for poor little Harriot; the latest account is that Sir Ev. Home is confirmed in his opinion of there being water on the brain. I hope Heaven, in its mercy, will take her soon. Her poor father will be quite worn out by his feelings for her; he cannot spare Cassy at present, she is an occupation and a comfort to him.

Letter LXXXIV – 1816

Chawton: Sunday (March 23).

I am very much obliged to you, my dearest Fanny, for sending me Mr. W.'s conversation; I had great amusement in reading it, and I *hope* I am not affronted, and do not think the worse of him for having a brain so very different from mine; but my strongest sensation of all is *astonishment* at your being able to press him on the subject so perseveringly; and I agree with your papa, that it was not fair. When he knows the truth he will be uncomfortable.

You are the oddest creature! Nervous enough in some respects, but in others perfectly without nerves! Quite unrepulsable, hardened, and impudent. Do not oblige him to read any more. Have mercy on him, tell him the truth, and make him an apology. He and I should not in the least agree, of course, in our ideas of novels and heroines. Pictures of perfection, as you know, make me sick and wicked; but there is some very good sense in what he says, and I particularly respect him for wishing to think well of all young ladies; it shows an amiable and a delicate mind. And he deserves better treatment than to be obliged to read any more of my works.

Do not be surprised at finding Uncle Henry acquainted with my having another ready for publication. I could not say No when he asked me, but he knows nothing more of it. You will not like it, so you need not be impatient. You may *perhaps* like the heroine, as she is almost too good for me.

Many thanks for your kind care for my health; I certainly have not been well for many weeks, and about a week ago I was very poorly. I have had a good deal of fever at times, and indifferent nights; but I am considerably better now and am recovering my looks a little, which have been bad enough – black and white, and every wrong colour. I must not depend upon being ever very blooming again. Sickness is a dangerous indulgence at my time of life. Thank you for everything you tell me. I do not feel worthy of it by anything that I can say in return, but I assure you my pleasure in your letters is quite as great as ever, and I am interested and amused just as you could wish me. If there is a *Miss* Marsden, I perceive whom she will marry.

Evening. – I was languid and dull and very bad company when I wrote the above; I am better now, to my own feelings at least, and wish I may be more agreeable. We are going to have rain, and after that very pleasant genial weather, which will exactly do for me, as my saddle will then be completed, and air and exercise is what I want. Indeed, I shall be very glad when the event at Scarlets is over, the expectation of it keeps us in a worry, your grandmamma especially; she sits brooding over evils which cannot be remedied, and conduct impossible to be understood.

Now the reports from Keppel St. are rather better; little Harriot's headaches are abated, and Sir Evd. is satisfied with the effect of the mercury, and does not despair of a cure. The complaint I find is not considered incurable nowadays, provided the patient be young enough not to have the head hardened. The water in that case may be drawn off by mercury. But though this is a new idea to us, perhaps it may have been long familiar to you through your friend Mr. Scud. I hope his high renown is sustained by driving away William's cough.

Tell Wm. that Triggs is as beautiful and condescending as ever, and was so good as to dine with us to-day and tell him that I often play at *nines* and think of him.

The Papillons came back on Friday night, but I have not seen them yet, as I do not venture to church. I cannot hear, however, but that they are the same Mr. P. and his sister they used to be. She has engaged a new maidservant in Mrs. Calker's room, whom she means to make also housekeeper under herself.

Old Philmore was buried yesterday, and I, by way of saying something to Triggs, observed that it had been a very handsome funeral; but his manner of reply made me suppose that it was not generally esteemed so. I can only be sure of *one* part being very handsome – Triggs himself, walking behind in his green coat. Mrs. Philmore attended as chief mourner, in bombazine, made very short, and flounced with crape.

Tuesday. – I have had various plans as to this letter, but at last I have determined that Uncle Henry shall forward it from London. I want to see how Canterbury looks in the direction. When once Uncle H. has left *us* I shall wish him with *you.* London has become a hateful place to him, and he is always depressed by the idea of it. I hope he will be in time for your sick. I am sure he must do that part of his duty as excellently as all the rest. He returned yesterday from Steventon, and was with us by breakfast, bringing Edward with him, only that Edwd. stayed to breakfast at Wyards. We had a pleasant family day, for the Altons dined with us, the last visit of the kind probably which *she* will be able to pay us for many a month.

I hope your own Henry is in France, and that you have heard from him; the passage once over, he will feel all happiness. I took my first ride yesterday, and liked it very much. I went up Mounter's Lane and round by where the new cottages are to be, and found the exercise and everything very pleasant; and I had the advantage of agreeable companions, as At. Cass. and Edward walked by my side. At. Cass. is such an excellent nurse, so assiduous and unwearied! But you know all that already.

Very affectionately yours,

J. AUSTEN.

Letters to Her Niece Anna Austen Lefroy, 1814–1816.

Letter LXXXV – 1814

MY DEAR ANNA,

I am very much obliged to you for sending your MS. It has entertained me extremely; all of us indeed. I read it aloud to your Grandmama and Aunt Cass., and we were all very much pleased. The spirit does not droop at all. Sir Thos., Lady Helen and St. Julian are very well done, and Cecilia continues to be interesting in spite of her being so amiable. It was very fit you should advance her age. I like the beginning of Devereux Forester very much, a great deal better than if he had been very good or very bad. A few verbal corrections are all that I felt tempted to make; the principal of them is a speech of St. Julian to Lady Helen, which you see I have presumed to alter. As Lady H. is Cecilia's superior, it would not be correct to talk of *her* being introduced. It is Cecilia who must be introduced. And I do not like a lover speaking in the 3rd person; it is too much like the formal part of Lord Orville, and I think it not natural. If *you* think differently, however, you need not mind me. I am impatient for more, and only wait for a safe conveyance to return this book.

Yours affectionately,

J. A.

Letter LXXXVI – 1814

August 10.

MY DEAR ANNA,

I am quite ashamed to find that I have never answered some question of yours in a former note. I kept it on purpose to refer to it at a proper time and then forgot it. I like the name "Which is the Heroine" very well, and I daresay shall grow to like it very much in time; but "Enthusiasm" was something so very superior that my common title must appear to disadvantage. I am not sensible of any blunders about Dawlish; the library was pitiful and wretched twelve years ago and not likely to have anybody's publications. There is no such title as Desborough either among dukes, marquises, earls, viscounts, or barons. These were your inquiries. I will now thank you for your envelope received this morning. Your Aunt Cass is as well pleased with St. Julian as ever, and I am delighted with the idea of seeing Progillian again.

Wednesday 17. – We have now just finished the first of the three books I had the pleasure of receiving yesterday. I read it aloud and we are all very much amused, and like the work quite as well as ever. I depend on getting through another book before dinner, but there is really a good deal of respectable reading in your forty-eight pages. I have no doubt six would make a very good-sized volume. You must have been quite pleased to have accomplished so much. I like Lord Portman[35] and his brother very much. I am only afraid that Lord P.'s good nature will make most people like him better than he deserves. The whole family are very good, and Lady Anne, who was your great dread, you have succeeded particularly well with. Bell Griffin is just what she should be. My corrections have not been more important than before; here and there we have thought the sense could be expressed in fewer words, and I have scratched out Sir Thos. from walking with the others to the stables, &c. the very day after breaking his arm; for, though I find your papa *did* walk out immediately after *his* arm was set, I think it can be so little usual as to *appear* unnatural in a book. Lyme will not do. Lyme is towards forty miles from Dawlish and would not be talked of there. I have put Starcross instead. If you prefer Exeter, that must be always safe.

I have also scratched out the introduction between Lord Portman and his brother and Mr. Griffin. A country surgeon (don't tell Mr. C. Lyford) would not be introduced to men of their rank, and when Mr. P. is first brought in, he would not be introduced as the Honourable. That distinction is never mentioned at

---

35 It must be remembered that there was no "Lord Portman" in 1814, the creation of that title having been in 1837.

such times, at least I believe not. Now we have finished the second book, or rather the fifth. I *do* think you had better omit Lady Helena's postscript. To those that are acquainted with *"Pride and Prejudice"* it will seem an imitation. And your Aunt C. and I both recommend your making a little alteration in the last scene between Devereux F. and Lady Clanmurray and her daughter. We think they press him too much, more than sensible or well-bred women would do; Lady C., at least, should have discretion enough to be sooner satisfied with his determination of not going with them. I am very much pleased with Egerton as yet. I did not expect to like him, but I do, and Susan is a very nice little animated creature; but St. Julian is the delight of our lives. He is quite interesting. The whole of his break off with Lady Helena is very well done. Yes; Russell Square is a very proper distance from Berkeley Square. We are reading the last book. They must be *two* days going from Dawlish to Bath. They are nearly 100 miles apart.

Thursday. – We finished it last night after our return from drinking tea at the Great House. The last chapter does not please us quite so well; we do not thoroughly like the play, perhaps from having had too much of plays in that way lately [vide *"Mansfield Park"*], and we think you had better not leave England. Let the Portmans go to Ireland; but as you know nothing of the manners there, you had better not go with them. You will be in danger of giving false representations.

Stick to Bath and the Foresters. There you will be quite at home.

Your Aunt C. does not like desultory novels, and is rather afraid yours will be too much so, that there will be too frequently a change from one set of people to another, and that circumstances will be introduced of apparent consequence which will lead to nothing. It will not be so great an objection to *me* if it does. I allow much more latitude than she does, and think nature and spirit cover many sins of a wandering story, and people in general do not care so much about it, for your comfort.

I should like to have had more of Devereux. I do not feel enough acquainted with him. You were afraid of meddling with him I dare say. I like your sketch of Lord Clanmurray, and your picture of the two young girls' enjoyment is very good. I have not noticed St. Julian's serious conversation with Cecilia, but I like it exceedingly. What he says about the madness of otherwise sensible women on the subject of their daughters coming out is worth its weight in gold.

I do not perceive that the language sinks. Pray go on.

Letter LXXXVII – 1814

Chawton: (Sept. 9).

MY DEAR ANNA,

We have been very much amused by your three books, but I have a good many criticisms to make, more than you will like. We are not satisfied with Mrs. Forester settling herself as tenant and near neighbour to such a man as Sir Thomas, without having some other inducement to go there. She ought to have some friend living thereabouts to tempt her. A woman going with two girls just growing up into a neighbourhood where she knows nobody but one man of not very good character, is an awkwardness which so prudent a woman as Mrs. F. would not be likely to fall into. Remember she *is* very prudent. You must not let her act inconsistently. Give her a friend, and let that friend be invited by Sir Thomas H. to meet her, and we shall have no objection to her dining at the Priory as she does; but otherwise a woman in her situation would hardly go there before she had been visited by other families. I like the scene itself, the Miss Leslie, Lady Anne, and the music very much. Leslie *is* a noble name. Sir Thomas H. you always do very well. I have only taken the liberty of expunging one phrase of his which would not be allowable – "Bless my heart!" It is too familiar and inelegant. Your grandmother is more disturbed at Mrs. Forester's not returning the Egertons' visit sooner than by anything else. They ought to have called at the Parsonage before Sunday. You describe a sweet place, but your descriptions are often more minute than will be liked. You give too many particulars of right hand and left. Mrs. Forester is not careful enough of Susan's health. Susan ought not to be walking out so soon after heavy rains, taking long walks in the dirt. An anxious mother would not suffer it. I like your Susan very much, she is a sweet creature, her playfulness of fancy is very delightful. I like her as she is *now* exceedingly, but I am not quite so well satisfied with her behaviour to George R. At first she seems all over attachment and feeling, and afterwards to have none at all; she is so extremely confused at the ball and so well satisfied apparently with Mr. Morgan. She seems to have changed her character.

You are now collecting your people delightfully, getting them exactly into such a spot as is the delight of my life. Three or four families in a country village is the very thing to work on, and I hope you will do a great deal more, and make full use of them while they are so very favourably arranged.

You are but *now* coming to the heart and beauty of your story. Until the heroine grows up the fun must be imperfect, but I expect a great deal of entertainment from the next three or four books, and I hope you will not resent these remarks by sending me no more. We like the Egertons very well. We see no blue pantaloons or cocks or hens. There is nothing to *enchant* one certainly in Mr. L. L., but we make no objection to him, and his inclination to like Susan is pleasing. The sister is a good contrast, but the name of Rachel is as much I can bear. They are not so much like the Papillons as I expected. Your last chapter is very entertaining, the conversation on genius, &c.; Mr. St. Julian and Susan both talk in character, and very well. In some former parts, Cecilia is perhaps a little too solemn and good, but upon the whole her disposition is very well opposed to Susan's, her want of imagination is very natural. I wish you could make Mrs. Forester talk more; but she must be difficult to manage and make entertaining, because there is so much good sense and propriety about her that nothing can be made very *broad.* Her economy and her ambition must not be staring.

The papers left by Mrs. Fisher are very good. Of course one guesses something. I hope when you have written a great deal more, you will be equal to scratching out some of the past. The scene with Mrs. Mellish I should condemn; it is prosy and nothing to the purpose; and indeed the more you can find in your heart to curtail between Dawlish and Newton Priors, the better I think it will be – one does not care for girls until they are grown up. Your Aunt C. quite understands the exquisiteness of that name – Newton

Priors is really a nonpareil. Milton would have given his eyes to have thought of it. Is not the cottage taken from "Tollard Royal"?

[Thus far the letter was written on the ninth, but before it was finished news arrived at Chawton of the death of Mrs. Charles Austen. She died in her confinement and the baby died also. She left three little girls – Cassie, Harriet, and Fanny. It was not until the 18th that Jane resumed her letter as follows:]

Sunday. – I am very glad, dear Anna, that I wrote as I did before this sad event occurred. I have only to add that your Grandmama does not seem the worse now for the shock.

I shall be very happy to receive more of your work if more is ready; and you write so fast that I have great hopes Mr. Digweed will come back freighted with such a cargo as not all his hops or his sheep could equal the value of.

Your grandmama desires me to say that she will have finished your shoes to-morrow, and thinks they will look very well. And that she depends upon seeing you as you promise before you quit the country, and hopes you will give her more than a day.

Yours affectionately,

J. AUSTEN.

Letter LXXXVIII – 1814

Chawton: Wednesday (Sept. 28).

MY DEAR ANNA,

I hope you do not depend on having your book again immediately. I kept it that your grandmama may hear it, for it has not been possible yet to have any public reading. I have read it to your Aunt Cassandra, however, in our own room at night, while we undressed, and with a great deal of pleasure. We like the first chapter extremely, with only a little doubt whether Lady Helena is not almost *too* foolish. The matrimonial dialogue is very good certainly. I like Susan as well as ever, and begin now not to care at all about Cecilia; she may stay at Easton Court as long as she likes. Henry Mellish will be, I am afraid, too much in the common novel style – a handsome, amiable, unexceptionable young man (such as do not much abound in real life), desperately in love and all in vain. But I have no business to judge him so early. Jane Egerton is a very natural comprehendable girl, and the whole of her acquaintance with Susan and Susan's letter to Cecilia are very pleasing and quite in character. But Miss *Egerton* does not entirely satisfy us. She is too formal and solemn, we think, in her advice to her brother not to fall in love; and it is hardly like a sensible woman – it is putting it into his head. We should like a few hints from her better. We feel really obliged to you for introducing a Lady Kenrick; it will remove the greatest fault in the work, and I give you credit for considerable forbearance as an author in adopting so much of our opinion.

I expect high fun about Mrs. Fisher and Sir Thomas. You have been perfectly right in telling Ben Lefroy of your work, and I am very glad to hear how much he likes it. *His* encouragement and approbation must be "quite beyond everything."[36] I do not at all wonder at his not expecting to like anybody so well as Cecilia *at first,* but I shall be surprised if he does not become a Susanite in time. Devereux Forester's being ruined by his vanity is extremely good, but I wish you would not let him plunge into a "vortex of dissipation." I do not object to the thing, but I cannot bear the expression; it is such thorough novel slang, and so old that I daresay Adam met with it in the first novel he opened. Indeed, I did very much like to know Ben's opinion. I hope he will continue to be pleased with it, and I think he must, but I cannot flatter him with there being much incident. We have no great right to wonder at his not valuing the name of Progillian. *That* is a source of delight which even *he* can hardly be quite competent to.

---

36 A phrase always in the mouth of one of the Chawton neighbours, Mrs. H. Digweed.

Walter Scott has no business to write novels, especially good ones. It is not fair. He has fame and profit enough as a poet, and should not be taking the bread out of the mouths of other people.

I do not like him, and do not mean to like *"Waverley"* if I can help it, but fear I must.

I am quite determined, however, not to be pleased with Mrs. West's *"Alicia De Lacy,"* should I ever meet with it, which I hope I shall not. I think I *can* be stout against anything written by Mrs. West. I have made up my mind to like no novels really but Miss Edgeworth's, yours, and my own.

What can you do with Egerton to increase the interest for him? I wish you could contrive something, some family occurrence to bring out his good qualities more. Some distress among brothers and sisters to relieve by the sale of his curacy! Something to carry him mysteriously away, and then be heard of at York or Edinburgh in an old great coat. I would not seriously recommend anything improbable, but if you could invent something spirited for him it would have a good effect. He might lend all his money to Captain Morris, but then he would be a great fool if he did. Cannot the Morrises quarrel and he reconcile them? Excuse the liberty I take in these suggestions.

Your Aunt Frank's nursemaid has just given her warning, but whether she is worth your having, or would take your place, I know not. She was Mrs. Webb's maid before she went to the Great House. She leaves your aunt because she cannot agree with the other servants. She is in love with the man and her head seems rather turned. He returns her affection, but she fancies every one else is wanting him and envying her. Her previous service must have fitted her for such a place as yours, and she is very active and cleanly. The Webbs are really gone! When I saw the waggons at the door, and thought of all the trouble they must have in moving, I began to reproach myself for not having liked them better, but since the waggons have disappeared my conscience has been closed again, and I am excessively glad they are gone.

I am very fond of Sherlock's sermons and prefer them to almost any.

Your affectionate Aunt,

J. AUSTEN.

If you wish me to speak to the maid, let me know.

Letter LXXXIX – 1814

Chawton: (Nov. 21).

MY DEAR ANNA,

I met Harriet Benn yesterday. She gave me her congratulations and desired they might be forwarded to you, and there they are. The chief news from this country is the death of old Mrs. Dormer. Mrs. Clement walks about in a new black velvet pelisse lined with yellow, and a white bobbin net veil, and looks remarkably well in them.

I think I understand the country about Hendon from your description. It must be very pretty in summer. Should you know from the atmosphere that you were within a dozen miles of London? Make everybody at Hendon admire *"Mansfield Park."*

Your affectionate Aunt,

J. A.

Letter XC – 1814

Hans Place (Nov. 28).

MY DEAR ANNA,

I assure you we all came away very much pleased with our visit. We talked of you for about a mile and a half with great satisfaction; and I have been just sending a very good report of you to Miss Beckford, with a full account of your dress for Susan and Maria.

We were all at the play last night to see Miss O'Neil in "Isabella." I do not think she was quite equal to my expectations. I fancy I want something more than can be. I took two pocket-handkerchiefs, but had very little occasion for either. She is an elegant creature, however, and hugs Mr. Young delightfully. I am going this morning to see the girls in Keppel Street. Cassy was excessively interested about your marriage when she heard of it, which was not until she was to drink your health on the wedding day.

She asked a thousand questions in her usual manner, what he said to you and what you said to him. If your uncle were at home he would send his best love, but I will not impose any base fictitious remembrances on you, mine I can honestly give, and remain

Your affectionate Aunt,

J. AUSTEN.

Letter XCI – 1814

Hans Place (Wednesday).

MY DEAR ANNA,

I have been very far from finding your book an evil, I assure you. I read it immediately, and with great pleasure. I think you are going on very well. The description of Dr. Griffin and Lady Helena's unhappiness is very good, and just what was likely to be. I am curious to know what the end of *them* will be. The name of Newton Priors is really invaluable; I never met with anything superior to it. It is delightful, and one could live on the name of Newton Priors for a twelvemonth. Indeed, I *do* think you get on very fast. I only wish other people of my acquaintance could compose as rapidly. I am pleased with the dog scene and with the whole of George and Susan's love, but am more particularly struck with your *serious* conversations. They are very good throughout. St. Julian's history was quite a surprise to me. You had not very long known it yourself I suspect; but I have no objection to make to the circumstance, and it is very well told. His having been in love with the aunt gives Cecilia an additional interest with him. I like the idea – a very proper compliment to an aunt! I rather imagine indeed that nieces are seldom chosen but out of compliment to some aunt or another. I daresay Ben was in love with me once, and would never have thought of *you* if he had not supposed me dead of scarlet fever. Yes, I was in a mistake as to the number of books. I thought I had read three before the three at Chawton, but fewer than six will not do. I want to see dear Bell Griffin again; and had you not better give some hint of St. Julian's early history in the beginning of the story?

We shall see nothing of Streatham while we are in town; Mrs. Hill is to lye in of a daughter. Mrs. Blackstone is to be with her. Mrs. Heathcote and Miss Bigg[37] are just leaving her. The latter writes me word that Miss Blackford *is* married, but I have never seen it in the papers, and one may as well be single if the wedding is not to be in print.

Your affectionate Aunt,

J. A.

---

[37] Sisters to Mrs. Hall.

Letter XCII – 1816

Chawton: Friday (Sept. 29).

MY DEAR ANNA,

We told Mr. B. Lefroy that if the weather did not prevent us we should certainly come and see you tomorrow and bring Cassy, trusting to your being good enough to give her a dinner about one o'clock, that we might be able to be with you the earlier and stay the longer. But on giving Cassy her choice between the Fair or Wyards, it must be confessed that she has preferred the former, which we trust will not greatly affront you; if it does, you may hope that some little Anna hereafter may revenge the insult by a similar preference of an Alton Fair to her Cousin Cassy. In the meanwhile we have determined to put off our visit to you until Monday, which we hope will be not less convenient. I wish the weather may not resolve on another put off. I *must* come to you before Wednesday if it be possible, for on that day I am going to London for a week or two with your Uncle Henry, who is expected here on Sunday. If Monday should appear too dirty for walking, and Mr. Lefroy would be so kind as to come and fetch me, I should be much obliged to him. Cassy might be of the party, and your Aunt Cassandra will take another opportunity.

Yours very affectionately, my dear Anna,

J. AUSTEN.

Letter XCIII – 1816

June 23.

MY DEAR ANNA,

Cassy desires her best thanks for the book. She was quite delighted to see it. I do not know when I have seen her so much struck by anybody's kindness as on this occasion. Her sensibility seems to be opening to the perception of great actions. These gloves having appeared on the pianoforte ever since you were here on Friday, we imagine they must be yours. Mrs. Digweed returned yesterday through all the afternoon's rain, and was of course wet through, but in speaking of it she never once said "it was beyond everything," which I am sure it must have been. Your Mama means to ride to Speen Hill to-morrow to see the Mrs. Hulberts, who are both very indifferent. By all accounts they really are breaking now – not so stout as the old Jackass.

Yours affectionately,

J. A.

Letters from Cassandra Austen to Fanny Knight, 1817

Letter XCIV – 1817*

[* This and the following letters were written after the death of Jane Austen, July 18.]

Winchester: Sunday.

MY DEAREST FANNY,

Doubly dear to me now for her dear sake whom we have lost. She did love you most sincerely, and never shall I forget the proofs of love you gave her during her illness in writing those kind, amusing letters at a time when I know your feelings would have dictated so different a style. Take the only reward I can give you in the assurance that your benevolent purpose *was* answered; you *did* contribute to her enjoyment.

Even your last letter afforded pleasure. I merely cut the seal and gave it to her; she opened it and read it herself, afterwards she gave it to me to read, and then talked to me a little and not uncheerfully of its contents, but there was then a languor about her which prevented her taking the same interest in anything she had been used to do.

Since Tuesday evening, when her complaint returned, there was a visible change, she slept more and much more comfortably; indeed, during the last eight-and-forty hours she was more asleep than awake. Her looks altered and she fell away, but I perceived no material diminution of strength, and, though I was then hopeless of a recovery, I had no suspicion how rapidly my loss was approaching.

I *have* lost a treasure, such a sister, such a friend as never can have been surpassed. She was the sun of my life, the gilder of every pleasure, the soother of every sorrow; I had not a thought concealed from her, and it is as if I had lost a part of myself. I loved her only too well – not better than she deserved, but I am conscious that my affection for her made me sometimes unjust to and negligent of others; and I can acknowledge, more than as a general principle, the justice of the Hand which has struck this blow.

You know me too well to be at all afraid that I should suffer materially from my feelings; I am perfectly conscious of the extent of my irreparable loss, but I am not at all overpowered and very little indisposed, nothing but what a short time, with rest and change of air, will remove. I thank God that I was enabled to attend her to the last, and amongst my many causes of self-reproach I have not to add any wilful neglect of her comfort.

She felt herself to be dying about half-an-hour before she became tranquil and apparently unconscious. During that half-hour was her struggle, poor soul! She said she could not tell us what she suffered, though she complained of little fixed pain. When I asked her if there was anything she wanted, her answer was she wanted nothing but death, and some of her words were: "God grant me patience, pray for me, oh, pray for me!" Her voice was affected, but as long as she spoke she was intelligible.

I hope I do not break your heart, my dearest Fanny, by these particulars; I mean to afford you gratification whilst I am relieving my own feelings. I could not write so to anybody else; indeed you are the only person I have written to at all, excepting your grandmamma – it was to her, not your Uncle Charles, I wrote on Friday.

Immediately after dinner on Thursday I went into the town to do an errand which your dear aunt was anxious about. I returned about a quarter before six and found her recovering from faintness and oppression; she got so well as to be able to give me a minute account of her seizure, and when the clock struck six she was talking quietly to me.

I cannot say how soon afterwards she was seized again with the same faintness, which was followed by the sufferings she could not describe; but Mr. Lyford had been sent for, had applied something to give her ease, and she was in a state of quiet insensibility by seven o'clock at the latest. From that time till half-past four, when she ceased to breathe, she scarcely moved a limb, so that we have every reason to think, with gratitude to the Almighty, that her sufferings were over. A slight motion of the head with every breath remained till almost the last. I sat close to her with a pillow in my lap to assist in supporting her head, which was almost off the bed, for six hours; fatigue made me then resign my place to Mrs. J. A. for two hours and a-half, when I took it again, and in about an hour more she breathed her last.

I was able to close her eyes myself, and it was a great gratification to me to render her those last services. There was nothing convulsed which gave the idea of pain in her look; on the contrary, but for the continual motion of the head she gave one the idea of a beautiful statue, and even now, in her coffin, there is such a sweet, serene air over her countenance as is quite pleasant to contemplate.

This day, my dearest Fanny, you have had the melancholy intelligence, and I know you suffer severely, but I likewise know that you will apply to the fountain-head for consolation, and that our

522

merciful God is never deaf to such prayers as you will offer.

The last sad ceremony is to take place on Thursday morning; her dear remains are to be deposited in the cathedral. It is a satisfaction to me to think that they are to lie in a building she admired so much; her precious soul, I presume to hope, reposes in a far superior mansion. May mine one day be re-united to it!

Your dear papa, your Uncle Henry, and Frank and Edwd. Austen, instead of his father, will attend. I hope they will none of them suffer lastingly from their pious exertions. The ceremony must be over before ten o'clock, as the cathedral service begins at that hour, so that we shall be at home early in the day, for there will be nothing to keep us here afterwards.

Your Uncle James came to us yesterday, and is gone home to-day. Uncle H. goes to Chawton to-morrow morning; he has given every necessary direction here, and I think his company there will do good. He returns to us again on Tuesday evening.

I did not think to have written a long letter when I began, but I have found the employment draw me on, and I hope I shall have been giving you more pleasure than pain. Remember me kindly to Mrs. J.

Bridges (I am so glad she is with you now), and give my best love to Lizzie and all the others.

I am, my dearest Fanny,

Most affectionately yours,

CASS. ELIZ. AUSTEN

I have said nothing about those at Chawton, because I am sure you hear from your papa.

Letter XCV – 1817

Chawton: Tuesday (July 29).

MY DEAREST FANNY,

I have just read your letter for the third time, and thank you most sincerely for every kind expression to myself, and still more warmly for your praises of her who I believe was better known to you than to any human being besides myself. Nothing of the sort could have been more gratifying to me than the manner in which you write of her, and if the dear angel is conscious of what passes here, and is not above all earthly feelings, she may perhaps receive pleasure in being so mourned. Had *she* been the survivor I can fancy her speaking of *you* in almost the same terms. There are certainly many points of strong resemblance in your characters; in your intimate acquaintance with each other, and your mutual strong affection, you were counterparts.

Thursday was not so dreadful a day to me as you imagined. There was so much necessary to be done that there was no time for additional misery. Everything was conducted with the greatest tranquillity, and but that I was determined I would see the last, and therefore was upon the listen, I should not have known when they left the house. I watched the little mournful procession the length of the street; and when it turned from my sight, and I had lost her for ever, even then I was not overpowered, nor so much agitated as I am now in writing of it. Never was human being more sincerely mourned by those who attended her remains than was this dear creature. May the sorrow with which she is parted with on earth be a prognostic of the joy with which she is hailed in heaven!

I continue very tolerably well – much better than any one could have supposed possible, because I certainly have had considerable fatigue of body as well as anguish of mind for months back; but I really am well, and I hope I am properly grateful to the Almighty for having been so supported. Your grandmamma, too, is much better than when I came home.

I did not think your dear papa appeared well, and I understand that he seemed much more comfortable after his return from Winchester than he had done before. I need not tell you that he was a great comfort to me; indeed, I can never say enough of the kindness I have received from him and from every other friend.

I get out of doors a good deal and am able to employ myself. Of course those employments suit me best which leave me most at leisure to think of her I have lost, and I do think of her in every variety of circumstance. In our happy hours of confidential intercourse, in the cheerful family party which she so ornamented, in her sick room, on her death-bed, and as (I hope) an inhabitant of heaven. Oh, if I may one day be re-united to her there! I know the time must come when my mind will be less engrossed by her idea, but I do not like to think of it. If I think of her less as on earth, God grant that I may never cease to reflect on her as inhabiting heaven, and never cease my humble endeavours (when it shall please God) to join her there.

In looking at a few of the precious papers which are now my property I have found some memorandums, amongst which she desires that one of her gold chains may be given to her god-daughter Louisa, and a lock of her hair be set for you. You can need no assurance, my dearest Fanny, that every request of your beloved aunt will be sacred with me. Be so good as to say whether you prefer a brooch or ring. God bless you, my dearest Fanny.

Believe me, most affectionately yours,

CASS. ELIZTH. AUSTEN.

Poetry, Backwards Letter Poetry*

[* Enclosed in one of the Letters of 1807.]

VERSES TO RHYME WITH "ROSE".

1. MRS. AUSTEN.

This morning I woke from a quiet repose,
I first rubb'd my eyes, and I next blew my nose;
With my stockings and shoes I then covered my
 toes,
And proceeded to put on the rest of my clothes.
This was finished in less than an hour, I suppose.
I employ'd myself next in repairing my hose.
'Twas a work of necessity not what I chose;
Of my sock I'd much rather have knit twenty
 rows.
My work being done, I look'd through the
 windows,
And with pleasure beheld all the bucks and the
 does,
The cows and the bullocks, the wethers and ewes.
To the library each morning the family goes,
So I went with the rest though I felt rather froze.
My flesh is much warmer, my blood freer flows,

When I work in the garden with rakes and with
 hoes.
And now I believe I must come to a close,
For I find I grow stupid e'en while I compose.
If I write any longer my verse will be prose.

***

2. MISS AUSTEN (CASSANDRA).

Love, they say, is like a rose;
I'm sure 'tis like the wind that blows,
For not a human creature knows
How it comes or where it goes.
It is the cause of many woes:
It swells the eyes and reds the nose,
And very often changes those
Who once were friends to bitter foes.
But let us now the scene transpose
And think no more of tears and throes.
Why may we not as well suppose
A smiling face the urchin shows?
And when with joy the bosom glows,
And when the heart has full repose,
'Tis mutual love the gift bestows.

***

3. MISS JANE AUSTEN.

Happy the lab'rer in his Sunday clothes!
In light-drab coat, smart waistcoat, well-darn'd
 hose,
And hat upon his head, to church he goes;
As oft with conscious pride, he downward
 throws
A glance upon the ample cabbage rose
Which, stuck in button-hole, regales his nose,
He envies not the gaiest London beaux.
In church he takes his seat among the rows,
Pays to the place the reverence he owes,
Likes best the prayers whose meaning least he
 knows.
Lists to the sermon in a softening doze,
And rouses joyous at the welcome close.

***

4. MRS. ELIZABETH AUSTEN.

Never before did I quarrel with a rose,
Till now, that I am told some lines to compose,
Of which I have little idea, God knows;
But since that the task is assigned me by those
To whom love, affection, and gratitude owes
A ready compliance, I feign would dispose
And call to befriend me the muse who bestows
The gift of poetry both on friends and foes.
My warmest acknowledgments are due to those

Who watched near my bed and soothed me to
 repose,
Who pitied my sufferings and shared in my woes,
And, by their simpathy, relieved my sorrows.
May I as long as the blood in my veins flows
Feel the warmth of love which now in my breast
 glows,
And may I sink into a refreshing doze
When I lie my head on my welcome pillows.

***

ON SIR HOME POPHAM'S SENTENCE, APRIL 1807.

Of a Ministry pitiful, angry, mean,
A gallant commander the victim is seen.
For promptitude, vigour, success, does he stand
Condemn'd to receive a severe reprimand!
To his foes I could wish a resemblance in fate:
That they, too, may suffer themselves, soon or
 late,
The injustice they warrant. But vain is my spite,
They cannot so suffer who never do right.

***

TO MISS BIGG, PREVIOUS TO HER MARRIAGE, WITH SOME POCKETHANDKERCHIEFS I HAD HEMMED FOR HER.

Cambrick! With grateful blessings would I pay
The pleasure given me in sweet employ.
Long may'st thou serve my friend without decay,
And have no tears to wipe but tears of joy.

***

ON THE SAME OCCASION, BUT NOT SENT.

Cambrick! thou'st been to me a good,
And I would bless thee if I could.
Go, serve thy mistress with delight,
Be small in compass, soft and white;
Enjoy thy fortune, honour'd much
To bear her name and feel her touch;
And that thy worth may last for years,
Slight be her colds, and few her tears.

Letter XCVI

YM RAED YSSAC,

I hsiw uoy a yppah wen raey. Ruoy xis snisuoc emac ereh yadretsey, dna dah hcae a eceip of ekac. Siht si elttil Yssac's yadhtrib, dna ehs si eerht sraey dlo. Knarf sah nugeb gninrael Nital. Ew deef eht Nibor yreve gninrom. Yllas netfo seriuqne retfa uoy. Yllas Mahneb sah tog a wen neerg nwog. Teirrah Thgink semoc yreve yad ot daer ot Tnua Ardnassac. Doog eyb, ym raed Yssac.

Tnua Ardnassac sdnes reh tseb evol, dna os ew od lla.

Ruoy etanoitceffa Tnua,

ENAJ NETSUA.

Books For ALL Kinds of Readers

At ReadHowYouWant we understand that one size does not fit all types of readers. Our innovative, patent pending technology allows us to design new formats to make reading easier and more enjoyable for you. This helps improve your speed of reading and your comprehension. Our EasyRead printed books have been optimized to improve word recognition, ease eye tracking by adjusting word and line spacing as well as minimizing hyphenation. Our EasyRead SuperLarge editions have been developed to make reading easier and more accessible for vision-impaired readers. We offer Braille and DAISY formats of our books and all popular E-Book formats.

We are continually introducing new formats based upon research and reader preferences. Visit our web-site to see all of our formats and learn how you can Personalize our books for yourself or as gifts. Sign up to Become A RHYW Registered Reader.

www.readhowyouwant.com